Reading Chinua Achebe

Studies in
African Literature
Series

James Currey Oxford
Heinemann Portsmouth, N.H.
EAEP Nairobi

Reading Chinua Achebe

Language & Ideology in Fiction

SIMON GIKANDI

Assistant Professor of Black Studies
University of Massachusetts, Boston

James Currey
OXFORD

Heinemann
PORTSMOUTH, N.H.

EAEP
NAIROBI

James Currey
an imprint of Boydell and Brewer Ltd,
PO Box 9, Woodbridge, Suffolk IP12 3DF, UK
and 668 Mount Hope Avenue, Rochester NY 14620-2731, USA
www.jamescurrey.com
www.boydell and brewer.com

Heinemann Educational Books, Inc
361 Hanover Street
Portsmouth, NH 03801-3912, USA

East African Educational Publishers
Mpaka Rd/Woodvale Grove
PO Box 45314
Nairobi

Transferred to digital printing

A catalogue record is available from the British Library

ISBN 978-1-85255-527-9 (James Currey)
ISBN 978-0-435-08057-0 (Heineman)

Library of Congress Catalog Card Number 90-26550

Typeset by Colset Private Ltd, Singapore
in 10/11 pt Paladium

This book is dedicated to
the
University of Nairobi

Acknowledgements

A book on Chinua Achebe and his seminal place in the development of an African narrative invites moments of reflection on my own involvement with African literature. I would like to thank Mr Geoffrey Kuira who, right out of Makerere University's Department of English, encountered me in secondary school, introduced me to African literature, and taught me how to read *Things Fall Apart*. It was my fortune to have been a student at the University of Nairobi at one of the most exciting periods in its history (the 1970s) and to have learnt, from all the members of the Department of Literature, about the importance of literary texts in the still unfinished quest for an African order of knowledge. To my teachers and fellow students at the University of Nairobi, I offer this book as my own contribution to that quest.

The book was completed when I was an Andrew Mellon Faculty Fellow at Harvard University and I would like to thank the Director of the Mellon Program, Dr Richard Hunt, and his staff for their generous help and assistance. Finally, a word of thanks to Gaurav Desai and my students at the University of Massachusetts at Boston for teaching me about the centrality of culture to our lives.

Contents

1
Reading Chinua Achebe

Nation Formation & the Novel

We are in a period so different from anything else that has happened that everything that is presented to us has to be looked at twice.

Chinua Achebe, Interview with Bill Moyers

Narrative, in short, introduces an opposing point of view, perspective, consciousness to the unitary web of vision; it violates the serene Apollonian fictions asserted by vision.

Edward W. Said, *Orientalism*

Language is our tool, and language is the tool of the politicians. We are like two sides in a very hostile game. And I think that the attempt to deceive with words is countered by the efforts of the writer to go behind the words, to show the meaning.

Chinua Achebe, *Times Literary Supplement*

I. The Anxiety of Writing

For many students and scholars of African culture, the inaugural moment of modern African literature was the publication of Chinua Achebe's *Things Fall Apart* (1958); since then the Nigerian novelist's reputation has never been hard to sustain. Achebe is read and discussed more than any other African novelist, and his works have come to constitute important interpretative spaces in the development and

1

critique of the postcolonial condition and its aesthetic. Nevertheless, Achebe has suffered the misfortune of being taken for granted: the intricate and deep structures that inform his narratives are rarely examined, except on an elementary introductory level, and the ideologies that inform his narratives and his theoretical reflections rarely seem to have the influence one would expect from Africa's leading novelist. Clearly, Achebe has been a victim of that kind of 'first' reading which Roland Barthes condemned as the consumption of the text, a reading which erases the problematics of the text and its contradictory meanings in its quest for the artifice of continuity.[1] My book is written in the belief that it is not enough to build Achebe's literary reputation on his pioneering status in the African tradition; his writings and thought must be placed in their proper perspective, placed in relation to both some important literary precursors and within the nationalist tradition that produced him. Only then can we begin to understand why the kinds of narratives Achebe inaugurated have acquired so much ideological import, why he is indispensible to understanding the colonial and postcolonial condition in Africa.

Achebe was not the first African literary figure: he is preceded on the scene of cultural production not only by the often invisible producers of our orature, but also by a myriad of writers who wrote in African languages, writers such as Mofolo in Sotho and Shaaban Robert in Swahili. Closer to home in Nigeria, Achebe's most significant precursor is Amos Tutuola. And yet, it is often said that modern African literature originates with Achebe. If this is the case, is Achebe's seminal status in African literary history due to his cultural influence, narrative prowess, or his mastery of the colonial language? The truth is, one would find it difficult to argue that Achebe has had more cultural influence in his time than his precursors, or that his narrative and poetic powers are more unique than those of his predecessors and contemporaries. What then is the historical significance of Achebe? Why do so many genealogies of African writing always seem to begin with him? Why isn't Amos Tutuola the father figure of modern African literature? And why has so much investment and prestige been attached to the novel form, the form of artistic practice which is the most alien to African cultures?

To raise these questions is no doubt to confront the whole issue about literary canonicity – the process and conditions in which some literary reputations are built and others denigrated – but it is also the first step in refocusing African literary history away from chronology, from some outdated assumptions that the growth of African literature was the natural product of our recent history, that writing and historical development necessarily go hand in hand. We must begin to probe the function of African literature as an instrument that wills new African realities into being, that imagines alternative configurations of our 'real histories' to either affirm or transcend them. We must develop

2

new ways of looking at African fiction as a narrative practice that revises and reverts the colonial discourses in which, to quote V.Y. Mudimbe, 'African worlds have been established as realities for knowledge;' for even in our postcolonial present, 'Africans themselves read, challenge, rewrite these discourses as a way of explicating and defining their culture, history, and being.'[2]

The theoretical supposition that African literature reflected what Mudimbe aptly calls the 'real universe, particularly the social relationships of production and the silent impact of ideological signalisations' has certainly not outlived its usefulness.[3] But if the African novel has become a formal instrument in the invention and reinvention of African cultures, it is surely because this form has sought to evoke worlds beyond its conditions of possibility, to will into being utopian worlds beyond colonial and neocolonial reification. In this sense Mudimbe is right to argue that 'the literary world could well be a mythical space' which, at the same time, 'unveils the concrete experience of human communities.'[4] However, some historical and chronological questions cannot be dismissed off-handedly: Why did many African writers decide to write novels in the last days of the colonial enterprise? What narrative ideologies, assumptions and presuppositions motivated this turn to the most Western of literary genres? These questions are important to understanding the genealogy of Achebe's novels and his quest for a postcolonial aesthetics.

The argument I want to make here is that Achebe's seminal status in the history of African literature lies precisely in his ability to have realized that the novel provided a new way of reorganizing African cultures, especially in the crucial juncture of transition from colonialism to national independence, and his fundamental belief that narrative can indeed propose an alternative world beyond the realities imprisoned in colonial and postcolonial relations of power. In other words, Achebe was possibly the first of our writers to recognize the function of the novel not solely as a mode of representing reality, but one which had limitless possibilities of inventing a new national community. In Achebe's works, questions of national identity are closely related to narrative strategies; fiction allows the writer to express a different vision and perspective.

In a recent interview, when Bill Moyers asked him to interpret a famous Igbo proverb – 'Wherever something stands, something else will stand beside it' – Achebe proceeded not only to explicate the dualities which this proverb stresses, but also to underscore the importance of 'a second point of view' in his own life and work.[5] Looking at an African world turned upside down during centuries of slavery and foreign domination, confronted with the cultural disorganization of this world, Achebe looks around and fails to see 'a space I want to stay in.' He then turns to narrative and the process of narration, as modes of rereading the world – of looking at everything twice – and as a space of imagining a different universe, of organizing ourselves in a world which holds many perils for black people. Literature, asserts Achebe, 'is one of the ways, I think – at least one of the ways available to the writer – to organize himself and his society to meet the perils of living.'[6] The inventive and reorganizational function of art is one which Achebe returns to often in his theoretical reflections on African literature. As he tells a convocation audience at the University of Ife in 1978, 'art is man's constant effort to create for himself a different order of reality from that which is given to him; an aspiration to provide himself with a second handle on existence *through his imagination.*'[7] Achebe's textual practice, then, aims to transform and reinvent the African world; the novelty of his narrative language derives from what Pierre Macherey would call its 'self-constituting power.'[8]

Indeed, the historical significance of Achebe's works lies in his ability to evolve narrative procedures through which the colonial language, which was previously intended to designate and reproduce the colonial ideology, now evokes new forms of expression, proffers a new oppositional discourse, thereby countering the 'permanence of vision' embedded in colonialist discourse.[9] As Iyay Kimoni has observed in another context, '[I]t took the arrival of the novel on the scene for the idea of the crisis of traditional society to hint at the possibility of the evolution of African culture towards a new form.'[10] And in seeking a new form of expressing African culture, Achebe and his contemporaries were also seeking a way out of the prisonhouse of colonialism. For these writers to evoke a new African identity – which is one of Achebe's declared goals and persistent themes – these writers had to take the colonial project into account; they had to interrogate its vision, ideologies, historical claims, and its theory of Africans. In Achebe's case, the imperative to confront the colonial project in its totality arises from the belief that '[C]olonization was the most important event in our history from all kinds of angles ... most of the problems we see in our politics derive from the moment when we lost our initiative to other people, to colonizers.'[11] Significantly, Achebe's return to the colonial archive is motivated by the need to imagine the future: taking colonialism into account (both in terms of writing about it and interrogating its claims), 'will help us to map out our plans for the future.'[12]

The inaugural function of Achebe's texts hence lies in his ability to relate the archaeological role of the novel – its narrative investigation of the social and historical conditions of African societies before and during colonization – with the utopian impulse that underlies the novel as a genre, that is, the desire for a mythical space in which a new society might be articulated. Indeed, a close examination of Achebe's theoretical reflections indicates a keen cognizance of this conjunction between the archaeological and the utopian – by using narrative to counter the fixed colonial vision of Africa, Achebe proposes

4

a new order of knowledge. There is certainly a sense in which Achebe's novels are concerned with the elaboration of a new knowledge on Africa, a knowledge which takes a dual path: first, it is reconstructed from latent meanings recovered from what colonialism had repressed and from the historical conditions colonialism itself has created; but this knowledge is also 'something newly raised up, an addition to the reality from which it begins.'[13] A close examination of Achebe's five novels points to a continuous and unwavering questioning of the conditions in which an African knowledge can be produced, the consciousness and problematics of such a knowledge, and its ideological function.

If the form of knowledge which Achebe's narratives propose does not seem to have the ideological resonance of some of his contemporaries, notably Ngugi and Soyinka, this has more to do with the forms his proclamations take rather than their weakness or lack of urgency. Neither Achebe's theoretical reflections nor his narrative practice seeks to produce or identify knowledge in terms of what Macherey calls 'quantative content'; rather Achebe's major works seek to delineate the conditions which make the emergence of an African knowledge possible or hinder its articulation. In his seminal reflections on this kind of knowledge in *A Theory of Literary Production*, Macherey argues that to identify the conditions which make a certain mode of knowledge possible, we should not consider this knowledge as a doctrine or system of answers; on the contrary, we should attempt 'to formulate the initial question which gives meaning to those answers':

> It is when the answers are mainly explicit that the question which gave rise to them is most often ignored; concealed under the answers, the question is rapidly forgotten. To discover the theory of a form of knowledge, that concealed central question must be rendered explicit. So rather than taking an inventory of critical doctrines, the questions which they are supposed to be answering must be disclosed.[14]

As I will show in this introduction, Achebe's works and thought always return to the forgotten questions of the African experience: Where, why, and when does colonialism begin to seize the initiative in the organization of African society (*Things Fall Apart* and *Arrow of God*)? How can an African nation and community be created in the marginal space between autonomy and the colonizing structure (*No Longer at Ease*)? What are the doctrines that inform the postcolonial situation and how can the pitfalls of national consciousness in Africa be represented without giving in to despair (*A Man of the People* and *Anthills of the Savannah*)? Furthermore, I want to insist that Achebe was possibly the first African writer to be self-conscious about his role as an African writer, to confront the linguistic and historical problems of African writing in a colonial situation, and to situate writing within a larger body of regional and global knowledge about Africa.

Achebe did not, of course, appear on the African literary scene as an orphan. As I have already observed, he had important precursors such as Amos Tutuola, Thomas Mofolo, Sol Plaatje, and Peter Abrahams whose pioneering status in the African literary project cannot be underestimated. And yet, it is fair to say that at the beginning of his career, Achebe felt impelled to define and redefine the project of African literature precisely because whenever he looked around him, he was confronted by the overwhelming hegemony of colonialist rhetoric on Africa – what he once called 'the sedate prose of the district-officer-government-anthropologist of sixty or seventy years ago'[15] – which the African intellectual has had to wrestle, like Jacob and the angel, at almost every juncture of our contemporary history. To invent a new African narrative was then to write against, and decentre, this colonial discourse as a prelude to evoking an alternative space of representation.

Above all, to produce a literature that was conscious of its Africanness, Achebe had to reread the canonical texts of colonialism to disperse their authority:

> I went to the first university that was built in Nigeria, and I took a course in English. We were taught the same kind of literature that British people were taught in their own university. But then I began to look at these books in a different light. When I had been younger, I had read these adventure books about the good white man, you know, wandering into the jungle or into danger, and the savages were after him. And I would instinctively be on the side of the white man. You see what fiction can do, it can put you on the wrong side if you are not developed enough. In the university I suddenly saw that these books had to be read in a different light. Reading *Heart of Darkness*, for instance, which was a very, very highly praised book and which is still highly praised, I realized that I was one of those savages jumping up and down on the beach. Once that kind of Enlightenment comes to you, you realize that someone has to write a different story. And since I was in any case inclined that way, why not me?[16]

The colonial text had made two erroneous assumptions which Achebe needed to reverse: one was that there was ideological continuity between the colonizer and the colonized, that the metropolis and the margin could be united by a common colonial culture; the second was that the colonized could always read the colonial text from a point of identification with the colonizer and hence not recognize their othering in the narrative.

For Achebe to learn how to read 'in a different light' was to recognize the plurality of meanings in the colonial text, his alienation in this text, and its inadequacy of representation. As a result, his novels are informed by a certain sense of mission which is also the source of narrative anxiety: on one hand, there is the novelist's self-consciousness about his role as a producer of a new African literature and the inventor of new forms through which African culture can adequately be represented; on the other hand, there is a certain kind of anxiety about the possibilities of an African literature in forms and languages borrowed from the European other. This anxiety often defines the different narrative strategies Achebe adopts in each of his novels. This anxiety has ideological and historical origins, too: we know, for example, that the young Achebe is not only a child of the colonial tradition but also comes of age at the height of African nationalism, a moment that promises a rupture in the colonial epistemology or a radical reversal of the colonial ideology. What does it mean for the young Achebe to abandon his undergraduate studies in medicine, to read English instead, and become a writer?

The answer can be found in the most consistent theme in Achebe's theoretical writings – the function of the writer as both the defender of a culture and the custodian of a national consciousness. A part of the writer's role, says Achebe, is 'to encourage the creation of an African identity.'[17] The 'fundamental theme' which the African writer must confront at the beginning of his or her career, Achebe informs us in 'The role of the writer in a new nation,' is the validation of the African culture denied by colonial historiography: 'African people did not hear of culture for the first time from Europeans; that their societies were not mindless but frequently had a philosophy of great depth and value and beauty, that they had poetry and, above all, they had dignity.'[18] Thus, the writer is implicated in the building and reconstruction of the new nation, in the quest for a new discursive field in which the integrity of the African people can be asserted. 'The worst thing that can happen to any people is the loss of their dignity and self-respect,' says Achebe. 'The writer's duty is to help them regain it by showing them in human terms what happened to them, what they lost.'[19]

Furthermore, in Achebe's writings, there is a fundamental link between the idea of the nation, the concept of national culture, and the quest for an African narrative. Fanon's famous dictum that the liberation of the nation is 'that material keystone which makes the building of a culture possible' finds its parallel in Achebe's desire to liberate the African mind from the colonial complex and the 'crisis of the soul' which it triggers in the colonized.[20] A writer, Achebe tells Donatus Nwoga in a famous interview, has the responsibility to unlock the colonial imprisonment of the African mind 'because unless our culture begins to take itself seriously it will never sort of get off the ground.'[21] Thus, the idea of a national culture that restores dignity to African peoples, describes and justifies, and praises 'the action through which that people has created itself and keeps itself in existence'[22] is an important function of Achebe's narrative and poetics.

The context in which national consciousness is written into fictional texts may change, but even after the disappointments of African independence and a civil war which almost tore his nation apart, Achebe will still insist that the first goal of African literature is its commitment to the notion of a national community. In 1964, Achebe insisted that '[A] national literature is one that takes the whole nation for its province and has a realised or potential audience throughout its territory' (MY, 56). In a 1980 interview with Kalu Ogbaa, Achebe wondered how one could 'transmit a national culture to Nigerians if not through works of imagination'; literature, he would add, 'is a life and death affair because we are fashioning a new man. The Nigerian is a new man. How do we get this into his mind?'[23] The last question points to the sources of Achebe's anxieties about writing: how can the idea of a national community – which is often taken for granted and propagated in narrative texts – be transferred into the body politic? Achebe's anxiety is exacerbated by the only too familiar fact that the nation in Africa is an arbitrary and often fictional colonial creation; the African writer's relationship to his nation is precarious; there is not always a determinate relationship between the idea of the nation and its terrain; and in the postcolonial situation where what Jean Franco calls 'the blueprints of national formation' have become a 'sceptical reconstruction of past errors', then the novel makes visible 'that absence of any signified that could correspond to the nation.'[24] Indeed, in the late 1960s, Achebe would find himself – consistently and true to form – committed to the idea of a nation even when the claims of that nation (in this case Biafra) were doubtful.

The important point, though, is that in the absence of real signifiers to correspond to the idea of the nation, African writers must often invent significant frameworks within which questions of cultural identity can be examined. If Achebe's commitment to Nigeria can be transferred – with ease and integrity – to Biafra, this should not be seen as an indication of the novelist's wavering allegiances, but of the shifting nature of African realities, and of the writer's need to shape his own thinking to come to terms with the African problematic; for Achebe, '[I]t is in the very nature of creativity, in its prodigious complexity and richness, that it will accommodate paradoxes and ambiguities' (HI, 110). And even when such paradoxes and complexities are signalized by tragic consequences, as in the case of the Nigerian civil war, the writer finds a constant factor in the idea and ideal of an African culture which he must realize in narrative practice. 'Most African writers write out of an African experience and of commitment to an African destiny,' says Achebe, 'For them this destiny does not include a future European identity for which the present is but an apprenticeship' (MY, 7). Narrative, in a different light, must have the power to point to a future world and destiny: 'We have to work with some hope that there is a new generation, a group of survivors who have learned something from the disaster. It is very important to carry the message of the disaster to the new dispensation. With luck, they will succeed.'[25]

In view of such a bold commitment to the utopian realization of Africa, why is Achebe considered to be a pessimistic writer? I would like to see this pessimism not as a symptom of Achebe's doubts about the African ideal and the dream of a national culture, but as an expression of his anxieties about the transference of his discourse on an African destiny from the imaginative realm, the mythical space, to the practices of everyday life. These doubts are, in turn, crystallized in Achebe's quest for the appropriate narrative form. Here, there is one overriding question: can an African culture, or an African mode of knowledge, be articulated in a European language, in European forms, and within the epistemological contexts of colonialism and post-colonialism? If so, can the resulting narratives still be considered African? Is what we call African literature and its critical discourse still determined by what Mudimbe calls 'its external conditions of possibility', and proceeds from 'the extension to Africa of Western fellowships of discourse'?[26] If so, then how is Africa to be represented in a literature of its own?

The truth is, Achebe's fiction is driven by uncertainty and anxiety about its relationship to the 'European identity' which it has set out to negate; in a sense, what has been called his pessimism is really his cognizance of the wide gap that separates the novelist's vision of an African order of knowledge and our present failure to wrench ourselves from the colonizing structures of old. It is Achebe's anxiousness about our 'failure of substance' that defines his narrative ideologies and practice. Furthermore, in striving to establish adequate forms and strategies for representing or reinventing the African experience, the writer must also interrogate the possibility of recovering an African aesthetic that might reinvigorate the borrowed colonial language and its narrative tradition. Throughout his works, Achebe will evoke the authority of Igbo culture and its aesthetic codes to recover what the colonizing structure has repressed and to legitimize his narrative strategies. Achebe's belief here is that there is 'a genuine need for African writers to pause momentarily and consider whether anything in traditional African aesthetics will fit their contemporary condition' (MY, 21). But, again, the two terms evoked – 'traditional African aesthetics' and the 'contemporary condition' – are placed in a state of undecidability: the traditional aesthetic, it could be argued, is precisely what colonial modernism and the postcolonial state have denigrated and renounced to create the contemporary condition.

Clearly, Achebe must negotiate both paradigms carefully for he is not one to fall easily into the romanticism of tradition or the mystification of our contemporary condition. He is categorical in his assertion that 'every literature must seek the things that belong unto its peace, must, in other words, speak of a particular place, evolve out of the necessities of its history, past and current, and the aspirations and destiny of its people' (MY, 7); but he also seems aware that Africa must be rescued not so much from itself or its history, as various schools of development and modernity claim, but from the discourse of the Western world which has fixed Africa as a fetish with the telescoping powers of what Edward Said would call a 'comprehensive vision' that does not allow for temporal and spatial transformations.[27]

II. The Interests of Narrative

In a brilliant discussion on how the Orient is 'translated into activity', Edward Said has argued that narrative is an important strategy for countering the essentialist and panoramic view which he aptly terms 'vision'. As a strategy of representation narrative counters the 'official' view of the colonized as ahistorical and hence fixed in time and space.[28] Said asserts that 'History and the narrative by which history is represented argue that vision is insufficient, that 'the Orient', as an unconditional ontological category does an injustice to the potential of reality for change.'[29] In an attempt to represent the colonized as a transparent entity which is, at the same time, immune to historical change and transformation, the colonizer fixes the colonized as a people without an objective history and hence subject to only those forms of change that come from outside, that is, from the colonial structures. In contrast, anti-colonial writers, seeking to assert the capacity of their people for change and transformation, return history to their people; narrative becomes the indispensible agent of history. For Achebe, 'It is the storyteller, in fact, who makes us what we are, who creates history. The storyteller creates the memory that the survivors must have – otherwise their surviving would have no meaning.'[30]

The important point to note here is that what is often at stake in Achebe's attempt to recover the integrity of African culture, and to negotiate the forces that block this process, is not the nature of African reality itself, but how Africa has been represented in European colonial discourse. Since the act of restoring the African self to history is itself dependent on a Western language, Western institutions, and Western intellectual categories, the question always arises: does the act of restoration lead to the constitution of a new culture or just a repetition – under the guise of nationalism – of colonialist discourse? Above all, how can a genuinely African literature develop under Western forms of domination that have continued even after political independence?

The truth is, Achebe's pronouncements on literature, like his fiction, are troubled by questions about the impulses and circumstances which lead to the development of a particular mode of writing. The preface to *Morning Yet on Creation Day*, to cite just one example, is concerned with the 'interest' of writing, a term which Achebe uses in 'both its senses': why do we find interest in a particular kind of writing and whose political interest does this writing serve? Let us look at the etymology of this world, 'interest,' to show how it is implicated in the ethics of writing. Although the OED gives numerous definitions of 'interest,' they all seem to fall into three categories: interest defines the relationship of one thing to another, and is hence a form of concernment; interest is also a form of commitment to a project or act; but it is also a form of compensation, or supplement, for a wrong done or for the loss of a valuable object. So, when Achebe calls attention to the 'interest' of writing, he possibly has all three meanings in mind.

In the first instance, the interest of writing denotes the author's implication in his own historicity – his definition by, and within, a collective memory and a communal regimen of truth. This form of concernment explains Achebe's astute claim that 'in our situation the great danger lies not in remembering but in forgetting, in pretending that slogans are the same as truth; and that Nigeria, always prone to self-deception, stands in great need of reminders' (MY, xiii). As a form of commitment, on the other hand, writing is propelled by the need to question its own contingency; instead of rushing to foreclose the issue – to become implicated in what Achebe calls 'the current national pastime of consigning ten years ago into pre-history' (MY, xiii) – writing calls attention to the historical moment; sustaining the 'problem' becomes more important than resolving it. In the third sense, writing functions as a form of compensation – what Jacques Derrida has called a 'supplement'[31] – for a historical experience that has been written out of existence in colonialist discourse or for the gap in the temporal development of Africa as it has been represented in the colonial text; narrative commemorates the African past.

I will hence argue that in every novel Achebe has written to date, what we know about Igbo or Nigerian culture is less important than how we know it; Achebe's narratives seek to create the initial situation in which the African problematic developed and to express the conditions in which knowledge about phenomena is produced. Rather than assume that experience is original and primary, Achebe calls attention to its existence as an effect of language and narrative strategies. He notes that '[E]xperience is necessary for growth and survival. But experience is not simply what happened. A lot may happen to a piece of stone without making it wiser. Experience is what we are able and prepared to do with what happens to us' (MY, xiii). In short, understanding is heightened by our awareness of the historical conditions that made a certain kind of experience possible; we need to be conscious of the strategic formations, or even styles, that have created Africa as an image and a reality in both Western and African eyes.

My theoretical position here is borrowed from Said, who argues limpidly that what is circulated and exchanged within a culture is not truth but representations: 'In any instance of at least written language, there is no such thing as a delivered presence, but a *re-presence*, or a representation.'[32] Indeed, what Achebe values most in the Igbo aesthetic, he says in an introduction to an exhibition of Igbo art, is the emphasis it places on process rather than product: 'Process is motion while product is rest. When the product is preserved or venerated, the impulse to repeat the process is compromised. Therefore, the Igbo choose to eliminate the product and retain the process so that every occasion and every generation will receive its own impulse and experience of creation.'[33] For this reason, my attention in this study will be focused on how realities are constructed through narrative and semiotic strategies, how ideology is produced by language and how language produces and reproduces ideology. In Edward Said's words, one way of getting hold of the postcolonial condition and its attendant debates 'is to analyze not its content, but its form, not what is said so much as how it is said, by whom, where, and for whom.'[34]

Furthermore, ideology as process and critique, rather than product and dogma, is the key to understanding Achebe's narrative strategies; for if there is an ideology of writing in his texts, as I will be arguing in the rest of this introduction, it is to be found in the author's acceptance, like the Mbari artists of his ancestry, of the precariousness and temporary nature of any artistic and intellectual project. Here, too, the key to Achebe's aesthetics is the ease with which he adopts his own contradictory postures and impulses. Consider his stand on epistemological categories and moral systems. Achebe often rejects, and sometimes scorns at, notions of 'universality and other concepts of that scope' (MY, 3) and any fight 'for the exclusive claim on righteousness and truth' (MY, 21). However, there are also occasions when his aesthetic props itself on absolute epistemological and moral categories, rejecting contingency and particularity: for example, in an interview with John Agetua, Achebe says that he never defines politics in a narrow sense – 'I'm talking of politics in a general sense which means, in my view, the ordering of society'; he then goes on to claim that '[T]here is a kind of law governing things in the world, the natural laws, the social laws.'[35]

Here, Achebe seems to have embraced the very universalism he had rejected previously, for how can one talk about a general law that governs things in the world unless one adopts universality as a philosophical category? The question, then, is this: how do we explain or resolve this contradiction in Achebe's thought? I do not think this contradiction can be resolved, and I do not think the resolution of contradications is important in Achebe's ideology or textual practice. As he has categorically stated, the Igbo aesthetic does not find value in any absolute resolution of the forces that inform human life and social practice; rather, '[I]t is the need and the striving to come to terms with a multitude of forces and demands which give Igbo life its tense and restless dynamism and its art an outward, social and kinetic quality.'[36]

The multiplicity of forces which Achebe's ancestors had recognized as crucial to any artistic project have become central to those African writers who were born in the heyday of colonialism and came of age in the period of decolonization, for such writers are defined both by the consciousness of colonialism – which fixed their identities as colonial subjects – and the failure of the colonizers to live up to their promise to turn them into what the Igbo call *oyin oji* (black Europeans) within the traditions and mythologies of empire. As an ideology bent on rejecting the mythologies of empire, nationalism offered the possibility of negating the colonial tradition:

> The Nationalist movement in British West Africa after the Second World War brought a mental revolution which began to reconcile us to ourselves. It suddenly seemed that we too might have a story to tell. *Rule Britannia* to which we had marched so unselfconsciously on Empire Day now stuck in our throat (MY, 70).

Because nationalism and narration will walk hand in hand in Achebe's novels, especially his early works, the conditions which make both paradigms possible need to be addressed.

III. Nation, Narration, and Colonial Self

In many influential studies, the history of African literature has been shown to have been determined by the interaction between the African cultural tradition and the socio-historical environment, which triggered a positive consciousness that needed to express itself in writing. For example, in his influential study of the West African novel, Emmanuel Obiechina set out to 'establish the determining background factors of the Western African novel': his study, he asserts, 'aims to show that the changing cultural and social situation in West Africa both gave rise to the novel there, and in far-reaching and crucial ways conditioned the West Africa novels' content, themes and textures.'[37] But as Mudimbe has argued, we too often take the conditions that enable African literature for granted when we tie it so closely to 'the concrete experience of human communities' without confronting its 'contradictory assumptions': 'What serious theory could support the fantastic liberties of our investigations in African literature, if, at least, on the one hand we do not agree on the urgency of analyzing the conditions of existence of this literature; and on the other hand we do not accept the hypothesis that present-day African criticism might not be an African practice at all?'[38]

My focus, then, is on the cultural and social factors that gave rise to Achebe's novels, the conditions of existence of his primary texts, and – more primarily – how these factors and conditions are (re)presented in narrative. In regard to the question of origins and literary tradition, I want to insist that it was the African writers' lack of a tradition, or rather their problematic relationship with the colonial tradition which constituted them, that necessitated the act of writing. Doesn't the African novel, despite its often cited claim to reconnect us to a past tradition, already involve, in its techniques and generic configurations, its themes and ideologies, an awareness of its indebtedness to an alien tradition and its absence of a native genealogy? Isn't the African novel a genre in exile, a reflection of the African writers' anxieties about their place in the colonial culture and their estrangement from the native traditions?

There is certainly no need to be defensive about the negative conditions that enable African fiction. For as Michel de Certeau has noted, there is a certain mode of writing which is generated by doubts about one's tradition and hence the need for a compensatory narrative:

> Writing is born of and treats of admitted doubt, of explicit division; in sum, of the impossibility of its own place. It articulates the constantly initial fact that the subject is *never authorized* by a place, that he could never be founded on an inalterable *cognito*, that he is always foreign to himself and forever deprived of an ontological ground, and hence is always *left over, superfluous*, always the *debtor of a death*, indebted in respect to the disappearance of a genealogical and territorial 'substance', and bound to a name lacking property.[39]

It is the writer's awareness of the lack of representation in what Fanon once called 'the settler's place'[40] that propels the colonized writer to seek an alternative narrative, a narrative which seeks not only to instal a cultural genealogy but also to mark a terrain with which the writer can identify. In this regard, argues Said, nationalism is essentially linked to exile: 'Nationalism is an assertion of belonging in and to a place, a people, a heritage. It affirms the home created by a community of language, culture and customs; and, by so doing, it fends off exile, fights to prevent its ravages.'[41]

Clearly, the African writer, exiled by the colonial culture in his or her own homeland, finds narrative to be a crucial instrument of reinventing a new community of language and culture. As Kwame Appiah has noted, an African literature was closely linked to the need by the first generations of African writers to invent an African literary tradition: 'We see the formation of a counterhegemonic discourse and the possibility of a counterhegemonic pedagogy as the decolonized subject people write about themselves, now, as the subject of a literature of their own.'[42] The desire for an African narrative, as I have already noted, is motivated by a negative consciousness – knowledge about its absence or loss. Amazingly, but not unsurprisingly, Achebe posits both the loss of, and desire for, a tradition as a certain kind of privilege.

Thus, in his autobiographical essay, 'Named for Victoria, Queen of England,' Achebe begins by showing how those Igbos who had accepted the colonial ideology – who included some of his ancestors – could not but see cultural alienation as a privilege. When Achebe was growing up, the line between Christian and non-Christian was definite and 'we tended to look down on the others. We were called in our language, "the people of the church", or "the association of God". The others we called, with the conceit appropriate to followers of the true religion, the heathen or even "the people of nothing" (MY, 65). This generation of Igbo Christians imitated and sustained a missionary discourse whose goal was to denigrate African traditions and hence effect what Mudimbe calls 'the conversion of African minds and space,'[43] but their conversion, in Achebe's view, pointed to 'ways in which the traditional society failed to satisfy everybody in it': 'Those people who found themselves out of things embraced the new way, because it promised them an easy escape from whatever constraints they were suffering under.'[44] But the dialectic of conversion and liberation would become more complex in the period of decolonization, for as I will show in my discussion of No Longer at Ease, the sons and daughters of the Igbo Christians who had renounced African traditions would become writers and nationalists bent on recovering and re-valorizing the traditions their fathers had denounced and desecrated.

The point is, we need to take Achebe seriously when he argues that it was precisely his alienation from his ancestral traditions that made him a writer. Distanced from what he sensed to be seminal to his native culture, Achebe saw the chasm between himself and Igbo traditions as a space in which he could reverse his cultural disjuncture into symbolic value. Hence his important comment, in an interview with Robert Serumaga, that it was his exclusion and distance from Igbo culture that 'made it possible for me not to take things for granted' (MY, 12). Finding himself situated at what he aptly calls 'the crossroads of cultures' (MY, 67) – at the point where the Igbo tradition intersects with the colonizing structure – Achebe adopts the crossroads as the point where even the most disparate paths inevitably meet to create something new. So the author's distance from his ancestral culture 'becomes not a separation but a bringing together like the necessary backward step which a judicious viewer may take in order to see a canvas steadily and fully' (MY, 68).

Is Achebe here claiming that the Igbo and colonial cultures mix and mingle at the crossroads in a mutual state of intelligibility? This might well happen in the writer's imagination, since he will find value in both the stories told by his relatives and his parent's books, but within a larger cultural context, the Igbo and colonial traditions exist in a state of contestation which Achebe's writing tries to mediate. Moreover, what exists at that point where the two arms of the cross meet is a void which narrative, in what I have already isolated as its compensatory function, must fill: 'I was brought up in a village and looking around you could see not the whole society, but you could see enough of what was left to be able to fill in the gaps', Achebe tells Duerden in another interview.[45] Narrative is the venerable symbolic process that fills in the gaps left open by everyday practice. Achebe recognizes that, for even his own children, being at the crossroads has both its perils and compensations when it comes to defining cultural traditions: 'They have to know more than either tradition, you see. This is the problem of being at the crossroads. You have a bit of both, and you really have to know a lot more than either. So their situation is not very easy. But it's very exciting. Those who have the energy and the will to survive at the crossroads become really very exceptional people.'[46]

Achebe's early works – notably *Things Fall Apart* and *Arrow of God* – function as mediating narratives; placed in that epistemological space between colonial modernity and African traditions, they seek to renegotiate the relationship between the two arms of the cross. Furthermore, like all literary texts committed to inventing a new tradition, Achebe's works are all experimental in nature: narrative strategies are shaped by the author's need to experiment with different forms of representation. And whatever their manifestations, these works always return to an incipient question – 'Where does the African writer come in all this?' (MY, 23). The quest for a new order of things, a new form for cultures in transformation seems to be the primary function of the African writer.

However, the process of narration is never clear-cut: often, in reflecting on the situation and function of the African writer, Achebe seems to sense confusion. Some African writers are seized by what he calls 'a spasmodic seizure of confidence' in which they proudly posit their writing as a complement to the European tradition in which they are either messiahs of emotion and soul, apropos negritude (MY, 23), or adopt their alienation as their *raison d'être* (MY, 26). In the midst of all this, the African narrative is improvisational: it must shift its forms and strategies to account for, and then represent, unstable cultural and social formations. There is, of course, another side to the coin: Africans, having been relegated to the status of inferiority in racist discourse on account of an absence of writing – now taken as what Henry Louis Gates calls 'the visible sign of reason itself'[47] – may approach this Western 'mythical practice' with temerity and doubt, a worse kind of anxiety, says Achebe, because it hinders our attempts to develop a literature of alteration:

Africa has had such a fate in the world that the very adjective *African* can still call up hideous fears of rejection. Better then to cut off links with this homeland, this liability, and become in one giant leap the universal man. Indeed, I understand the anxiety. But running away from myself seems to me a very inadequate way of dealing with an anxiety. And if writers should opt for such escapism, who is to meet the challenge? (MY, 27)

For Achebe, the best kind of writing must transcend the anxieties of its conditions of possibility and meet the African challenge. And so it would appear that at a time when much Western writing strives to transcend the authorial function, when modernist and postmodernist writing has freed itself from what Foucault calls 'the dimension of expression', and texts strive to create a space 'into which the writing subject constantly disappears',[48] Achebe's works exalt the act of writing itself and its manifest powers as a way of dealing with our anxieties of selfhood and our crisis of culture.

IV. The Project of African Literature

The literary enterprise is, of course, a source of anxiety in itself, for what enabled Achebe and his contemporaries to become writers, as he so aptly notes in 'What do African Intellectuals Read?' is accessibility to the Western Library and Dictionary (MY, 40). And let's not forget that in post-Enlightenment Europe, the Library and Dictionary, as regimes of truth and knowledge, are instruments of Western conquest. Moreover, because African writers were privileged in their societies by virtue of having mastered the Western cultural tradition and its literary canon, an African narrative is generated by what Appiah characterizes, in a term already popularized by Kane in *Ambiguous Adventure*, as a situation of double ambivalence: 'their ambiguous relations to the world of their foremothers and forefathers and to the world of the industrialized countries is part of their distinctive cultural (dis)location.'[49] In fact, writing is a symptom, and the result of, this (dis)location. This kind of cultural (dis)location has placed the African writer in what Victor Turner once characterized as the space of liminality, 'a period of structural impoverishment and symbolic enrichment': 'To be outside of a particularized social position, to cease to have a specific perspective, is in a sense to become (at least potentially) aware of all positions and arrangements and to have a total perspective.'[50] Spaces of transition and liminality are certainly indispensable to Achebe's narrative project.

Indeed, as we will see in the following chapters, Achebe locates his major novels in temporal breaks which, nevertheless, offer the possibilities of constructing a new discourse on Africa: *Things Fall Apart* and *Arrow of God* are located in the period of transition from the Igbo system of knowledge and political economy to the colonial one; *No Longer at Ease* mediates the shift from colonialism to independence; and both *A Man of the People* and *Anthills of the Savannah* represent the political and cultural crisis that marks the transition from the colonial system to a postcolonial situation. These narratives are also forms of finding a detour around 'the forms and formulations of the colonial culture' whose 'aims were somewhere the means of trivializing the whole traditional mode of life and its spiritual framework.'[51]

Let us be more specific: Achebe's motivation for writing *Things Fall Apart* was, to put it mildly, his dissatisfaction with the 'superficial picture' of the African character in Joyce Cary's *Mister Johnson*.[52] The genesis of this colonialist literature and the ideologies that succour it have been studied in eminent works by Jablow and Hammond, JanMohammed, Mudimbe and Miller: these writers have all raised important questions about the powerful influence Africa has exerted on the European imagination and the relationship between writing about Africa and the colonial enterprise itself.[53] For example, Miller has shown how European utterances on Africa – what he calls 'Africanist discourses' – are more about European ideas and concerns rather than African ones, for the gesture 'of reaching out to the most unknown part of the world and bringing it back as language . . . ultimately brings Europe face to face with nothing but itself, with the problems its own discourse imposes.'[54] And yet this discourse of European desire, however unreal and phantasmagorical it is, cannot be ignored by the African writer because it exists, indeed draws its authority, from its function as an instrument of European power over Africa. It must, therefore, be written against.

First of all, this discourse, from its Hegelian manifestations in European historiography to movies such as *Out of Africa* begins by denying the existence of an African subject; the African is a naked body which must be written into being by the colonizer; and even then, this African figure is always a broken image in the mirror since it will never satisfy the colonizer's desire to see himself or herself reflected in the other; in this tradition of colonialist discourse, notes Achebe, the African is 'an unfinished European' (MY, 3). Secondly, this unfinished product, this broken image in the mirror, is a reflection of 'the desire – one might indeed say the need – in Western psychology to set up a foil to Europe, a place of negations at once remote and vaguely familiar in comparison with which Europe's own state of spiritual grace will be manifest' (HI, 2). This European discourse on Africa must be countered because of its clear function as a tool of Western hegemony. In discussing the relationship between power and knowledge in the colonizing structure, Achebe asserts that for the colonial mind, a claim to know 'native psychology and institutions,' is already a form of control – 'understanding being a precondition for control and control constituting adequate proof of understanding' (MY, 5).

The third reason why colonialist discourse must be denied its authority is a logical consequence of the first two: the colonial academy marshalls a large body of knowledge to represent the African as a way of managing the 'people without history.' In the words of Governor Clifford of Nigeria, writing in 1923, the 'scientific study of tribal origins and institutions is vital to successful administration.'[55] And thus ethnography and colonialism will walk hand in hand claiming to restore the African to history, but in the process evoking a mythical Africa which 'as setting and backdrop . . . eliminates the African as human factor' (HI, 8). In any case, Achebe conceives African writing as a project that seeks to reinvent Africa within a context that 'identifies the dual sources of the situation of the modern African text.'[56] His commitment is defined by a simple question: what does it mean to be an African writer today and what does African connote to the Other?

> I'm an Igbo writer, because this is my basic culture; Nigerian, African and a writer . . . no, black first, then a writer. Each of these identities does call for a certain kind of commitment on my part. I must see what it is to be black – and this means being sufficiently intelligent to know how the world is moving and how the black people fare in the world. This is what it means to be black. Or an African – the same: what does Africa mean to the world? When you see an African what does it mean to a white man?[57]

'What does Africa mean to the world today?' This is the central question that characterizes Achebe's mode of being, the nature of his texts, and his vision. When he talks about an 'African experience,' he does not assume that this Africa exists independently of the colonial discourse that invented the continent in the first place; writing is a practice geared toward the appropriation of Africa from colonialist rhetoric, but this Africa, too, must be invented. Hence Achebe's belief that every literature speaks of a particular place and evolves out of the necessity of its history and the destiny of its people (MY, 7). The words 'necessity' and 'destiny' have a particular resonance in Achebe's critical vocabulary: one connotes what needs to be done, the other what is desired. Necessity is undoubtedly a reference to the different historical and cultural contexts that have moulded the writer's vision; destiny, on the other hand, expresses the writer's desire to transcend historical necessity – the 'deep rooted need to alter things within that situation, to find for myself a little more room than has been allowed me in the world' (MY, 14). To write is to demand one's space and terrain.

And what makes this demand so fascinating is that in spite of Achebe's indebtedness to an alien form (in this case the novel) and language, he still dreams of recovering an African aesthetics. It is not enough, says Achebe, to try to establish the 'truth' about Igbo culture through alienated systems of thought and method; 'anyone seeking an insight into their world must seek it along their own way' (MY, 94). For Achebe, duality is the condition for signification in Igbo culture, and as my reading will show, in his fiction, too. We have already seen this duality embodied in the idea of the crossroads, but it is also represented in other signs and concepts such as the marketplace and the concept of *chi* in Igbo cosmology. In a masterful reading of Onitsha market and its literature, Achebe provides pointers to the nature of his own writing by insisting that, in seeking to establish why 'pamphlet literature' developed in Onitsha, it is not enough to evoke geographical, political, economic and 'other rational explanations,' for there will 'always remain an area of shadows where some (at least) of the truth will seek to hide' (MY, 90). The unnameable, the area of shadows where truth hides itself from the analyst, the unconscious side of history, 'the esoteric region from which creativity sallies forth at will to manifest itself' – or even the Fanonist 'zone of occult instability' – is the region where the imagination thrives (MY, 90).

Indeed, Onitsha becomes, in Achebe's analysis, a space defined by 'a play of differences'[58]: the town is located at the place where the Niger 'has answered many names, seen a multitude of sights'; its claim to difference might not be justified by historical data, but it feels 'different from the peoples and places in its vicinity' (MY, 90). Above all Onitsha is, like the figure of the crossroads, a site of temporal differences, duality, and reversal;[59] '[I]t can be opposite things at once': 'It sits at the crossroads of the world. It has two faces – a Benin face and an Igbo face – and can see the four directions, either squarely or with the tail of an eye' (MY, 90-1). As a place of exchange, Onitsha rejects singular meanings; as a historical phenomena, the town stands as the mark of the cash nexus that dominated the colonial economy, an economic system which weakened traditional Igbo modes of production, and yet sustained essential mechanisms of this culture, including the extended family. A similar kind of duality and reversal will be evident in Achebe's novel.

Duality appeals to Achebe precisely because it produces a multiplicity of meanings and indeterminate zones of representation which generate narrative invention. In another sense, I believe, this duality allows the author, like his Igbo ancestors, to contest the central claims of Western metaphysics and its dependence on 'Reason.' As Derrida aptly puts it: 'Metaphysics – the white mythology which reassembles and reflects the culture of the West: the white man takes his own mythology, Indo-European mythology, his own *logos*, that is the *mythos* of his idiom, for the universal form of that he must still wish to call Reason.'[60] Such a claim will not make sense to the Igbo mind which thrives on a temporal reversal of concepts and categories. For the Igbo, says Achebe, there are no fixed taxonomies: 'Wherever Something stands, Something Else will stand beside it. Nothing is absolute. *I am the truth, the way and the life* would be called blasphemous or simply absurd for is it not well known that a man may worship Ogwugwu to perfection and yet be killed by Udo' (MY, 94). We will later see how dualism – what Cole and Aniakor aptly call 'the dynamic relationship between opposites'[61] – generates the Achebe novel.

Achebe's evocation of an African, or rather Igbo aesthetic, is already an attempt to deal with a more central problem in his works – the question of history and historiography. The intellectual influence in this regard is Fanon who had argued that the 'cultured individuals of the colonized race,' in their demand for national culture, situate their action and take their stand 'in the field of history.'[62] In fact, in one of his early essays, Achebe had seen the task of the writer in a new nation as analogous to that of those historians who 'everywhere are rewriting the stories of the new nations – replacing short, garbled, despised history with a more sympathetic account.'[63] Now, the key point in this assertion is not Achebe's claim that our history has to be rewritten to be recovered from the colonial tradition, but the important collapsing of the terms 'history' and 'story.' Colonial historians argued we had no history because they did not consider our stories to be history, but what is the difference between history and story? Well, it seems that the West has finally caught up with us because, as de·Certeau and others have argued so eloquently, historiography already bears in its name 'the paradox – almost an oxymoron – of a relation established between two antinomic terms, between the real and discourse.'[64]

Thus, Achebe's archaeology of the African past,' apart from trying to make the crucial connection between the real and discourse, is an attempt to evoke our stories to contest the claims of their history. And yet, it is within the confinements of colonial history that Achebe's narrative revolution has to take place. There is a simple reason for this – colonialism engenders the most radical reorganization of African society in recent times. This important point has been made more clearly by Mudimbe in his study of the colonizing structure and the question of marginality in *The Invention of Africa*:

> Although in African history the colonial experience represents but a brief moment from the perspective of today, this moment is still charged and controversial, since, to say the least, it signified a new historical form and the possibility of radically new types of discourses on African traditions and cultures.[65]

African cultures are negated within these historical forms, but it is within them that new traditions must evolve and a new identity be constructed. If colonial history is a means of transforming 'non-European areas into fundamentally European constructs', as Mudimbe has argued, and of transforming 'the space of the other into a field of expansion for a system of production',[66] the anti-colonial writer and the nationalist had to have a common ideological agenda: They needed to alter the arrangement which kept them and their people out in the rain and the heat of the sun' (MY, 15). For Achebe, altering the European arrangement of Africa is an important narrative function.

Now, Achebe is aware that colonialist criticism has the tendency to dismiss the African novel 'on the grounds that it is a peculiarly Western genre'; but isn't the African writer's appropriation of the privileged discursive instruments of the West what gives the African novel its subversive force? To answer his critics, Achebe finds a masterful analogy in Afro-American cultural formation:

> Did not the black people in America, deprived of their own musical instruments, take the trumpet and the trombone and blow them as they had never been blown before, as indeed they were not designed to be blown? And the result, was it not jazz? Is any one going to say that this was a loss to the world or that those first negro slaves who began to play around with discarded instruments of their masters should have played waltzes and foxtrots and more Salvation Army hymn tunes (MY, 17)?

The power of a form – whether it is music or fiction – does not solely lie in its claim to be original, but in its irruption of the already-written discourse. The borrowed instrument – which the dominant culture has discarded because it was supposed to have outlived its usefulness – is bent around and used against the culture that produced it.

Thus, the novel may be the genre that is most alien to African cultures, but it is also the most amenable to representing the historical transformations and contradictions engendered by the colonial enterprise. The world of the novel, argues Culler, is a world of semiotics – 'the creation and organization of signs not simply in order to produce meaning but in order to produce a world charged with meaning.'[67] Achebe's novels are dominated by signs and symbols of culture which always beg for multiple interpretations. Such signs, as I will show in my reading of *Things Fall Apart* and *Arrow of God*, are marshalled to serve two opposed functions: first, signs of everyday life (greetings, chalk drawings, foot etc.) are intended to call our attention to the Igbo people as a community with its own sense of order and disorder, and its own unknowable occult zones. The need to show the colonized culture as unknowable is particularly important because colonial power, and its attendant economy of representation 'produces the colonized as a fixed reality which is at once an 'other' and yet entirely knowable and visible.'[68] Second, the novel allows the author to produce a semiotic machine that displaces hegemonic ideologies and creates alternative systems of meaning.

In this context, my reading of Achebe's fiction in the chapters that follow assumes that they are cultural texts that seek, in Bakhtin's words, to explore 'the details and subtleties of ideological structures.'[69] If in the foregoing pages I have sought to highlight the relationship between Achebe's novels and other writing practices and ideologies, it is because my ultimate goal is to return his texts to the ideological environment that produced them. However, I share Bakhtin's premise that literature is not a slave of any ideological environment but a sector within an ideology:

> Literature is one of the independent parts of the surrounding ideological reality, occupying a special place in it in the form of definite, organized philological works which have their own specific structures. The literary structure, like every ideological structure, refracts the generating socioeconomic reality, and does so in its own way. But, at the same time, in its 'content,' literature reflects and refracts the reflections and refractions of other ideological spheres (ethics, epistemology, political doctrines, religion, etc). That is, in its 'content' literature reflects the whole of the ideological horizon of which it is itself a part.[70]

My concern is definitely with the mechanisms which Achebe's texts use, in their 'own way,' to refract, rather than simply imitate, the socioeconomic realities that generated them in the first place. My premise is that the 'way' of the text and its 'content' meet and become inseparable on the ideological horizon.

Moreover, form and content will be shown to have become dissolved, at least in the methods of reading I adopt, on the narrative and linguistic level. I will be arguing that in every text Achebe has written narrative strategies and linguistic structures are closely related; language and the ideologies that sustain it are key thematic concerns in Achebe's novels, closely aligned with, and often a symptom of, the 'crisis of the soul' he writes about and the cultural transformations that mark his fiction. If I may borrow Lévi-Strauss's formulation, language is a condition of culture: 'language can be said to be a condition of culture because the material out of which language is built is of the same type as the material out of which the whole culture is built.'[71] If Igbo culture 'lays a great deal of emphasis on differences, on dualities, on otherness,' as Achebe tells Ogbaa, then language in this culture will undoubtedly signify those conditions.[72]

But I suspect Achebe would also agree with Barthes's notorious claim that 'A writer is someone to whom language is a problem, who experiences its profundity, not its instrumentality nor its beauty.'[73] In any case, to reread Achebe, we must return his texts to their conditions of possibility or ideological environment – to the sometimes uninterrupted but also often displaced history of Igbo and Nigerian culture – and restore 'to the surface of the text the repressed and buried reality of this fundamental history'[74] and discuss the linguistic and narrative forms in which it is represented.

2
Writing, Culture & Domination

Things Fall Apart

Another reason for insisting upon exteriority is that I believe it needs to be made clear about cultural discourse and exchange within a culture that what is commonly circulated by it is not 'truth' but representations ... language itself is a highly organized and encoded system, which employs many devices to express, indicate, exchange messages and information ... In any instance of a written language, there is no such thing as a delivered presence, but a re-presence, or a representation.

— Edward Said, Orientalism

I. The Generation of a Cultural Text

So far we have seen how the theoretical questions that have haunted Achebe's writing career – the writer's relationship with his dual traditions, the value of history, and the possibilities of an African literature in a colonial language – are all prompted by the desire to initiate a discourse of resistance and to re-present Africans other than they have been presented in colonialist discourse. The 'deeper meaning of teaching' as a function of the fictional enterprise, Achebe tells Nwoga in 1964, involves the writer in a radical reorientation of cultural discourse as it presently exists: 'what I think a novelist can teach is something very fundamental, namely to indicate to his readers, to put it crudely, that we in Africa did not hear of culture for the first time from Europeans.'[1] However, this limpid theoretical position on the function of the novel as a form of cultural intelligibility, like many of the reflections on narrative examined in the previous section, comes after the fact – Achebe will have been a novelist for many years before he becomes a critic of his own writings.

Indeed, when he turns his attention to the conditions in which his first novel was produced, there is a highly important tentativeness in the author's theoretical position: 'Although I did not set about it consciously in that solemn way, I know that my first book, *Things Fall Apart*, was an act of atonement with my past, the ritual return and homage of a prodigal son.'[2] Two things need to be stressed here: first, the 'solemn' (as opposed to gentile) motives for writing the novel are unconscious, they are only clear after the event; second, writing is an act of ritual atonement, a compensation for something already lost. There is still a larger question that needs to be addressed as a way of clarifying my reading agenda: how is a particular mode of writing established, especially when a writer feels – as Achebe did at the beginning of his career – that he had no positive literary models to emulate or precursors with which to identify? In view of his self-conscious desire to produce an African literature which will use the language of the hegemonic culture to express the desire for cultural liberation, Achebe cannot start writing until he locates himself in a strategic linguistic and ideological position in relation to something else – an obscurant colonial tradition. The narrative of liberation derives its power from the tradition it seeks to reject, revise, or appropriate and set in a different direction.

Indeed, as Roland Barthes has observed, resisting the dominant tradition is an important precondition for modern literature: 'For a century now, every mode of writing . . . has been an exercise in reconciliation with, or aversion from that objectified Form inevitably met by the writer on his way, and which he must scrutinize, challenge and accept with all its consequences, since he cannot ever destroy it without destroying himself as a writer.'[3] The pertinence of this assertion, in relation to the writer in a colonial situation, is already evident in Achebe's description of writing as an act of ritual atonement. To write is to reconcile oneself to a past foreclosed by the experience of colonialism; it is an archaeological gesture that seeks to recover the historicity of Igbo life and culture. But before this act of restitution becomes possible, it must overcome the 'objectified Forms' of colonialist discourse, the representation of Africa as what Hammond and Jablow have succinctly called 'a field for the free play of European fantasy.'[4]

And so in reading *Things Fall Apart* we must not only reflect on the social and historical conditions that created this text, but also recall what was written before it, for to clear what Bloom would call 'imaginative space for himself,' the writer must confront and contest his precursors.[5] As a form of ritual atonement, writing is here posited as an act of cultural misappropriation, for when a text is haunted by unpleasant cultural memories, as most anticolonial texts are, then 'its role is to re-utter definitively discourse whose presence has become tyrannical, tinselly discourse, fossilized discourse.'⁶ Failure to interpret Achebe's novel against the tyrannical discourse of colonialism always provides some fascinating misreadings such as Wole Soyinka's claim – in his attempt to show that Achebe unintentionally bolsters Negritude – that 'Things Fall Apart is content to portray a tragic passage in history and leave it thus.'⁷ However, Achebe is not content to let things express themselves, for as we have already seen in the epigraph from Edward Said's important text on 'Orientalism', writing is already a form of representing something which predates it.⁸ ·

As I hope to show in this chapter, Achebe develops techniques – and promotes ideologies – whose primary purpose is to contest, and wrestle with, the silent shadows and forms of colonialist discourse. He has become (if I may borrow John Hearne's expression) an African Jacob wrestling with the Angel of Western history.⁹ My contention here is that if we do not tune our ears to the written and unwritten discourse that blocks Achebe's attempt to recover the essential forms of Igbo culture in Things Fall Apart – whether we believe such a recovery possible or not – then we will often miss the value of the novel as a form of cultural formation. The first question we need to take up, then, relates to the strategies Achebe develops to reply to his colonialist precursors, or rather to turn the Western fantasy on Africa upside down, a gesture of reversal which, I will insist, makes it possible for Achebe to initiate narratives of resistance. A reading of Things Fall Apart which fails to relate it to the discourse that shadows it, misses the revolutionary nature of Achebe's text.

Consider, then, the famous opening paragraph of the novel:

> Okonkwo was well known throughout the nine villages and even beyond. His fame rested on solid personal achievements. As a young man of eighteen he had brought honour to his village by throwing Amalinze the Cat. Amalinze was the great wrestler who for seven years was unbeaten, from Umuofia to Mbaino. He was called the Cat because his back would never touch the earth. It was this man that Okonkwo threw in a fight which the old man agreed was one of the fiercest since the founder of their town engaged a spirit of the wild for seven days and seven nights.¹⁰

A reading of this paragraph which is not informed by what I have called the silent discourse of colonialism (silent only because it is not in the text itself) and the exterior historical circumstances of Achebe's text, will be condemned to repeat the dead generic conventions of the novel. In other words, the most obvious elements in this description – the introduction of a hero, his placement in a temporal and dramatic situation, and his dynamic relationship with a discernible culture – are things which the novel, especially in the tradition of realism, takes for granted. But if we read this paragraph within a larger discursive context, then the same elements acquire a different meaning and insist on being read as marks of difference *vis-à-vis* the colonial discourse that has fixed Africans as a people without history.

Now, it is true that in the above passage Achebe seems to eschew judgements: in fact, his representations here and elsewhere are intended to naturalize Okonkwo's situation, to show him and his village in terms which have often been described as universal. Thus, while many other novelists might be tempted to highlight Okonkwo and his culture, Achebe adopts an algebraic strategy: this is a dramatic moment, but nothing about it is exotic or out of place. But even in this rejection of exoticism, Achebe is contesting the representation of African in the novels of Conrad and Cary who have the propensity to represent the continent as either a blank space or a monstrous presence. Thus, the ordinariness of the language in the above description represents a strategic decision, on Achebe's part, to move his novel away from the phantasmal images of Africa in colonialist fiction and rhetoric. Achebe also needs to contest such colonialist writing because what it represses in the African – subjectivity, history and representation – are the key ingredients in the reconstruction of African cultures.

To understand the narrative techniques which Achebe adopts in *Things Fall Apart*, we need to examine the ways in which the colonial tradition represses the African character, African history, and African modes of representation. In the first case, in the discourse against which Achebe writes – a discourse which is evident not only in the African romances of Cary but also in the 'scientific' reports of government anthropologists – Africa is represented as what David Caroll aptly calls 'a landscape without figures, an Africa without Africans.'[11] The African has no character because he or she exists solely as a projection of European desire. Secondly, the African has no sense of history: as the famous British imperial historian, Margery Perham, writes in her study of Lord Lugard and the invention of Nigeria, the Igbo and other groups in the South East of Nigeria 'have no history before the coming of the Europeans.'[12] Thirdly, not only can these people not represent themselves (since they have no tradition of writing), there is a sense in which colonialist discourse derives its authority from the claim that the Igbo, and other African peoples, cannot be represented. As Christopher Miller asserts in his incisive reading of Conrad's *Heart of Darkness*, 'Africanist writers felt themselves to be cut off from comprehension in some way; but they would thematize this by depicting the African mind as cut off from representation and signification.'[13] 'We are cut off from the comprehension of our surroundings,' cries the narrator in Conrad's novel. But the European has a certain advantage over the 'native' cut off from similar situations: the former can rationalize and hence represent what is absent; the latter do not even understand their mental confinement, since they are not even aware of their 'objective' history.

27

Let us bring this paradox closer to Achebe's home. Let us see how it functions in the anthropological writings of G.T. Basden, a missionary turned anthropologist who was not only a friend of Achebe's father, but as Robert Wren has shown, a person who provided an important intertextual reference for Achebe.[14] In the preface to his 1921 account, *Among the Ibos of Nigeria*, Basden claims that his authority as a writer derives from his 'actual experience' of the Igbos. Nevertheless, Basden hastens to add, 'it is a practical impossibility for the European to comprehend fully the subtleties of the native character,' for the African, unlike the European, lacks logic, the key ingredient that makes understanding, and hence representation, possible:

> Let not this be thought strange, for the black man himself does not know his own mind. He does the most extraordinary things, and cannot explain why he does them. He is not controlled by logic: he is the victim of circumstance, and his policy is very largely one of drift. The will of the tribe or family, expressed or implied, permeates his whole being, and is the deciding factor in every detail of his life.[15]

For Achebe to write, he must show that the very things that are supposed to cut the African off from representation – the absence of reason and logic and the dominance of collective consciousness – exist only in the mind of the colonialist writer and have no 'fidelity to some great original.'[16] Certainly, Okonkwo knows his mind, as do many other characters in the book; in fact, his tragedy arises, contrary to Basden's assertion above, from pursuing the logic or his own existence too much, pushing the communal ethos to the limits and hence undermining it in the process. I will return to this question later in this chapter. What I want to emphasise here is the importance of the African's ostensible lack of subjectivity, history, and reason to *Things Fall Apart*: writing the novel in reverse (in a manner of speaking) Achebe generates his narrative by restoring the same (absent) elements to the African character and his or her community.

Thus, if we return to the opening paragraph of *Things Fall Apart*, keeping in mind the unspoken opposition between Achebe's literary ideology and colonialist discourse, we can see how things which we initially took for granted have acquired greater significance. The novel begins by creating a unique subject (Okonkwo) who is placed within a functional, cultural and temporal situation. Throughout the novel, the narrator will underscore the tripartite relationship between the subject, culture, and time. Okonkwo is unique because of his extraordinary capacity for self-engenderment – represented here by his wrestling prowess – but his subjectivity is only possible because of the cultural framework in which he is cast. This explains the curious linkage in the first paragraph between the character and the founding of Umuofia: Okonkwo's wrestling victory is a temporal marker, a reminder of a distant time in which Umuofia itself was founded; it is the evocation of a historicity and, as it were, a mode of cultural production.

Achebe evokes this temporal situation not merely to show that the Umuofians are a people with a history, but also to address one of the central problematics in the Igbo epistemology – the question of origins and foundations. A leading historian of Igbo history has framed the problem in this way: 'No historical question arouses more interest among the present-day Igbos than the enquiry, "where did the Igbo come from" . . . It is as if the question of origins contained, somewhere, a key to the elusive problem of Igbo identity.'[17] The opening of *Things Fall Apart* can be read as an imaginary response to the problems of genealogy and cultural identity which have haunted Igbo culture: here, Okonkwo, the cultural hero, can be seen as a surrogate founding father, comparable to the original founder of the village; his context, Umuofia, has a definitive consciousness of its genealogy which is represented by its magic and war-medicine: '. . . its most potent war-medicine was as old as the clan itself. Nobody knew how old' (p. 8).

The novel is indeed dominated by a sense of things happening or taking place historically: the main events in the narrative follow a logical sequence; the village social structure and its system of exchange and beliefs follows an established calender, a signifier of the culture's sensitivity to the process of time and the fundamental connection of people, things and words. Thus, the feast of the new yams is the form in which Igbo culture is represented in time because: 'The new year must begin with tasty, fresh yams and not the shrivelled and fibrous crop of the previous year' (p. 26). Later in the novel, in a dramatic rendering of the *egwugwu* – 'the spirits of the ancestors' (p. 62) – administering justice, we are told that the nine *egwugwu* 'had grown out of the nine sons of the first father of the clan' (p. 63). In a sense, Achebe is keen to demonstrate a fundamental linkage between a mode of production, a system of beliefs and a kinship structure.

What we are dealing with here is not merely a re-enactment of the past, although the novel is often read as such, but a discourse on the nature of history and its meaning to the people who live it. Indeed, as Henderson observes in his seminal study of temporality among the Onitsha Igbo, traditions of origins represent 'a reasonable coherent system of constitutive symbolism, a system that contains evidence not only of what the community meant to its people but also of the development of that meaning over time.'[18] Even the narrative techniques which Achebe adopts underscore this sense of the temporal: the novel opens by placing Okonkwo in the present, but immediately represents shifting time frames – we are taken back to the time when Okonkwo was eighteen, to the ancient founding of Umuofia, and back to the present again (p. 3). More importantly, the narrator often uses utterances that place characters in a temporal context, such as the diegetic connection between Okonkwo as a young man and as an elder: 'That was many years ago, twenty years or more, and during this time Okonkwo's fame had grown like a bush-fire in the harmattan' (p. 3). So, we always read the novel with a parallel sense of the present (the enunciating moment) and the past (the enunciated situation).

Moreover, as George Lukacs argues in *The Theory of the Novel*, time is a constitutive principle of the novel as a genre: narration and plotting are both predicated on a notion of time as duration; time passes and in the process triggers a multiplicity of oppositions, between character and society, nature and culture, movement and stasis.[19] And if we recall Miller's apt observation that 'narrative is the translation of time into language', and the Conradian representation of Africa as a 'perpetual childhood', a place trapped in the past, then we will appreciate Achebe's insistence on the constitutive power of time in his text.[20] Far from offering us what Soyinka calls 'a poignant affirmation of a basically secure, traditional society,'[21] *Things Fall Apart* is a narrative of a community where 'everyone speaks from somewhere which always indicates a historicity, a becoming, and their questions.'[22]

As a matter of fact, Umuofia's attempt to represent itself as an organic and unchanging community is always confronted with, and often challenged by, temporal and spatial progression. Similarly, characters find it difficult to follow an established routine in their quest for self-fulfillment. For example, very early in the book Okonkwo's first efforts to reinvent himself are questioned by time: the year he borrows yams from Nwakibie is described as 'the worst year in living memory. Nothing happened at its proper time; it was either too early or too late' (p. 16). Time, as we will see later, frustrates the character's vision of a natural order of things, of life as a logical process in which hard work leads to success; instead of being an ally of nature, time disrupts the natural process and thus almost destroys the political economy (that of the yam) which makes 'manhood' possible.

Thus, although the process of time signifies Umuofia's historicity and emphasizes the Igbo conception of history, this is not always a positive process. Indeed, the overwhelming sense of spatial and temporal progress we have when we read the first part of the book is radically reversed in the second part: now, in exile, Okonkwo conceives time in a less eschatological sense, as a process of loss and denial. Okonkwo will work hard to try and rebuild his life in exile: '[B]ut it was like beginning life anew without the vigor and enthusiasm of youth' (p. 92). Time is henceforth measured by the standard of exile – 'It was in the second year of Okonkwo's exile that his friend, Obierika came to visit him . . .' (p. 96) – a figure of displacement rather than fulfilment.

Significantly, the same negative conception of time determines the representation of the Igbo community from the moment Okonkwo is exiled. 'Abame is no more', Obierika tells Okonkwo during the former's visit to Mbaino, 'Abame has been wiped out' (p. 97). Hitherto, communities previously represented as presences (known because of their magic or wrestlers), will acquire historical significance as absences or displaced terrains. Okonkwo's identity had previously been shaped by his dominance over Umuofia, and his success 'over time'; now he has become decentred, defined often by his temporal belatedness: 'Seven years was a long time to be away from one's clan. A man's place was not always there waiting for him' (p. 121). In the meantime, Umuofia has changed in ways the hero could not have anticipated and he no longer beats to the drum of time. But if Okonkwo's destruction is aided by historical change, as I will argue later in this chapter, he has given Achebe the opportunity to denigrate the whole colonial ideology that the Igbo are a people without a sense of history. Okonkwo's tragedy, and the social transformation of Umuofia, takes place in dramatic moments marked by time and historicity.

II. The Spirit of Things

The immense popularity of *Things Fall Apart* has largely been due to Achebe's evocation of an 'authentic Igbo world', and countless interpretations of the novel have been written to confirm and celebrate the author's reproduction of an 'authentic' Igbo culture and its essences. Indeed, Achebe has encouraged this mode of reading his novels by emphatically claiming that what he is doing 'is presenting a total world and a total life as it is lived in that world . . . I am writing about my people in the past and in the present, and I have to create for them the world in which they live and move and have their being.'[23] And yet, however appealing this mimetic claim might be, however tantalizing the notion of an empirical order reproduced in narrative might be to the reader of Achebe's texts, it must be resisted because it is not possible for the writer to appeal to an original notion of Igbo culture; like many other cultural products, the Igbo world is only accessible to us as it has been represented by others. Igbo reality, insofar as it is available to Achebe, comes to him (and hence the reader) mediated by the novelist's sources, both Igbo and colonial. This is why it is important for us to remember Said's stricture that the object of a reading is not a truth; rather, 'the things to look at are style, figures of speech, setting, narrative devices, historical and social circumstances, *not* the correctness of the representation nor its fidelity to some great original.'[24]

In examining the ways Achebe (re)presents Igbo culture, then, my primary concern here are the semiotic codes which Achebe evokes to represent his people, codes which are important not only because they evoke the schemas and grammar of this culture, but also point to the ways it represents and interprets itself. The Igbo world which Achebe seeks to represent in this novel is dependent on certain signs and images, a collection of social codes and signs, which are central to the development of meanings in *Things Fall Apart*. The codes are important in Achebe's attempt to evoke, through narration, what Michel Foucault calls 'the empirical order'. According to Foucault, '[T]he fundamental codes of a culture – those governing its language, its schemas of perception, its exchanges, its techniques, its values, the hierarchy of its practices – establish for every man, from the very first, the empirical order with which he will be dealing and within which he will be at home.'[25] As a hermeneutical text – one that refers to 'those elements by which it is constituted and communicated'[26] – isn't *Things Fall Apart* also a commentary on Igbo culture and the conditions that enable or restrict it?

We can address this question, in the first instance, by showing how Achebe's text painstakingly represents Igbo culture – in different scenarios and historical situations – in the process of providing interpretations about itself, or reflecting on the primary linguistic codes that govern it. The book is packed with countless semiotic codes – from the mundaneness of the breaking of kola nuts (p. 5) to the dance of the ancestral spirits (p. 62). Some of these signs are intended to provide a cultural background to the characters, but they should not be reduced to 'local colour'; rather, they are Achebe's ways of pointing to the values that govern this society; signs are already posited as ideological symbolizations of a cultural order and its spirit of things. Thus, the simple gesture of breaking kola nuts and drawing lines on the floor is a form of communication between characters and their ancestors (p. 5); the painting of walls with red earth and the drawing of 'patterns on them in white, yellow and dark green' (p. 27) is itself a homage to the earth goddess Ani. One can quote endless examples from the text, but what is more pertinent here is the function these signs serve in the culture itself. For these signs constitute the very grammar of the Igbo world: they function as objects of knowledge which represent either meanings which have become so natural that ordinary people can recognize them, or more hermetic meanings which need to be uncovered by specialists, the diviners and the *egwugwu*.

For the Igbo, signs have an affinity to, indeed signify, a cosmology – what Victor Uchendu calls 'an explanatory device and a guide to conduct' and 'an action system'; as an explanatory system, 'Igbo cosmology theorizes about the origin and character of the universe.'[27] The 'logocentric' linkage between language and being becomes in effect a precondition for an empirical cultural order in *Things Fall Apart*, and there are persistent appeals to a natural order of things and a natural knowledge. Early in the text, for example, when Udo's wife is killed in a neighbouring village, we are told that the neighbouring clans 'naturally knew' about Umuofia's magical powers; when the transgressing village compensates Umuofia with a lad of fifteen and a virgin, '[T]he elders, or *ndichie*, met to hear a report of Okonkwo's mission. At the end they decided, as everybody knew they would, that the girl should go to Ogbuefi Udo to replace his murdered wife' (p. 9). So the meeting of the elders is, strictly speaking, a formality; they put into effect a cultural practice which follows a pre-determined order of knowledge. When worshippers go to 'seek knowledge' at the shrine of the Oracle Agbala, they are also seeking an interpretation for the already 'written' codes of culture and even nature. When Unoka goes to consult the oracle of Agbala, for example, the priestess is agitated by the very thought that Okonkwo's father does not know how to interpret his own situation: 'You have offended neither the gods nor your fathers. And when a man is at peace with his gods and his ancestors, his harvest will be good or bad according to the strength of his arm. You, Unoka, are known in all the clan for the weakness of your machete and hoe ... Go home and work like a man' (p. 13). In effect, the priestess reaffirms truths which are already common knowledge. However, the priestess's utterances combine the voices (and truths) of nature, culture and the cosmos: 'She was full of the power of her god, and she was greatly feared' (p. 12). Her voice is also an important link between the ideal order of nature and the ideal of 'manhood' which is enhanced by that order; she hence scorns Unoka because of his deviation from an empirical system which manifests itself in human labour (p. 13).

Of course, the relationship between being, language, and nature is one which recent literary theory has sought to negate in radical and sometimes unconvincing ways. In his criticism of the 'logocentric tradition', for example, Derrida has scorned the heritage of 'that logocentricism which is also a phonocentricism: absolute proximity of voice and being, of voice and the meaning of being, of voice and the ideality of meaning.'[28] However, in *Things Fall Apart*, Achebe seems to be making a case for the absolute and inescapable linkage between being and voice. After all, the most obvious sign of the destruction of Igbo culture and its authority is the repression of Igbo voices at the end of the novel when colonialism imposes its grammatology and henceforth represents the African as a subject with neither a voice nor a logos. Clearly, writing in the colonial situation, as an act of restitution, demands a process of reversal – the reconstitution of the repressed being and its voice. In *Things Fall Apart*, the act of narration is often a celebration of the power of the Igbo voice.

The central symbolic function of the circle of culture in the novel is closely aligned to the power of the Igbo voice.[29] This circle of culture, which is evident – and often described – whenever Umuofia meets, functions as a synecdoche of Igbo culture and a symbol of its cosmological configuration; it is the sign of 'an organic community' and even contains within its formation a philosophy of language. Thus, the circle is preceded, or summoned into being, by the beating of the drums; these drums provide listeners with the surrogate language of the cosmos. When the drums beat in a persistent and unchanging tone, we are told, '[T]heir sound was no longer a separate thing from the living village. It was like the pulsation of its heart. It throbbed in the air, in the sunshine, and even in the trees, and filled the village with excitement' (p. 31). The concept of language as a form of power and possession has already been underscored earlier in the book when it is suggested that the diviner of Agbala speaks a different language when she is 'full of the power of her god' (p. 12). Now, as Umuofia congregates around the sacred silk-cotton tree, the drummers 'were possessed by the spirit of the drums' (p. 33). The phonocentric language of the drum has hence transferred the community to what Soyinka would call its 'pristine existence': at this 'fourth stage', language has become 'the embryo of thought and music where myth is daily companion.'[30]

In ideological terms, the circle has a dual function: it allows Umuofia to evoke its identity in an organic world of resemblance, similitude, and order; but it also allows the narrator to expose the elements of alienation and disjunction which this order seeks to conceal. For in this circle that celebrates unity and totality, '[I]t was clear from the way the crowd stood or sat that the ceremony was for men. There were many women, but they looked on from the fringe like outsiders' (p. 62). In view of this deliberate exclusion of women from the circle of culture, how do we interpret its claim to represent wholeness and communal identity? There are two possible readings: On the one hand, we could argue that the circle is no longer a sign of cultural totality but of a lost or desired utopian ideal, holding to its desire for totality against social practices which have marginalized women. On the other hand, we can read this circle as the symbol of phallocentricism – meanings are defined and controlled by men and cultural identity is only achieved through the exclusion of women.

I will deal with the latter proposition later in this chapter. What I want to show here is how Igbo culture has created a regime of meanings which gives its members insight into their conditions of existence, and yet this insight is achieved through omission or a certain kind of blindness. Can culture have value without a blindspot? There is no doubt that before 'things fall apart' in Umuofia, the circle of culture is shown to have ideological value because it represents the ideal, or possibly the illusion, of completeness and identity. This is why it is important for the women, although they are excluded from the inner circle, to have a presence on the fringes of the ceremony (p. 62); we are reminded that there are even ceremonies, such as the *uri*, in which 'the central figures were the bride and her mother' (p. 77). Thus, cultural circles have ideological value because they are complete: at Obierika's daughter's wedding, the in-laws 'sat in a half-moon, thus completing a circle with their hosts' (p. 81); when Uchendu's son marries, the members of the *umuada* 'sat in a big circle on the ground and the bride sat in the centre with a hen in her right hand' (p. 93). The completion of the circle denotes a harmonious relationship between the various elements who make up a family or kinship group.

Conversely, the first manifestation of cultural crisis in the novel will be the break-up of this circle: those people who are excluded from it, because they are not considered to be full members of the community (the *osu*, for example), will become the colonizer's weapon of exposing the contradictions which Umuofia sought to repress (p. 101). When Okonkwo returns to Umuofia after seven years of exile, he will no longer have a place in the circle of the 'nine masked spirits' (p. 121); when he kills the court messenger, Umuofia, which had come together in a circle to make a last stand breaks down into 'tumult' (p. 144). Umuofia is, of course, defeated because it is disunited, and this disunity has important implications for the way the culture understands its own nature and situation. The hermeneutical circle – the process by which the culture understands and interprets itself – is predicated on a relationship of parts to the whole. In David Couzens Hoy's words, 'part and whole are related in a circular way: in order to understand the whole, it is necessary to understand the parts, while to understand the parts it is necessary to have some comprehension of the whole.'[31] And so, what we see in this breaking up gesture is not merely the disintegration of a culture but also the fundamental ideology on which it was built – the appeal to unity and totality. What we witness at the end of the novel is the collapse of what Sahlins calls 'meaning' as a 'symbolic scheme' which invokes the unity of the cultural order: 'And it is this meaningful system that defines all functionality . . . for functional value is always relative to the given cultural scheme.'[32] When Umuofia's scheme of meanings is colonized, the function of its culture is rapidly eroded.

But the central metaphors of a culture, such as the signs and circles we have examined so far, are closely aligned to a mode of production, or a system of exchange. Indeed, through an analysis of the production of wealth and the system in which this wealth is exchanged, we can derive a grammar of culture in *Things Fall Apart*. Consider, for example, the notion of the market in Igbo culture. Elizabeth Isichei tells us that among the Igbo, the market is already a field of symbolic meanings, 'an institution which marries the dimensions of space and time.'[33] In *Things Fall Apart*, the market is shown to be a sign of wealth and of hidden cosmological powers: the market place is the field in which goods are exchanged and meanings are constructed and communicated (p. 8); it is also the place in which 'the spirits of the ancestors' emerge from the 'other' world (p. 62). The market, in other words, is a field in which the spirit of things themselves is shown to be at work, a spirit which expresses 'all the threads of which the social fabric is composed'; because a market is a microcosm of the community it serves, it is a total social phenomena in which 'all kinds of institutions find simultaneous expression: religious, legal, moral, and economic.'[34]

Above all, the market is the visible symbol of economic and spiritual power:

> The people of Umuike wanted their market to grow and swallow up the market of their neighbours. So they made a powerful medicine. Every market-day, before the first cock-crow, this medicine stands on the market-ground in the shape of an old woman with a fan. With this magic fan she beckons to the market all the neighbouring clans. She beckons in front of her and behind, to her right and to her left (p. 79).

The people of Umuike have found an appropriate symbolic expression of their economic dominance; here, the exchange of goods is represented as if it is both 'a hidden presence and visible signature of all the wealth of the world.'[35] Thus, the discourse on wealth which permeates *Things Fall Apart* has close affinity to Achebe's economy of representation and even narrative techniques. Wealth is not only the mark of dominance and presence in this culture, it is a precondition for self-engenderment and subjectivity.

Wealth is a visible sign of communal and individual value, and both are tied up with a complexity of other symbolic meanings. The following description of Okonkwo's household is illustrative:

> Okonkwo's prosperity was visible in his household. He had a large compound enclosed by a thick wall of red earth. His own hut, or *obi*, stood immediately behind the only gate in the red walls. Each of his three wives had her own hut, which together formed a half moon behind the *obi*. The barn was built against one end of the red walls, and long stacks of yam stood out prosperously in it . . . Near the barn was a small house, the 'medicine house' or shrine where Okonkwo kept the wooden symbols of his personal god and of his ancestral spirits (p. 10).

Here, we can see the truism of Foucault's argument that wealth is linked to 'an entire praxis, to a whole institutional complex' and is the function 'that permits the attribution of one sign to another sign, of one representation to another, and the function that permits the articulation of the elements that compose the totality of representations.'[36] The description begins by stressing the visibility of Okonkwo's prosperity – the materiality of wealth is important because items of exchange have no value unless they are visible as tangible entities. But the physical presence of things is not enough in itself; their materiality always raises a troublesome question: what is the source of this prosperity and what are its techniques of signification? It is on the symbolic level that the material and spiritual value of things is closely related: Okonkwo's compound is large (size is equated with value) and its thick walls are made of red earth, the symbol of the earth goddess Ani, the source of all prosperity; his three wives and the yams are commodities, but their value is primarily symbolic not functional. In effect, the material symbols of wealth are reinforced, in terms of their social meaning and value, by the symbols of Okonkwo's 'personal god and of his ancestral spirits'.

Furthermore, wealth has evoked a certain domain of discourse, complete with a specialized language and a privileged set of signs which are the key to understanding the Igbo grammar of culture in *Things Fall Apart*. The wealthy man has huge barns, many wives and many children; he also wears titles as signs of the authority and power that comes with prosperity. Thus, wealth – expressed through its titles – mediates human relationships. In textual terms, wealth has value only because it has developed an intelligible symbolic system; in Achebe's novel, and in the Igbo culture in general, the yam sits at the centre of this system. As Isichei has reported, the introduction of the yam into the Igbo economy 'formed the basis of Igbo civilisation; it was of supreme importance and was given ritual and symbolic expression in many areas of Igbo life.'[37] Indeed, in its dual denotative and connotative value, as Sunday Anozie has shown in his discussion of the semiotics of the yam, this commodity has the power of a metatheory: the nature and meaning of the yam is the key to understanding, and explaining, Igbo cultural formation and the value of the self in this culture.[38]

'I have cleared a farm but have no yams to sow,' the young Okonkwo tells Nwakibie. 'I know what it is to ask a man to trust another with his yams, especially these days when young men are afraid of hard work' (p. 15). Neither ownership of land nor labour have value until they have produced yams. There is another important point, too: the man who possesses yams has power over the one who has none. The yam, 'the king of crops, was a man's crop', and is hence an instrument of class and gender domination (p. 16). The symbolic value of the yam is also apparent in its mediation of other aspects of cultural formation: the yam controls or explicates the temporal process and mediates between nature and culture; the feast of the New Yam denotes the transition of one period to another; success and failure are measured in terms of the yam-value. Thus, the tragedy of the year of drought is most manifest in the way the earth 'burned like hot coals and roasted all the yams that had been sown'; when the rains fall at the wrong time, the yams put on 'luxuriant green leaves, but every farmer knew that without sunshine the tubers would not grow' (p. 17). Without good yams, the year and the harvest are miserable occasions 'and many farmers wept as they dug up the miserable and rotting yams. One man tied his cloth to a tree branch and hanged himself' (p. 17).

Since subjectivity, or rather manhood, is determined by the possession of yams, the failure to acquire the commodity denotes the lack
of self-worth. The yam even mediates desires: one may want to have
women and children and titles, but these important things cannot be
acquired without yams. In fact, for Okonkwo, the yam expresses both
his drive to reject his father's legacy, and his need to have his son
Nwoye function as a surrogate Okonkwo: 'Yam stood for manliness,
and he who could feed his family on yams from one harvest to another
was a very great man indeed. Okonkwo wanted his son to be a great
farmer and a great man. He would stamp out the disquieting signs of
laziness which he thought he already saw in him' (p. 23-4). In essence,
the yam is a symbol of this culture's 'productive forces'.

Now, if we accept Cabral's claim that the mode of production is 'the
principal factor in the history of any human group,' then we can
see why colonization in the novel is predicated on the usurpation of
'the free operation of the process of development of the *productive
forces*.'[39] If the discourse on wealth discussed above establishes a
hierarchy of autonomous values and structures; the introduction of the
colonial political economy and its symbolic complexes disturbs and
denigrates the taxonomy in which the yam links men's labour to wealth
and power. The process of conversion which the missionary advocates
is strategically important precisely because it simultaneously questions
the old hierarchy of values and meanings and recentres those which
had been marginalized:

> None of his converts was a man whose word was heeded in the
> assembly of the people. None of them was a man of title. They were
> mostly the kind of people that were called *efulefu*, worthless empty
> men. The imagery of an *efulefu* in the language of the clan was a
> man who sold his machete and wore the sheath to battle. Chielo,
> the priestess of Agbala, called the converts the excrement of the
> clan, and the new faith was a mad dog that had come to eat it up
> (p. 101).

The Achilles heel in the Igbo epistemology, as will become clearer
in my discussion of *Arrow of God*, is its blindness, or refusal to
contemplate, its own ethnocentrism. In the above quotation, the
culture assumes (as will its colonial adversary) that its mode of
knowledge is natural and that its hierarchy of values is fixed. But as
Ross Chambers has reminded us, 'meaning is not inherent in discourse
and its structures, but contextual, a function of the pragmatic situation
in which the discourse occurs.'[40] Thus, the *efulefu* are only worthless
within the Igbo system of meaning; liberated from it by the colonial
church, they will become the new leaders of the emerging (colonial)
community.

Things Fall Apart

III. The Social Construction of Okonkwo

The issues of language and ideology which are so crucial to Achebe's texts are best illustrated through a close examination of Okonkwo's ambivalent relationship with the social grammar of his culture. The symbolic structures which the culture has invented to represent itself acquire ideological value by repressing differences and contradictions; language, considered, in John Thompson's words, as 'a phenomenon which is enmeshed in relations of power, in situations of conflict, in processes of social change,'[41] also reproduces the aberrations and disjunctions of a culture. In general terms, Okonkwo acquires his heroic and tragic status by becoming alienated from the very values he espouses and uses to engender himself. For this reason, Okonkwo would appear to function as what Abiola Irele has called 'a symbolic receptacle, the living theatre of a social dilemma'.[42] But it is not enough to see Okonkwo as a symbolic receptacle of Umuofian values gone awry; I would prefer to stress the point where, in Irele's terms, 'his actions become a pure contradiction of the values they are meant to defend.'[43] As a matter of fact, as I hope to show in this section, Okonkwo invents himself through a process that subtly contradicts the central tenets of his culture.

Consider, then, the duality involved in Okonkwo's construction as a subject: at the beginning of the novel he is represented as a cultural hero equivalent to the founder of Umuofia, and in this sense he would appear to be a symbolic receptacle of the village's central doctrines. But Okonkwo is notably characterized by his displacement from the Umuofia mainstream; undoubtedly, the most obvious symbols of the character's displacement from his culture are his linguistic parapraxes (slips of the tongue). In a community in which mastery of figurative language is the core to social survival and control – 'Among the Ibo the art of conversation is regarded very highly, and proverbs are the palm-oil with which words are eaten' (p. 5) – Okonkwo's stammer is a tragic flaw. Furthermore, his power as a wrestler and warrior is closely linked to this failure of language: 'He had a slight stammer and whenever he was angry and could not get his words out quickly enough, he used his fists' (p. 3). Thus, physical aggression has become a substitute for verbal communication. Okonkwo has repressed linguistic competence as a subconscious way of negating the image of his father, Unoka, who is shown to have 'a sense of the dramatic' and to be a verbal virtuoso. Displacement – 'the operation whereby affect is transferred from an unacceptable object to an acceptable one'[44] – is at work here. For Okonkwo, verbal language is an affect associated with the failed father; violence and power are, to him, more acceptable forms of affect.

This does not mean that Okonkwo has negated those values of his culture – especially the humane and aesthetic – associated with his father; as we will see when we examine the nature of his repression, Okonkwo has a 'soft' (Unoka) side to him. The problem is that he cannot adopt such values publicly without being identified with his father. But can Okonkwo find a detour around the father's failure and hence deny his own prehistory? The truth is, Okonkwo's failure to come to terms with Unoka displaces him from an important side of Igbo culture – the 'female side'. And by repressing the memories and images that remind him of his father, the subject has cut himself off from the 'preconscious' side of his people's culture. The preconscious is an important ingredient of any form of self-realization because, as Claude Lévi-Strauss notes in *Structural Anthropology*, it is 'the individual lexicon where each of us accumulates the vocabulary of his personal history.'[45]

The relevance of this discussion is that Okonkwo's self-representation as a self-made man is an illusion. He claims that he has invented himself from zero ground, that he has rejected his paternity as a precondition for this self-invention; but his consciousness will still continue to be dominated by Unoka because he can only define himself against the negative forces represented by his dead father. So the unconscious links Okonkwo to Unoka in ways he would hate to contemplate; the laws that structure the son's conscious acts have been predetermined by the father. Thus, Okonkwo's heroism appears to be the opposite of Unoka's cowardice, but both traits develop from the same anxiety: Okonkwo 'was a man of action, a man of war. Unlike his father he could stand the look of blood' (p. 7). The fear that dominates Okonkwo's life, and largely shapes his behaviour, is not solely the fear 'of failure and of weakness'; '[I]t was the fear of himself, lest he should be found to resemble his father' (p. 10). Everything Okonkwo does seeks to compensate for the father's lack: other sons built on their father's images and memories but Unoka died a death which was considered to be 'an abomination to the earth' (p. 13); patriarchy is considered to be a reproduction of a given identity, but Okonkwo does not inherit its properties – 'He neither inherited a barn nor a title, nor even a young wife' (p. 13).

To borrow Kaja Silverman's formulation, the blockage of Okonkwo's 'originally desires' initiates 'a series of displacements which continue through the entire life of the subject and structure that subject's psychic reality.'[46] Every step Okonkwo makes to distance himself from his original scene of denial, is already marked by the presence of his father. We are told, for example, that 'to lay the foundations of a prosperous future' Okonkwo worked 'like one possessed' – 'And indeed he was possessed by the fear of his father's contemptible life and shameful death' (p. 13). If we keep in mind that Unoka, in spite of his failure to live up to the ideology of wealth which the culture promotes, represents an indispensable side of Igbo life (the artistic and humanistic, if you want), then Okonkwo's absolute negation of the father complicates his relationship with his community.

Now, Okonkwo's relationship with his society has generated a lot of critical debate and provoked some divergent opinions, but there is agreement on at least one point – Okonkwo is alienated from the central tenets of Igbo life in the process of trying to perfect them, to live up to their original or pure intentions. Indeed, Harold Scheub has made the claim that Okonkwo is opposed to many Igbo traditions.[47] However, this assertion needs to be qualified – Okonkwo is not opposed to the tenets that govern Umuofia's life, but the community's failure to live up to the ideal or original intentions of such values. Because of his inflexibility, Okonkwo will not allow for the simple fact that communities develop value systems to serve pragmatic interests. So if his social conformism degenerates to what Irele calls 'an inverted sort of nonconformity' and 'his concern for a public image takes him to a point where his actions become a pure contradiction of the values they are meant to defend,'[48] it is because he will not allow for the contradictions that make ideologies possible.

In this respect, Scheub is right to argue that what Okonkwo promotes and defends as the values of Umuofia are really projections of his desires; thus '[A]ll events and characters come to be seen by Okonkwo within the context which *he* has created.'[49] In essence, Okonkwo's Umuofia is an imaginary construct and the relationship between ideology and the imaginary explains a lot about his constitution. In his essay 'Ideology and ideological State apparatus', Louis Althusser defines ideology as the representation of the imaginary relationship of individuals to their real conditions of existence:

> All ideology represents in [sic] its necessarily imaginary distortion not the existing relations of production (and the other relations that derive from them), but above all the (imaginary) relationship of individuals to the relations of production and the relations that derive from them. What is represented in ideology is therefore not the system of the real relations which govern the existence of individuals, but the imaginary relation of those individuals to the real relations in which they live.[50]

What this suggests, and is borne out by Okonkwo's experiences, is that a subject is defined by his or her culture, but this definition is not mediated by the real conditions of existence, but the ideal images which the culture develops to promote itself. Okonkwo's mistake, it appears, is his commitment to those ideal images ('imaginary relationships') which his culture promotes but also blocks.

There is a famous scene in the book which illustrates this paradox clearly. After the killing of Ikemefuna, Okonkwo goes through a period of depression during which he seems, in his mind, to be succumbing to the 'feminine values' he has tried to repress all his life. Several days later he goes to visit his friend Obierika and asks the latter why he refused to participate in the killing of the boy. Obierika replies: '[B]ecause I did not want to,' a response that surprises Okonkwo because in his reading of his community's cultural codes, 'the authority and decision of the Oracle', is paramount. Obierika reminds Okonkwo that his participation in the killing of the boy, who had become almost a son to him, will not please the Earth because it is 'the kind of action for which the goddess wipes out whole families' (p. 46). This remark represents the kind of interpretative dilemma which makes Okonkwo impatient with the society whose values he is trying to defend: 'The earth cannot punish me for obeying her messenger . . . A child's fingers are not scalded by a piece of hot yam which its mother puts into its palms' (pp. 46-7). Obierika had found a loophole in the earth's laws, and was hence able to wriggle out of carrying out the Oracle's directives, but Okonkwo's monological view of things has not trained him for such acts of equivocation.

In the above example, it appears that the hero is alienated by the ideology and language that defines him; he is too faithful to the collective mythology, and his interpretation of linguistic and ideological codes is too literal. However, the converse is also true, for in moments of excess, Okonkwo negates the fundamental laws that govern social relationships in his community: he beats his wife during the holy week and will not stop it 'half-way through, not even for a fear of a god' (p. 21). This act of transgression is unprecedented, as is Okonkwo's suicide at the end of the novel. And thus, the subject who goes out of his way to fulfill the canonical laws, is also the first to transgress them to satiate his imaginary relationship with the great cultural ideal.

Nevertheless, there is nothing unusual about this contradiction, especially if we remember that it is a condition of ideology itself. What after all is ideology, asks Althusser in his 'Bertolazzi and Brecht', 'if not simply the "familiar", "well-known", transparent myths in which a society or an age can recognize itself (but not know itself), the mirror it looks into for self-recognition, precisely the mirror it must break if it is to know itself?'[51] When the old gods are desecrated by followers of the new religion, Okonkwo insists on violent action to punish the transgressors (pp. 112-13) and cannot understand Mbanta's hesitancy in the face of this new menace. You see, for him the authority of the old gods is transparent; it is the mirror that has given him a cultural image; only the old truths are sensible and comprehensible. But the people of Mbanta and those of Umuofia hesitate because they seem to realize that the mirror that reflects their values also conceals what is unseen and unspoken: as Uchendu puts it, 'There is no story that is not true . . . The word has no end, and what is good among one people is an abomination with others' (p. 99). It is this 'otherness' that ideology does not allow into the discourses of culture.

We could argue that Okonkwo has to break the mirror of ideology to know himself, but this task will be left to Ezeulu, the intellectual in *Arrow of God*. Okonkwo's problem is more elementary – it concerns repression, desire, and reversal. In Scheub's apt phrase, Okonkwo is 'a man drawn by a dream and driven by fear, the latter providing much of the substance of the dream.'[52] Before we examine this linkage between fear and dreams, let us examine a few examples of repression in Okonkwo's character. Let us recall that beneath Okonkwo's spartan image, there is concealed a gentler element which he goes out of his way to repress. We are told, for example, that Okonkwo is fond of his surrogate son, Ikemefuna, but he cannot express this fondness openly because he 'never showed any emotion openly, unless it be the emotion of anger' (p. 20); when he transgresses the sacred week, he is 'inwardly repentant', but he 'was not the man to go about telling his neighbors that he was in error' (p. 22); he adores his daughter Ezinma, but 'his fondness only showed on very rare occasions' (p. 32). Furthermore, Okonkwo's unconscious desires would appear to be signified by a drive to engage in the very activities which the public image of a cultural hero has denied him.

What is initially repressed, Silverman reminds us in her reading of Freud, 'is the subject's desire to engage in some sort of forbidden activity, generally of a quite specifically sexual nature' (p. 78). And while sexuality is not a latent theme in *Things Fall Apart*, it affects the social construction of Okonkwo in a very subtle way. First of all Unoka was a sensual man, clearly identified with erotic forces (p. 4), and thus when Okonkwo buries the image of his father, he buries with it his own sexual drives. Nevertheless, he must find alternative, or rather more acceptable means of expressing this sexual drive: the beating of the drums; the call to battle makes him tremble 'with the desire to conquer and subdue. It was like the desire for a a woman' (p. 30). His favourite stories 'of the land – masculine stories of violence and bloodshed' (p. 37) are a form of substitution; here, Okonkwo's sexual desires are represented through other channels.

From these examples, it would appear that Okonkwo has repressed a significant part of himself to sustain the public image of a heroic man and in the process his ideals become perverted. One could even argue that Okonkwo lives against his true nature, and has created a personal ideology of self which, nevertheless, undermines the selfhood it is supposed to sustain. This last point becomes pertinent if we recall Freud's assertion that 'dream-work' 'restricts itself to giving things a new form,' and to effect these new forms it relies on 'a *displacement of physical intensities* to the point of a transvaluation of all psychic values.'[53] In his quest for new ways to express Umuofia's ideals, Okonkwo will not allow for the possibility of a logical relationship between old ideals and new historical forms, but neither will he countenance the ambivalence that is such a crucial element of Igbo culture and values. I want to argue that the ambivalence which

Okonkwo refuses to countenance is the key to Achebe's narrative strategies in *Things Fall Apart*.

IV. Narrative and the Uses of Ambivalence

Writing, Barthes reminds us in *Writing Degree Zero*, is 'essentially the morality of form, the choice of that social arena within which the writer elects to situate the Nature of his language.'[54] To the extent that Achebe has situated his language at the intersection of the colonial and Igbo traditions, and the multiplicity of contradications that define both value systems, ambivalence is a central element in the techniques he uses. A great deal of critical literature has tried to show how coherent and logical the ideology and form of *Things Fall Apart* are, but as I have shown in the previous two sections, Achebe's text is informed by a complex set of semiotic oppositions and processes of displacement and substitution; thematically, the novel draws its power from ambivalences in the Igbo culture it dramatizes. As we saw in the introduction, this ambivalence is captured by the Igbo proverb which Achebe believes is the *raison d'être* of his people's culture – 'When something stands, something else stands beside it.' In this section, I want to discuss the formal (or textual) manifestations of Achebe's ambivalent ethics and how this affects his narrative strategies.

Consider, for example, narrative voice in the novel. One of the problematics of the text, one which many critics have noted but not always clearly explained, concerns the status of the narrator and his or her authority. The common consensus is that the narrator represents the collective voice. Thus, concludes Carroll, the narrative voice is 'that of a wise and sympathetic elder of the tribe who has witnessed time and time again the cycle of the seasons and the accompanying rituals in the villages.'[55] Innes shares this basic assumption when she declares that 'the narrative voice is primarily a recreation of the persona which is heard in tales, history, proverbs and poetry belonging to an oral tradition'; this is the voice of 'the epic poet whose society is as yet unproblematic.'[56] There are two fundamental problems with these assertions. Firstly, the narrator in *Things Fall Apart* has no persona at all; there is no evidence in the text to characterize him/her in terms of gender or age, nor is there a voice in the text which can be characterized as that of a 'narrator agent' – defined by Prince as 'a character in the situations and events recounted and has some measurable effect on them.'[57] Secondly, the whole notion of a collective voice, in the terms it has been presented by Innes, rests on an untenable epistemological assumption – that this narrator exists in an unproblematic society and that he or she represents that society's communal interests and ideological views. My readings in the previous sections have clearly demonstrated that precolonial Umuofia is a society with various voices and conflicting interests.

My main contention, then, is that since *Things Fall Apart* is a hetero-diegetic narrative – one in which the narrator is not a character in the narrated situations and events – our concern should not be with the personality of this narrator, nor his/her identity; rather, our emphasis should be on how this narrator functions in the text and on his/her shifting focalization, the different perspectives 'in terms of which the narrated situations and events are presented.'[57] A shift in the perspective of the narrator is of paramount importance in Achebe's works because it is the technique that enables him to sustain his ambivalent ethics. Indeed, as Taiwo has succinctly noted, the use of 'varied points of view' enables the reader of Achebe's novels to discover that 'no one point of view is wholly acceptable and that, to reach a satisfying conclusion, several points of view have to be taken into consideration.'[58]

The most fascinating form of focalization in the novel is that which highlights the narrator's double voice; here the narrator seems to promote one perspective or world view but in the process also calls our attention to the negative side of this point of view. Readers of the novel will recall the first and quite lengthy introduction of Okonkwo's father Unoka (pp. 3-4) which seems, on one level at least, to denigrate the dead musician for having deviated from the materialistic ethic that governs the culture. If we pay close attention to the tone of the narrator, we cannot fail to notice his or her contemptuous dismissal of Unoka: 'In his days he was lazy and improvident and was quite incapable of thinking about tomorrow . . . Unoka was, of course, a debtor, and he owed every neighbour some money, from a few cowries to quite substantial amounts' (pp. 3-4). The succession of negatives in the first part of the description suggests the narrator's intolerance with Unoka. It is as if this narrator, in promoting the Umuofian ideals from which Unoka has ostensibly deviated, completely identifies with Okonkwo's ideological posture – the man who pursues leisure also negates the task of producing wealth and is thus useless to the community. The second part of the description presents Unoka as a debtor, setting the scene for the next paragraph which shows Unoka finding happiness only in drinking and music. Debt and pleasure are hence linked by the narrator as forms of social deviance; Unoka will die an abomination to the earth simply because he is not involved in productive activity.

However, the narrator's condemnation of Unoka is not total, for in the midst of the above censure, and in the process of tracing the musician's deviation from cultural orthodoxy, the narrator also introduces the repressed ethics of Igbo culture – expressed through art and music – which are linked to a 'femininity' which is marginalized and yet is crucial to the existence of the culture. I would even suggest that one of the reasons the villagers continue lending Unoka money is because they accept the value of the pleasure principle which he represents. The narrative voice thus leaves a gap in which it is possible to actually synthesize pleasure and labour: this 'third position' is exemplified by Okoye who was a musician but 'was not a failure like Unoka' (p. 5). What I want to emphasize with this example, however, is the narrator's position as a propitiator of cultural values: the speaker condemns Unoka's laziness but also acknowledges the value of pleasure.

In the above example, the narrator can be located ideologically: he or she is aligned with the Igbo conceptual system. However, there are also instances when the narrative voice establishes a definite distance from the communal ethos, or rather describes it as if he or she were external to the diegetic position. When the narrator qualifies his presentation of Okonkwo's inheritance by saying that '[F]ortunately, among these people a man was judged according to his worth and not according to the worth of his father' (p. 6), we can notice a shift in the relationship between addresser and addressee: the narrator adopts distance and represents the Igbo as if they were an anthropological 'other.' Another example of this is the assertion that 'Among the Igbo the art of conversation is regarded very highly, and proverbs are the palm-oil with which words are eaten' (p. 5); here, too, the narrator speaks of the Igbo as if he or she was not one of them.

Of course, one could argue that in both these two examples what has changed is the addressee, rather than the speaker. In this case, the audience is the 'other' – readers with no familiarity with the central doctrines of Igbo culture. This may well be the case; but the position of the addressee in the narrative does not explain those situations in which the narrator, to provide commentary on Umuofia, takes the culture he is describing for granted and assumes that the reader is privy to its innermost secrets. When the cry of Chielo, the priestess of Agbala breaks 'the outer silence of the night', the narrator hastens to assure the reader that 'There was nothing new in that. Once in a while Chielo was possessed by the spirit of her god and she began to prophesy' (p. 70). In this instance, both narrator and the object of discourse are placed on the same level; the only possible outsider is the reader who needs to be reassured about the event narrated.

But even in those instances when the narrator identifies with his or her objects of discourse – writing from within the culture, as it were – it would be a mistake for the us to characterize the narrative voice as the collective voice, for there will be instances when the narrator will enter the discourse of the 'other' and represent it from within. Take, for instance, that dramatic moment in the novel when one of the Christian converts tries to explain the concept of *osu* to Mr. Kiaga:

'You do not understand,' the convert maintained. 'You are our teacher, and you can teach us the things of the new faith. But this is a matter which we know.' And he told him what an *osu* was.

He was a man dedicated to a god, a thing set apart – a taboo for ever, and his children after him. He could neither marry nor be married by the free-born . . . (p. 111)

Since the speaker in both paragraphs is the convert, the most immediate question here is this: why is one part of his speech in quotation marks and not the other? Clearly, by presenting the convert's speech as indirect discourse, the narrator has endowed this discourse with narratorial authority. That is, the character's words, when represented without quotation marks, have more credibility because they are shared by the narrator. In all the above cases, the narrative position in *Things Fall Apart* functions in complex and often ambivalent ways.

The same kind of ambivalence can also be demonstrated on a semantic level. How does the culture produce its central meanings? Who is authorized to speak and when? The most talked about semantic process in the novel is that of the proverb, which has variously been discussed as a Herskovian 'grammar of values' (Lindfors), metaphor (Harrow), or even epistemology (Obiechina).[59] All these excellent discussions have shown us how proverbs constitute an enunciative modality in the novel which is, nevertheless, linked to an increasingly problematic semantic process. The only point I want to add here, as far as proverbs are concerned, is that they also function as a form of metacommentary: proverbs are figures of thought which comment on the logic of the culture and its discourse; they provide censure and guidance; but they also provide a cultural text from which the individual can read the rules that govern society and the conditions in which such rules are established. As the saying goes, 'an old woman is always uneasy when dry bones are mentioned in a proverb' (p. 15).

The mode of discourse in which the proverb is dominant is one in which there is a clear identity between signs and their signifier, between the value of the object and the utterance; for those who understand its meaning, the proverb is a means of intelligibility; you cite it to make complex phenomena easier to understand, or to endow simple things with the authority of tradition. Thus, when Okonkwo calls another man a woman in a communal meeting, the oldest man present 'said sternly that those whose palm-kernels had been cracked for him by a benevolent spirit should not forget to be humble' (p. 19). This statement is not wholly true, as the narrator reminds us, but, momentarily at least, it succeeds in humbling Okonkwo. Its real meaning is in its effect.

Often, meanings evolved in one mode of discourse have more power than those developed in another: In the culture represented in *Things Fall Apart*, the proverb and the masculine story have more authority than songs and feminine stories. Moreover, such dominant meanings are achieved through the exclusion of ambivalences and con-tradictions. Okonkwo, who is a strong advocate of the dominant ideology in Umuofia, cannot comprehend semantic aberrations, such as Obierika's reinterpretation of the oracle's words in the Ikemefuna episode, or his friend's questioning of some of the laws concerning titles (p. 48). There is an even more illustrative example: Ogbuefi Ndulue dies, and as soon as his first wife hears of the death, she too collapses. This double death, says Obierika, is evidence of the closeness between the couple: 'I remember when I was a young boy there was a song about them. He could not do anything without telling her' (p. 48). Okonkwo, who strongly believes that 'manhood' is only achieved through the exclusion of women, is flabbergasted: 'I thought he was a strong man in his youth' (p. 48). He is not convinced that a man can be strong and still have the 'same mind' as his wife.

Still, Achebe emphasizes many ideological contradictions in Umuofia and uses semantic ambiguity to represent them. The most obvious relationship between ideology and semantics can be found in the author's representation of patriarchy in the novel. Umuofia is feared by its neighbours for its power and magic, 'and its priests and medicine-men were feared in all the surrounding country,' but the 'active principle in that medicine had been an old woman with one leg' (p. 9); yams are the signs of manhood, but they can only grow at the will of Ani, the earth goddess. So, whichever way you look at it, the female principle – which is repressed in the quest for power and wealth – is central to the constitution of the community. In addition, the culture's duality toward women is brought out in the words it has fashioned to explain the order of things: the word *agbala*, we are told, is an aspersion when it is used to describe 'a man who had taken no title' (p. 10); but the key hermeneutical agent in Umuofia, the Oracle of the Hills, is called Agbala (p. 12). Thus, Agbala, as god and woman, has a certain power over men like Okonkwo: 'Beware of exchanging words with Agbala,' the hero is reminded by Chielo, the priestess. 'Does a man speak when a god speaks?' (p. 71).

But why is it, that even as the text draws our attention to the power of Agbala (and hence of women in general), that the culture at the same time blocks this power, refuses to accept the manifest role played by women? In an important discussion of the rules of exclusion in his book *The Archaeology of Knowledge and the Discourse on Language*, Foucault concludes that 'in every society the production of discourse is at once controlled, selected, organised and redistributed according to a certain number of procedures, whose role is materiality.'[60] Igbo society has already developed zones of prohibition and exlusion to deal with the unknown and the unseen: these zones include the evil forest, the ritual slaves, and even subjects of sacrifice. The language and ideology of exclusion is empowering because it allows the culture to control its material conditions. But when these spaces of exclusion are appropriated by the colonizing structure, and their meanings are reversed, a semantic crisis develops.

For example, the new Christian missionaries arrive in Mbanta and request a place to settle; the elders of the clan give them the evil forest which is 'alive with sinister forces and powers of darkness', assuming that this is an offer which 'nobody in his right senses would accept' (p. 105). Of course, the missionaries will not be destroyed by the evil forest because this is not their zone of prohibition; by surviving in the evil forest, the missionaries call the Mbanta rules of prohibition into question. From this moment on, the evil forest will mean different things to different people: to the missionaries, it will be home; to the people of Mbanta, it will be a dangerous dumping ground. However, this ambivalence, this dispersal of meanings, will have deprived the site of its powerful ritual authority: only those who believe in the evil forest can be affected by it.

Toward the end of the novel, we can see the beginning of a semantic reorganization as linguistic value shifts from the Igbo structures to colonial ones. In the old world, meanings were defined, as we saw above, by some identity between words and things; in the new economy of representation, there are new phenomena and experiences, where things have no words to signify them. Victims of the new colonial legal system, for example, 'have not found the mouth with which to tell of their suffering' (p. 125); arrested by the new government, Okonkwo and five other village elders 'found no words to speak to one another' (p. 138); and when Okonkwo commits suicide, his friend, Obierika, one of the most accomplished masters of the word in the village, strives to communicate with the District Commissioner, but his 'voice trembled and choked his words' (p. 147). At the beginning of the novel, Okonkwo was one of the few characters who found it difficult to find words to describe things; now, it seems, parapraxes have become a communal phenomenon. Furthermore, in the last few paragraphs of the novel, there is a significant shift from speech – which was the pride of Igbo culture – to writing, the mythical practice of Western history. The new District Commissioner will write a book on 'the pacification' of the people of Nigeria in which Umuofia's hero will get 'a reasonable paragraph, at any rate' (p. 148).

But there is something strange about the ending of the novel: why does Achebe give the colonizer the last word in an anti-colonial text? Gareth Griffiths has argued that both the Commissioner and Achebe 'seek to reduce the living, oral word of Umuofia to a series of words on the written pages; and they are English words, for Achebe as well as for the commissioner . . . Achebe is aware that in gaining the voice to speak he reveals his involvement with the destruction which he records.'[61] But if we see writing as a process which is tied up with questions of power and knowledge, as I have argued throughout this chapter, it is a mistake to confound Achebe and the Commissioner as writers liberated or entrapped by writing in a colonial language. Both writers use the same language and mode of representation, but their ideological function is obviously different and this difference needs to be stressed. The District Commissioner writes to compress the history of Umuofia into a general text of colonization; Achebe writes to liberate his people from that text and to inscribe the values and ideological claims of Igbo culture in the language and form that sought to repress it. The ultimate irony of his novel is that although the Commissioner has the final word in the fictional text, Achebe – the African writer who has appropriated a Western narrative practice – writes the colonizer's words and hence commemorates an African culture which the colonizer thought he had written out of existence.

3
The Language
of the Dancing Mask

Arrow of God

Mmuo, ana amasighi amasi
(Spirit, your secrets are never completely known)

– Igbo saying

What always interests us is the sense concealed in the proclamation.
If we cannot agree about the nature of the secret, we are nevertheless
compelled to agree that secrecy exists, the source of the interpreter's
pleasures, but also of his necessary disappointment.

– Frank Kermode, *The Genesis of Secrecy*

I. The Figure of the Mask

Although *Arrow of God* is a sustained representation of the struggle
for power and authority between the African and colonial traditions,
and within the Igbo culture itself, the figure of the dancing mask, which
characterizes key moments of interpretation in the novel, marks
Achebe's deeper involvement with the Igbo aesthetic and its modes of
interpretation. For if narrative strategies in *Things Fall Apart* are
motivated by the author's desire to narrate what Fanon characterized
as the manichean relationship between the colonizer and the colonized,
and to set up the binary oppositions between the Igbo tradition and

European culture, narration in *Arrow of God* is a process that evokes the dualities that characterize Igbo culture in the moment of colonial domination.[1] The goal of narration now is not to show us where 'the rain began to beat us,' but to express the ways in which authority – including the authority of language and power – has become dispersed among contending social forces.

Narration in *Arrow* is geared toward the representation of the Igbo world as 'an arena for the interplay of forces,' as 'a dynamic world of movement and of flux,' in which previously repressed social differences and opposed interests are exposed when colonialism supersedes the old value systems.[2] As we saw in the Introduction, Achebe's concern with contradictions and cosmic dualities is indebted to Mbari, the famous Igbo process of artistic production. For the Mbari artist and his audience, Achebe observes in a discussion of the writer and his community, there is no general agreement on what constitutes a good work of art – '[B]ut they are all interested in the process by which material becomes art and the meaning of the final outcome'. Above all, Mbari art derives its power from its position of authority in the everyday life of the people: because it is at the centre of the life of the people, Mbari art can 'fulfil some of that need that first led man to make art: the need to afford himself through his imagination an alternative handle on reality.'[3] But for the community in *Arrow of God* – and thus, too, the narrator and reader – the necessity of art and the meaning of reality have changed; there is neither certainty about the direction of the cultural process under colonialism, nor any sense of conviction about the final outcome of the history initiated by the colonizer. As a result, the most obvious question in the novel revolves around the meaning and value of the African experience during the 'second phase' of the colonial encounter: how does the artist function in a culture which has been disturbed through the imposition of foreign value systems?

Because Achebe can no longer evoke the communion between the artist and his people as the condition that enables 'good art,' as the Mbari artists before him might have assumed, I want to argue that *Arrow of God* is a novel predicated on the loss of narrative and linguistic authority, set in a situation where meanings cannot be taken for granted. In this novel, Achebe must find narrative paradigms which express the displacement of Igbo authority, the loss of that kind of linguistic empowerment which, as we saw in the last chapter, has previously been predicated on traditional sources of meaning. Mbari has analogies for this process of displacement, too: it is manifested in the mask, the figure of duality, the kernel where the contradictory forces of a culture, its self-assertion and dissimulation, are all represented. As Jonathan Peters has aptly noted, the central theme in *Arrow of God* – the question of power – 'is always related to the presence of masks.'[4]

Let us then look at the function of the figure of the dancing mask, as a prologue to analyzing narrative strategies in *Arrow of God*. Let us begin by discussing the duality of the mask, especially its symbolization of traditional authority and Igbo forms of closure, and also its open-ended function as a force of change and transformation. The relationship between tradition and change is particularly important in *Arrow of God*, not only because it is one of Achebe's main ideological concerns, but also because it is at the centre of the Mbari process which has influenced his modes of narration. In his seminal study of the Igbo aesthetic, Herbert M. Cole has observed that the Mbari process is 'an interplay between the united but separable concepts of change and continuity': 'The history of all mbari, as well as the development of a single one, can be visualized as a dialogue between a conservative adherence to a tradition and a series of breaks with that tradition.'[5] However, in the context of colonialism, as Achebe shows in *Arrow of God*, what constitutes tradition, and the authority this tradition holds, has been put in doubt. So, many of the tensions that arise in Umuaro can be related to one simple question: where do the allegiances of different characters and social groups lie when important ritual acts cannot guarantee security and continuity?

As a metaphor and paradigm, the mask is often used in *Arrow of God* to express the tension between tradition and transformation. For example, Ezeulu justifies his decision to send one of his sons to the colonial school by evoking the figure of the mask: 'the world is like Mask dancing,' he says. 'If you want to see it well you do not stand in one place.'[6] Here, Ezeulu is not merely using the mask metaphor to rationalize his decision to hedge his bets on the meaning of the future; he is also, perhaps unconsciously, expressing his own doubts about the survival of Igbo culture in the face of the colonial challenge. Indeed, Ezeulu – who as the priest of Ulu is supposed to be the guardian of the past and the rituals that represent it, and thus the guarantor of continuity – is often motivated by his own doubts about the survival of his culture in the face of the colonial occupation. By citing a traditional metaphor of the mask, Ezeulu is able to express his desire for cultural transformation and to mask this desire at the same time. For as Duerden has noted in his study of African art, masks are figures of ambiguity which 'contain empty spaces into which the observers project or "dream" their own definition.'[7]

Furthermore, Ezeulu often uses his own personification as a mask to conceal his intentions, or to define and redefine his role in a changing historical context. From the opening scenes of Achebe's narrative, the priest is presented posing as a masked figure, often caught in contemplation of his invisible powers or his dream of transcendence. For instance, after a discussion with his elder son, Edogo, on the differences between 'the face of a deity and the face of a Mask,' we have a mask-like portrait of Ezeulu '[L]ooking outwards,': 'As was usual with him on these occasions his mind seemed to be fixed on distant thoughts' (p. 5). Ezeulu's gesture of 'looking outwards' is a way of trying to understand and define his self and function as the minister of Umuaro's most powerful god; but like a mask, he never lets those around him share his uncertainty and vulnerability. Thus, Ezeulu's sense of tragedy arises from the fact that, like a mask, his character is unknown both to his community and to himself; he functions in a state of crisis in which even his commitment to his traditional priestly functions is a source of anger and anguish: 'Every time he prayed for Umuaro bitterness rose into his mouth, a great smouldering anger for the division which had come to the six villages and which his enemies sought to lay on his head' (p. 6). Ulu was created by the six villages to evoke their identity and unity; the god's priest has now become the symbol of disunity and division. Ezeulu's new context is also 'masked' in the sense that colonialism, by changing the traditional relationship between the priest and his people, creates a situation of duality and reversal.

Achebe's representation of Ezeulu as a masked figure will masterfully evoke this process of institutional transformation and its inherent contradictions. For in a very significant way, as Franco Monti has observed, the masked figure is involved in a struggle to identify with 'universal, divine forces or demonic forces' and to reject contingent conditions.[8] Remember that at the centre of the crisis that pits Ezeulu against Umuaro is the need to distinguish the universal from the historical: Umuaro demands that the priest bear witness to the desires and interests of his community; the priest insists that there exists a universal truth irrespective of the context of utterance or the interests of meaning (p. 7). Curiously, Ezeulu's adoption of a universal doctrine of truth in the land dispute is not entirely disinterested; his reputation, in the colonizer's eyes, as 'the only witness of truth' (p. 7) masks a more secular desire: a disinterested version of history conceals his sense of temporal dislocation and crisis, his discontent with both the past and what he scornfully refers to as 'the new age' (p. 14).

Indeed, Ezeulu's discontent with the undefined nature of his power, both in the past and present, is a form of masking; it marks what Monti would call 'a desire to break out of the human constriction of individuals shaped in a specific and immutable mould and closed in a birth-death cycle which leaves no possibility of consciously chosen existential adventure.'[9] Every stage of Ezeulu's life, as we will see in closer detail below, masks an existential adventure – his desire to transcend the worldly. As Achebe puts it so aptly in an interview with Egejuru, 'Ezeulu transcends the local very often without actually being certain of what is going on' because he has 'a kind of instinct for the ultimate things'.[10] And as Wole Soyinka has noted in a controversial discussion of *Arrow of God*, 'this priest aspires to no less than cosmic

control.'[11] My contention, however, is that Ezeulu's quest for 'ultimate things' or 'cosmic control' is exposed, in the course of the novel,
as a subtle mask for his more pragmatic desire for secular authority.
The figure of the mask enables the priest to combine the spiritual and
the secular and thus conceal his worldly interests. Thus, when Ezeulu
salutes Umuaro like 'an enraged mask' (p. 18) during his bitter encounter with Nwaka, we are not sure whether he is defending his spiritual
authority or his secular influence.

In any case, through the representation of Ezeulu as a mask, Achebe
has created two paradigms which are crucial to his narrative strategies
and ideologies – the mask as the depository of essential values and as
a figure of duplicity. Ezeulu serves both functions well because, as he
reminds us later in the book, he is a figure of duality: 'I am Known
and at the same time I am Unknowable' (p. 132). The desire for clear
meanings in Achebe's text will always come up against this dualism.
Furthermore, the figure of the mask provides an important pointer on
how we should interpret *Arrow of God* in particular and Achebe's
novels in general. What does it mean to read a story, or to interpret
a mask? The text provides us with a dramatic response to this question
during the 'coming to earth' of a new mask in which two of Ezeulu's
sons, Edogo and Obika, are intimately involved, but in contrastive
ways. In this scene, which comes towards the end of the novel, Obika's
generation is bringing out a mask as a sign of its entry into Umuaro
culture and its systems of power and authority. Since Obika is a leader
of this group, he will certainly play an important role in protecting the
mask and participating in the sacrifices that consecrate it. What is far
more important is the fact that early in the novel, Obika has been
introduced to us as a masked figure. We are told that Obika walks
through the night singing or speaking in a voice which carries over like
the disguised utterance of the masked figure in an Igbo secret society;
his 'manly voice rose louder and louder into the night air as he
approached home. Even his whistling carried farther than some men's
voices' (p. 7). The stress on Obika's masculinity is important here: of
all of Ezeulu's sons, he is the one closely associated with his father's
secular power and authority; in this regard, he is shown to mirror the
potential for danger and excess concealed in Ezeulu's 'unknowable'
side. In his affirmation of penile power, Obika will almost bring disaster to his family and community; in his zeal to affirm his masculinity,
he will destroy himself.

But in using Obika as a mirror image of Ezeulu's desire for paternal
domination and secular authority, Achebe is also keenly aware of the
kind of artistic powers the Igbo have evolved to counter excess
authority. The moral and transcendental side to Ezeulu is reflected in
his elder son, Edogo, the carver of the mask and the interpreter of its
social semiotics. More importantly, Edogo mirrors the tentativeness
which the Igbo value in their culture, a state of mind which Ezeulu's

authoritarian streak seems to reject. At a crucial moment in the novel, when the community has become divided into warring factions immutable in their ideological positions, Edogo watches the mask he carved and is overwhelmed by doubts about his own product. The owners of the mask are satisfied with the work of art, but the artist is disappointed with his labour; he cannot be sure about the success of his product until he sees the mask performing its function: 'he must see the Mask in action to know whether it was good or bad, so he stood with the crowd' (p. 200).

Edogo's doubts are not entirely assuaged by the mask in motion, nor by the praises people heap on it:

> Many people praised the new mask but no one thought of compar-ing it with the famous Agaba of Umuagu, if only to say that this one was not as good as that. If Edogo had heard anyone say so he might have been happy. He had not set out to excel the greatest carver in Umuaro but he had hoped that someone would link their two names. He began to blame himself for not sitting in the *okwolo*. There, among the elders, was a more likely place to hear the kind of conversation he was listening for. But it was too late now (p. 200).

Edogo's doubts and sense of uncertainty, it would appear, are the dis-appointments of art itself. The carver's state of mind underscores the important point, which Achebe seems to have derived from the Igbo aesthetic, that narrative cannot meet its horizon of expectations and must hence always be found wanting. Narrative cannot find solace in the kind of ultimate things which Ezeulu seeks relentlessly.

Edogo's reflections force us to pose an interesting question: where does the authority of ambiguity in narration lie? If we take Edogo's mask as analogous to the narrative text, then isn't it possible for us to argue that the authority of art does not derive from a consensus about its meanings, but from its defiance of conventions of meaning and representation? Edogo's mistake was to have assumed, especially when he was carving the mask, that his relationship to previous authority, to a traditional regimen of meaning, had empowered him. In the dark hut where he had retreated to carve the mask, we are reminded, he was surrounded by 'older masks and other regalia of ancestral spirits, some of them older than even his father. They pro-duced a certain ambience which gave power and cunning to his fingers' (p. 51). When the mask is put on display, however, the artist discovers that he cannot be empowered by any comparative relation-ship to a previous tradition, as he would have liked, for his work has acquired a life of its own, has indeed violated and defied all previous authorizations. The value of the mask – and by analogy, narrative – lies in this act of transformation, this revolutionary break from what Garrett Stewart calls 'inherited and hierarchical time, its centrifugal break against inertia, its spin from a vacated center'; this spin allows narrative 'to redraft all history.'[12]

II. Narration and Authority

We can clearly see the function of the mask as a paradigm for narration in *Arrow of God* if we recall the investment both writers and readers of fiction have traditionally put into the tripartite relationship between the narrator, reader, and social referent. Jonathan Culler's reflections on this process provide some useful insights:

> One might say that all claims made for the novel as a humanizing influence, as a purveyor of vicarious experience, as a tool for refining and extending our awareness of the possibilities of life, assume a cyclical movement on the reader's part between text and world. The first step takes him from text to that of which it speaks. He must identify in the world the referents towards which the text gestures.[13]

The problem in Achebe's text, of course, is that the referent to which the text gestures is not stable nor easily knowable. This is not only because of the shifting relationship between the known and the unknowable which Achebe has borrowed from the Igbo aesthetic, but also the more immediate fact that the theme of this novel is the collapse of the Igbo referent and its authority under colonialism. If the traditional authority of narrative has been derived from an intelligible world (in his *Structuralist Poetics*, Culler makes a now famous claim that the novel is 'the primary semiotic agent of intelligibility'[14]), what happens when this world, and its semiotic system, are in a state of crisis? How do you narrate a world in which things have fallen apart?

Achebe's response to the problems of narrating a situation of historical instability is to show how narrative can derive its power from the crisis of meaning and interpretation which it tries to overcome; as readers we must recognize the complexity of the situation that necessitates the story. For example, in reading a character like Ezeulu, Achebe tells Nwachukwu-Agbada in an interview, we must recognize the complexity of life and history for '[W]hat we try to encapsulate perhaps, is merely to help us in our understanding of life; it is not to delude us into thinking that this is a final answer.'[15] Achebe would perhaps share Edward Said's view that narrative is bound by its authority and molestation. In the first case, notes Said, 'narrative fiction asserts itself psychologically and aesthetically through the technical efforts of the novelist. Thus in the written statement, beginning or inauguration, argumentation by extension, possession and continuity stand for the world *authority*.'[16] But the power and effort to produce and elaborate meanings is always mitigated by a process of disturbance, a sense of disillusionment, of the author's, narrator's, or even reader's awareness of the incompleteness of their own project. Said concludes, then, that '[T]o speak of authority in narrative prose fiction is always inevitably to speak of the molestations that accompany it.'[17]

Achebe's narrative strategies in *Arrow of God* could well be explained by his belief that the function and authority of narrative derives from its consciousness of failure and loss, of the gap that separates an ideal desired and a reality encountered. As he tells Ogbaa, there would be no need for writers if things were perfect; writing is motivated by writers' visions of a world 'which is better than what exists; it is because they see the possibilities of man rising higher than he has risen at the moment that they write. So, whatever they write, if they are true practitioners of their art, would be in essence a protest against what exists, against what is.'[18] Thus, narration demands strategies that simultaneously represent that which exists, is found wanting and thus must be transcended, and the ideal that is desired. Between the two axis, there is a semiotic crisis that must be negotiated.

It is not difficult to see how this semiotic crisis presents Achebe with the conditions and constraints of narration, the play between narrative authority and molestation. In the famous gesture that opens the novel, Ezeulu watches for signs of the new moon three days early because he knows that even with the authority of prophesy bestowed on the priest of Ulu, one cannot take such signs, or their meanings, for granted. The moon has a determinate meaning in Umuaro's temporal process because it determines the movement of the seasons; however, such authoritative meanings are also subject to molestation: 'sometimes the new moon hid itself for days behind rain clouds so that when it finally came out it was already halfgrown. And while it played its game the Chief Priest sat up every evening' (p. 1). The narrative begins, then, with a significant question mark being put on the priest's claim to any cosmic knowledge.

Indeed, a few moments later the narrator contrasts Ezeulu's assumed authoritative meanings with his consciousness of error and disillusionment, and then proceeds to highlight the priest's doubts about his own selfhood: gazing at the new moon, Ezeulu has to face the possibility that his sight is 'no longer as good as it used to be'; but he will not, of course, accept such a likelihood and the loss it denotes – 'for the present he was as good as any young man, or better because young men were no longer what they used to be' (p. 1). In both these assertions, there is a definite tension between the ideal image that Ezeulu holds about himself and his subliminal knowledge that such an ideal image might not be sustained at all because times have changed. For this reason, Ezeulu's assertions about his power and prowess are questioned by the context in which they are made. Thus, his control over the temporal process (the moon and the seasons) would appear to be a manifestation of the priest's power over his community, but the moon that appears that night 'was as thin as an orphan fed grudgingly by a cruel foster-mother' (p. 1) as if to mock Ezeulu's notion of his own powers.

Achebe's narrative strategy, then, is to emphasize the duality of meanings in his text as a way of evoking the hermeneutical crisis in Igbo culture. Whenever Ezeulu considers the 'immensity of his power,' we are told, 'he wondered whether it was real': does the priest have real authority over the temporal process or is he merely a watchman? The response to this question is narrated in a style which calls attention to the ambiguity of meaning that runs through *Arrow of God*:

> No! the Chief Priest of Ulu was more than that, must be more than that. If he should refuse to name the day there would be no festival – no planting and no reaping. But could he refuse? No chief priest had ever refused. So it could not be done. He would not dare.
>
> Ezeulu was stung to anger by this as though his enemy had spoken it.
>
> 'Take away that word *dare*, ' he replied to his enemy. 'Yes I say take it away. No man in all Umuaro can stand up and say that I dare not. The woman who will bear the man who will say it has not been born yet' (p. 3).

The passage opens with an utterance which is not attributed directly to either narrator or character, and hence belongs to what is known as free indirect discourse.[19] What is important about this form of utterance, at least in this context, is the way it calls attention to the duality of voices in the narrative. While the first paragraph in the above quotation might be attributed to the narrator because it does not contain the tags and quotation marks which might clearly attribute the utterance to Ezeulu (as does the third paragraph), it nevertheless expresses the character's thoughts. The speaker of the first paragraph might very well be the narrator expressing Ezeulu's thoughts. The important point, though, is that we cannot be sure about the origin of the utterance. In free indirect discourse, as Michal Ginsburg has stated, 'two voices, that of the character and that of the narrator, co-exist in a structure of undecidability, where one cannot opt for either one or the other as being the "meaning" of the utterance.'[20]

Certainly, Ezeulu's mistake throughout the narrative is to assume that meanings develop from clear reservoirs of knowledge while the narrator seems to emphasis the dispersed sources of such meanings in Umuaro. We are told, for example, that Ezeulu's mind, 'never content with shallow satisfactions crept again to the brinks of knowing' (p. 4); ironically, the phrase, 'a brink of knowing' indicates that the kind of total knowledge Ezeulu seeks is still out of his reach. Indeed, Ezeulu's quest for stable meanings is contradicted by the authorial representation of the Igbo system of knowledge. The priest seems certain that his son Nwafo has been chosen to succeed him ('Although he was still only a child it looked as though the deity had already marked him out as his future Chief Priest' [p. 4]), but the narrator cautions that one can never be sure about such things – 'When the time came that Ezeulu was no longer found in his place Ulu might choose the least likely of his sons to succeed him. It has happened before' (p. 4). When the major decision is made, Ezeulu will be absent from the system of meanings dominated by the god he serves.

What begins to become clear from this point onwards is that the narrator rejects the kind of totality and sense of order we associate with the omniscient narrator, preferring to emphasise the tentativeness and indeterminancy of Igbo culture. In contrast, although characters in narratives are often inhibited by a limited knowledge and perspective, Ezeulu seems determined to assume what Culler calls the 'viewpoint of experience and wisdom' usually reserved for the narrator.[21] Consider, then, the priest's famous reflections on the question of truth: after the dispute between Umuaro and Okperi, Ezeulu contents himself with the thought that he was the only 'witness to the truth' because, as we have already seen, he believes truth to be universal and self-evident. But the narrator also forces us to question this assumption when he relates the fact that Ezeulu's truth was authorized by the white man – 'He had called Ezeulu the only witness of truth' (p. 7). So, which truth are we talking about here? The white man's truth? Okperi's truth? Umuaro's truth? Ezeulu's drive for monological meanings does not allow for such destabilizing questions.

The point of all this is that the narrative process in *Arrow of God*, unlike that in *Things Fall Apart*, is not generated by any sense of a past tradition with stable systems of meaning; rather, a continuous crisis of meaning and authority becomes the precondition for narration. *Things Fall Apart* opened with the celebration of a tradition that authorizes cultural meanings (the founding of the community and the rise of its cultural hero); *Arrow of God* begins in *medias res*, in a social hiatus when there is genuine confusion about community values and meanings. When the causes of social conflict in Umuaro are finally unravelled in Chapter Two, the narrator cannot affirm the authority of a past social order, while the main character is obsessed with the present state of disorder. Ezeulu claims that 'the ways of the new age' must bewilder the dead fathers of Umuaro; he is convinced that his community is being punished for having challenged its founding god; what he leaves out here is the fact that his priestly authority and the doctrines that have sustained it so far are being questioned, too. Thus, the initial conflict in the novel – a dispute about the 'truth' on the ownership of a piece of land – becomes effectively a mandate on the authority of the Chief Priest of Ulu. From this point on, a consistent pattern emerges in the narrative: every major scene is triggered by a dispute over meaning and authority.

What one may call a conflict of interpretations comes early in the novel when Akulalia and his company are sent as emissaries to Okperi. Their host, Otikpo, asserts that the messengers have come on the wrong day: 'Everybody in Igboland knows that Okperi people do not have other business on their Eke day' (p. 22). In turn, Akulalia responds that 'Your habits are not different from the habits of other people' (p. 22). Two ethnocentric positions are apparent here: one asserts that Okperi phenomenon is known everywhere because of its uniqueness; the other responds that all cultural systems are the same. The end result is, of course, familiar to readers of the novel: Akulalia destroys Ebo's ikenga, the symbol of paternal authority and masculine power (p. 25); Ebo in turn kills Akulalia, thus triggering the war between the two communities.

However, the war between the two communities is not important in itself. In narrative terms, its value lies in its function as a symptom of the larger crisis of authority and meaning which I have been tracing in my discussion so far. My working hypothesis is borrowed from Said: 'Authority and its molestations are at the root of the fictional process; at least this is the enabling relationship that most fiction itself renders.'[22] My concern here is not solely what authorizes Achebe's fiction; I am more interested in the authority on which different individual and communal fictions in *Arrow of God* are constructed. Nwaka appeals to the authority of tradition and communal mythology; he evokes Umuaro's sense of nationalism and uses his eloquence to stir 'many hearts' (p. 26). In contrast, Ezeulu evokes the authority of his god 'the deity that destroys a man when his life is sweetest to him': 'Today the world is spoilt and there is no longer head or tail in anything that is done. But Ulu is not spoilt with it' (p. 27). So, Ezeulu stands for a truth he believes is sanctioned by a deity which still retains its integrity despite the chaos in the world. But what authority or influence does this deity or his priest have when the community becomes divided and the opposing faction begins to question his sacred functions? This question becomes irrelevant when the colonial authorities enter the scene and sit in judgement over the warring communities; from this point, the only sanctioned cultural text – and social fiction – is that backed by the power of the colonial state (pp. 28-9).

But every fiction is underwritten by an irrational and subconscious system of meanings based on paranoia and projection, the struggle by the self to create an image which ends up questioning the character's claim to have mastered reality. This process is evidently at work in the colonizer's attempts to come to terms with the African order of things. Captain Winterbottom is clearly the new source of power in the region, but his authority is precarious precisely because it is founded on fantasy rather than reality. In short, his representation of African culture expresses his alienation in it rather than the mastery and control which is manifested by his exercise of power. In effect,

The Language of the Dancing Mask

Winterbottom is imprisoned by what he assumes to be his knowledge of Africa. On the surface, Winterbottom's notions of Africa seem to be represented with power and authority; like Ezeulu's pronouncements, they don't allow for doubts. Consider the judicial cadence of his sentences represented in free direct discourse as if to emphasise their magisterial source: 'this treacherous beguiling wind was the great danger of Africa'; 'Africa never spared those who did what they liked instead of what they had to do'; 'He would wonder what unspeakable rites went on in the forest at night, or was it the heart-beat of the African darkness' (p. 29).

The ostensible absence of a mediating narrator beguiles the innocent reader into believing that the character's perceptions are unquestionable. But this situation is only momentary, for no sooner have we begun to wonder why the colonizer is allowed to get away with all this nonsense, than we realize the highly ironic game Achebe is playing with Winterbottom. For one, Winterbottom's judicious 'facts' about Africa are subjected to authorial mockery: 'Then one night he was terrified when it suddenly occurred to him that no matter where he lay at night in Nigeria the beating of the drum came with the same constancy and from the same elusive distance. Could it be that the throbbing came from his own heartstricken brain?' (p. 30). How was it that concrete meanings about Africa slip away from this 'hardened coaster,' the man 'on the spot who knew his African' (p. 56)? By forcing the reader to pose this question, Achebe has masterfully deprived Winterbottom's discourse of its factual or scientific claims and exposed it as an example of what Christopher Miller has called Africanist discourse – 'ideas received from always anterior sources, which cannot be located; hearsay from "one who has witnessed" but remains absent; hints, rumors, and reports, which frustrate the reading process.'[23]

Clearly, the reading process in *Arrow of God* should not be frustrated by Achebe's reproduction of the colonizer's discourse: the narrator assumes the voice and perspective of the colonizer so that he can mimic the colonial utterance from within, so to speak. By reciting and retextualizing colonial ideologies and discourses, as they are circulated in government houses or represented in manifestoes such as George Allen's *The Pacification of the Lower Niger*, Achebe subverts them by reducing them to clichés and dead language (see pp. 32–8). Parody is an important device in this respect because it allows Achebe to appropriate colonialist discourse and to subvert it at the same time. Take the following quotation from Allen's treatise, for example:

> For those seeking but a comfortable living and a quiet occupation Nigeria is closed and will be closed until the earth has lost some of its deadly fertility and until the people live under something like sanitary conditions (p. 33).

This sentence opens the only passage in Allen's book that stirs Tony Clarke presumably because it strikes him as original. The reader, of course, will not read this passage with enthusiasm; the prose is dead and unoriginal, echoing, as it does so strongly, Conrad's *Heart of Darkness*.

There is another point which needs to be stressed about the narrator's treatment of official discourse: the similarity between Ezeulu's language and Winterbottom's discourse is striking. The language the two adversaries (and one time 'friends') will speak is that of dominant discourse. As I will show in greater detail below, Ezeulu speaks the language of paternal power; his utterance – the statement or word of the father – is supposed to be unquestionable and absolute. Consider that instance early in the novel when Edogo tries to argue the distinction between the face of a deity and that of a mask? Ezeulu cuts his son short with a totalitarian statement: 'It is not me you are talking to. I have finished with you' (p. 5). This kind of speech act closes off all further discourse as if to underscore the point that the priest of Ulu is always right. Even Ezeulu's public utterances always end with an abrupt closure of other opinions (p. 18). Winterbottom's utterances don't alow for doubts either: 'There was no doubt whatever in the mind of Captain Winterbottom that Chief Ikedi was still corrupt and high-handed only cleverer than ever before' (p. 58).

In both cases, what we are dealing with is what Terdiman has called 'the speech of the cliché, the language of the received idea, the discourse whose domination resides in its appearance of ubiquity and inevitability.'[24] Indeed, how often do both Ezeulu and Winterbottom assume that their opinions are drawn from higher sources of truth and will hence be sanctioned by inevitable outcomes? They both assume that there is no alternative to their utterances or actions. When one of Ezeulu's sons entraps the royal python in a box and almost suffocates it, Ezeulu knows that the transgression is a serious matter, but 'the ill will of neighbours and especially the impudent message sent by the priest of Idemili left him no alternative but to hurl defiance at them all' (p. 59). This gesture is then transformed into an ubiquitous event: 'It is good for a misfortune to happen once in a while,' Ezeulu says, 'so that we can know the thoughts of our friends and neighbours' (p. 59). Similarly, Winterbottom decides to make Ezeulu a chief on the assumption that his interpretation of Igbo culture is correct: 'The prefix *eze* in Ibo means king. So the man is a kind of priest-king' (p. 107). Out of this ubiquitous misunderstanding arises the event that locks Winterbottom and Ezeulu in hermeneutical and political combat.

In contrast, Achebe's narrator has adopted a critical stance *vis-à-vis* the above monological claims and created a situation in which ideological utterances can be decentred. Indeed, one obvious conclusion we can draw from my discussion so far is that there is no dominant perspective in *Arrow of God*; the narrative shifts its locus of meaning between different contesting communities (Umuaro, Okperi, the colonial government office) and individuals (Ezeulu, Nwaka, Winterbottom etc.). Moreover, we need to underscore the ways in which a crisis of authority or meaning shapes narratives in general and Achebe's novel in particular. In his 'Structural analysis of narratives,' Roland Barthes has observed that the form of narrative is characterized by two powers – 'that of distending its signs over the length of the story and that of inserting unforeseeable expansions into these distortions.'[25] What I have discussed above are some of the ways in which Achebe, by questioning the meanings and authority which his characters adopt, distends his narrative. Indeed, the key to understanding *Arrow of God*, from a narrative perspective at least, is the reader's realization that meanings which characters assumed were fixed are quite unstable and there is no longer a narrative sequence that confirms what we thought was true. A revealing example of this point is the set of ironies that inform each of Ezeulu's actions: he thought he was extending his powers when he sent Oduche to the Christian school, only to discover that the boy is already beyond his absolute control (p. 42); another son, Obika is whipped by a white man in spite of the power the priest thinks he holds in the village (p. 88).

So far I have been examining narrative strategies in *Arrow of God* from the perspective of Achebe's subjects. This is not enough, for as we saw in the introduction, Achebe would agree with Frederic Jameson's conclusion in *Marxism and Form* that 'all narrative must be read as a symbolic meditation on the destiny of the community.'[26] In *Arrow of God*, the community has constructed narratives to maintain its sense of order (and disorder) and to retain its essential vision against the threats posed by colonialism. But the question to pose here is this: what does it mean to interpret narrative from the perspective of the community? Once again, the function of order and disorder in the shaping of narrative becomes crucial. In an interesting reading of Sartre's theory of narrative, Culler makes an observation which is pertinent to my reading here:

> Nineteenth-century fiction, Sartre observes, is told from the viewpoint of experience and wisdom and listened to from the viewpoint of order. Order is everywhere. The narrator evokes the spectacle of a past disorder, but it cannot cause uneasiness because he has understood it and will bring his audience to understand also.[27]

So far, we have seen that all of Achebe's stories are told from the perspective of disorder rather than order; what we need to explore more closely now is the perspective from which the community perceives itself in its own narratives. What kind of narratives do the community evoke? There are two possible answers to this question: the first one is that the community creates narratives to compensate for threatening disorder, so that art comes to serve as what Lévi-Strauss calls 'the fantasy production of a society seeking passionately to give symbolic expression to the institutions it might have had in reality.'[28] The second view is that narrative exposes the inner contradictions that inform every social order.

Actually, both functions seem to be at work in *Arrow of God*. Let us examine the first major narrative spectacle in the book, the festival of purification in Chapter Seven. In the colourful and spectacular scene that opens the chapter, the market is a symbol of confluence, of group identity and kinship ties: 'A stranger to this year's festival might go away thinking that Umuaro had never been united in all its history' (p. 66). The ceremony of purification represses differences and divisions and highlights the symbolic unity that, had things been equal, would have held the community together. Thus, the 'voice of the market' is the fantastical expression of collective voices which are here amplified as one individual voice: 'Every woman of Umuaro had a bunch of pumpkin leaves in her right hand; any woman who had none was a stranger from the neighbouring villages coming to see the spectacle. As they approached Nkwo its voices grew bigger and bigger until it drowned their conversation' (p. 68). Nkwo drowns and thus blends the voices of natives and strangers, not to mention different castes and social classes; the language of the drum recognizes the six villages as one and equal (pp. 68–9); Ezeulu enacts the past of Umuaro as the representative figure of the community, retracing the struggles the six villages had to go through before they completed the full circle which signifies a communitas (p. 72).

But to the reader of the novel, who has already witnessed the deep divisions in Umuaro, all this evocation of unity and identity is a fantastic reproduction of an order that does not exist in reality, for even within the collective utterance ('the voice of the market') there are some disturbing dissonances which the narrative exposes even as it celebrates the symbols of unity. Nwaka's wives stand out as if to resist any co-option into the order of equivalence:

> Each of them wore not anklets but two enormous rollers of ivory reaching from the ankle almost to the knee. Their walk was perforce slow and deliberate, like the walk of an Ijele Mask lifting and lowering each foot with weighty ceremony. On top of all this the women were clad in many coloured velvets. Ivory and velvets were not new in Umuaro but never before had they been seen in such profusion from the house of one man (p. 68).

Clearly, Nwaka's wives have pushed the notion of spectacle to further heights and appropriately adopted the extravagant Ijele Mask as their model. This kind of mask, suggests Attah, marks the 'historical process of increasing secularization of masking in the twentieth century' which is 'paralleled by a progressive aggrandizement in forms and character types.'[29] So, while Ezeulu engages Umuaro's history on the ritual level, enacting the past in a process of repetition which affirms spiritual continuity, Nwaka's wives are involved in the converse process: they celebrate wealth and secular power, and hence affirm a process of change and cultural transmutation.

The above contrast between Nwaka and Ezeulu should not be seen to signify a set of binary oppositions in which one character is identified with change and the other one with continuity. As a matter of fact, these roles are sometimes interchangeable, for both characters will invoke change when it serves their interests and fall back on tradition when it is necessary to do so. What is important for our discussion here is how the struggle between the two men is a symptom of a breakdown in the framework of ideology in Umuaro. Obiechina is right to argue that 'Nwaka's subversion of the Chief Priest's power succeeds because of the encroaching changes which are working towards a realignment of relationships and a readjustment of attitudes.'[30] Although Ezeulu is cast in the festival of purification as the representative of his community, this should not disguise the obvious fact that, like Okonkwo before him, he is alienated from Umuaro in significant ways, thus allowing Nwaka to speak for the mainstream. True, Ezeulu has 'a deep sense of obligation to the values and integrity of his culture'[31]; but he also wants to acquire more personal power to break the constraints put on him by tradition so that he can effect change in Umuaro. For this reason, Ezeulu is even prepared to sacrifice his son Oduche on the altar of white power: 'Shall I tell you why I sent my son? Then listen. A disease that has never been seen before cannot be cured with everyday herbs' (p. 133). However, this act, which divides Ezeulu from his community (p. 143), does not win him favour with white power either.

Amazingly, this division has already been inscribed in Ezeulu's functions as a priest. JanMohammed asserts that 'Ezeulu's ultimate alienation from self and society lies in his rather complex search for power,' and goes on to insist that it is impossible 'to determine whether his desire to control others is an idiosyncratic product of his personality or whether it is a natural extension of the socio-religious power vested in the hereditary priesthood.'[32] Actually, it is possible to show that Ezeulu's desire for power is both personal and cultural, and can easily be explained by his sense of inadequacy about both his strength of character and communal function.

This point is hinted earlier in the novel when Ezeulu reflects, rather defensively, about the nature of his power, but it is crystallized in an interesting discussion, in the middle of the book, of the relationship between the Chief Priest of Ulu and his half-brother, Onenyi. The tension between the two men revolves around the division of power between the priesthood and medicine, both important components of Igbo social organization. We are reminded that 'there were few priests in the history of Umuaro in whose body priesthood met with medicine and magic as they did in the body of the last Ezeulu. When it happened the man's power was boundless' (p. 147). Ezeulu's problem, and that of his half-brother, is that none could inherit the boundless powers of their father; they both have to live with 'the splitting of the powers between them' (p. 147). In *Arrow of God*, the question of power, its division and loss, needs to be examined more closely for it is primary to the ideology of the text and the narrative forms we have been discussing.

III. Language, Power, and Knowledge

In an intricate discussion of the function of social division in the establishment of a social order in his *Outline of a Theory of Practice*, Pierre Bourdieu has observed that although a sense of crisis is an important condition for questioning doxa, it is not a sufficient condition for evoking a critical discourse.[33] Or, as Achebe shows in *Arrow of God*, it is one thing for a culture to be cognizant of its crisis, it is another to postulate alternatives to this crisis. Of course, Achebe's primary concern in this novel is not to postulate an alternative order of things; his narrative is content to show how the Igbo doxa is questioned and devalued from both within its own taxonomy and from outside, to show what historical and cultural conditions make it possible for a certain kind of discourse on African societies and cultures to emerge. As I have argued elsewhere, it is in the process of narrating how an African tradition is superseded by the colonial order that Achebe keeps on returning to questions of language, power, and knowledge.[34]

Indeed, David Carroll has rightly described *Arrow of God* as a political novel 'in which different systems of power are examined and their dependence upon myth and ritual compared. Of necessity, it is also a study in the psychology of power.'[35] But in order to pursue and build on this assertion, we need to pose two questions: Why does the discourse of power become so urgent in the historical period in which the novel is set? In what ways does the revolution in modes of production engendered by colonialism affect the use of language (or utterances), cause them to deviate from the Igbo norm, and how does the literary text represent this process? In trying to answer these questions, let's keep in mind Foucault's important postulation that 'one cannot speak of anything at any time; it is not easy to say something new.'[36] In reflecting on the nature of his power, in both a collective and subjective sense, Ezeulu, like many of his compatriots, is trying to develop a new grammar for saying something radically new - the culture of colonialism.

However, for Achebe to emphasise the problem of power in Igbo culture at the dawn of colonialism, he must also call attention to the conditions that make it necessary for his culture to represent things other than as they have been represented before. Moreover, as the Igbo try to respond to the colonial episteme, they must also turn inwards and question the authority on which their own system of knowledge has been built. For under the system of warrant chiefs instituted by the colonial government in pursuance of its dubious doctrine of 'indirect rule,' as Simon Ottenberg has noted, '[T]he traditional system of control was weakened, and confusion arose as to who possessed authority. These factors helped permit the rapid rise of the new educated and acculturated Ibo into positions of authority.'[37] Thus, as we have already seen, the hierarchy of power and knowledge had become dispersed and divided between several centres of meaning such as Ezeulu/ Idemili (Nwaka), Goodcountry/Unachukwu, Winterbottom/Clarke. In a sense, this dispersal of linguistic and other authority does not lead to a sharing of power; on the contrary, any loss of authority by the old power structures creates 'a ferment in the structure of traditional authority itself.'[38]

Having dealt with the ferment in traditional authority and the ideological struggles it triggers in *Reading the African Novel*, my concern here is to examine the ways in which ideology is transformed into a symbolic system, of how cultures in contention manipulate signs and transform meanings from one communicative system to another.[39] My basic premise here is provided by Volosinov who argues that '[T]he domain of ideology coincides with the domain of signs. They equate with one another. Wherever a sign is present, ideology is present, too. *Everything ideological possesses semiotic value.*'[40]

In *Arrow of God*, the narrator's focus is, of course, on the deviation or distortion of Igbo signs from their original ideological meaning or intention; the novel is full of signs whose power is in the process of being shattered.[41] The most dramatic example of this shattering of symbols of power is the destruction of Ebo's ikenga at the beginning of the conflict between Umuaro and Okperi: the splitting of the ikenga is presented as an act of transgression and violation, so unheard of and unwarranted in the traditional symbolic system that Ebo, the victim of this dastardly act, does not want to believe in what he sees with his own eyes: 'At his shrine he knelt down to have a close look. Yes, the gap where his *ikenga*, the strength of his right arm, had stood stared back at him – an empty patch, without dust, on the wooden board' (pp. 24–5).

To understand the implications of the gap or empty patch which Ebo sees where his ikenga once stood, we have to remember the important ideological value the culture invests in this symbol. Cole and Aniakor have clearly shown how the ikenga functions as a symbol of male power and patriarchy:

> The primary diagnostic of all *ikenga* is a pair of horns, and the primary meaning of horns to the Igbo is power, especially masculine

power – spiritual, economic, social, military, and political – that
a:e amplified and specified by other symbols present, especially the
recurrent knife and head, and of course ritual.[42]

The ikenga is the symbolic manifestation, not only of the idea of mate-
rialism and progress, says Nwala in *Igbo Philosophy*, but also of a
more profound idea of temporality underlying Igbo metaphysics;
behind the love of achievement and progress 'is the idea of a never-
ending life *ndu* which is sustained by both material and spiritual forces
. . . Thus, in the ikenga the human, the natural, and the supernatural
forces in the philosophy of the people are united.'[43] What is crucial in
the destruction of Ebo's ikenga is that Akulalia, who knew very well
the holistic value his culture invested in the ikenga, could have the
moral courage to destroy such a sacrosanct symbol. The crisis of
authority which colonialism triggers in Igbo culture has clearly opened
a gap – a space of doubts and blasphemy – which makes this kind of
abomination possible.

In the same vein, Oduche – the young son whom Ezeulu has sent
to the colonial school – can have the audacity to try and kill the royal
python because he is now in a universe of meanings 'in which the
python has no symbolic value. As Goodcountry, the catechist, points
out to the new converts to Christianity: 'You address the python as
Father. It is nothing but a snake that deceived our first mother Eve.
If you are afraid to kill it do not count yourself as a Christian' (p. 47).
Nothing seems to illustrate the denigration of traditional power and
its cultural referents in Umuaro more than the notion implied in the
above assertion: for an Igbo to be a true Christian, and hence have
authority in the new value system, he or she is asked to denigrate the
spiritual foundations of his or her people's culture.

As an intellectual, Achebe says in admiration, Ezeulu realizes the
dilemma this shift in power and semiotic values poses for his culture:
'He saw what was happening, he saw that change was inevitable –
unlike the intellectual today who perhaps doesn't see that the change
has in fact happened – he saw this and he asked himself, "How do I
use this new force, while still retaining my position, and make it my
own?" '[44] If this is the case, then a more elementary question needs to
be posed: why does Ezeulu fail in this quest for what one may call a
third discourse between rigid traditionalism and colonial hegemony?
The obvious answer is that he fails to recognize that the relationship
between words, power, and knowledge is intricate and is often determined by the context in which utterances are made rather than the
meaning of things in themselves. Achebe tells us that Ezeulu has 'a kind
of instinct for the ultimate things'[45]; what the priest fails to realize,
however (as the final outcome of the novel will show so clearly), is
that there is already a struggle over the meaning of utterances in
Umuaro. If we take the basic semiological assumption that 'a word

69

changes meaning according to the position of the person who uses it,'[46] then Ezeulu's tragedy arises from his failure to realize that his position in Umuaro was weakened the moment he sided with his people's enemies in the land dispute with Okperi.

This point can be discussed more lucidly if we trace the transformation of Ezeulu's utterances in the novel. Let us begin with some reflections on the nature and power of utterances in cultural systems in general. In oral cultures, we are reminded by Jack Goody, knowledge is predicated on, and exemplified by, speech; through the intervention of spoken words, knowledge that is acquired through speech functions as a form of action.[47] Speech as form of knowledge and action is what the narrator of *Arrow of God* has in mind when he or she informs us that '[U]tterance had power to change fear into a living truth' (p. 90). Depending on the status and social position of a speaker, an utterance is endowed with particular kinds of powers. Thus, notes Cole in 'Ibo art and authority', the right to speak, which is 'virtually limited to holders of high titles in some areas,' is the primary constitution of leadership, 'since the decisions made in a meeting are in effect the constitutions and laws of the town and are implemented by the authority of the meeting as a whole.'[48]

Indeed, the best indication of how power is shifting from Ezeulu to his adversaries is how the latter begin to be associated with eloquence. For example, at an important public meeting, Nwaka's discourse 'totally destroyed Ezeulu's speech' and he carried the day; Nwaka's power derives both from his wealth, no doubt, but also from his oratorical prowess – he is called 'Owner of Words by his friends' (p. 40). By the same token, the growing influence – and attraction – the Christians have for many people seems to stem from their eloquence in 'the language of the white man' which is now associated with 'more knowledge' (p. 46). While it is true that Ezeulu understands the dynamics of power and knowledge in Umuaro, he still believes that his position as a priest and a father still sanctions the power of his utterances. In particular, he believes that so long as he utters the truth, people will come around to his point of view sooner or later.

But speech does not function this way: however important the position of the speaker may be, 'speech acts' draw their 'elocutionary force' from the addressee or audience.[49] Ezeulu's problem, then, is that he often speaks in vain because his utterances no longer have an elocutionary force. Consider the famous encounter between Ezeulu and Nwaka on the land dispute with Okperi. Ezeulu tries to win the crowd to his side by appealing to universal values (the notion of 'an unjust war,' for example), and the authority of tradition passed from his father (p. 15). In both cases, Ezeulu assumes that the truth is fixed in both time and value. In contrast, Nwaka appeals to the more immediate interests of Umuaro (the need for a piece of land as a symbol of wealth and power); more significantly, he asserts that truth and knowledge are not fixed: 'Wisdom is like a goatskin bag; every man carries his own. Knowledge of the land is also like that. Ezeulu has told us what his father told him about the olden days. We know that a father does not speak falsely to his son. But we also know that the lore of the land is beyond the knowledge of many fathers' (p. 16). By the time Nwaka has finished telling his version of the story, the community has given him 'power to carry on' (p. 17).

There is another reason why Ezeulu's discourse fails to persuade his listeners: so consumed is he with the truthfulness of his position that he rarely countenances the fact that other utterances are made from equally authoritative (that is, truthful) positions. In other words, Ezeulu will not accept a basic premise, recently articulated by John Frow, that resistance is 'written into the structure of all discourse': 'If power is no longer thought of simply as a negative and repressive force but as the condition of production of all speech, and if power is conceived of as polar rather than monolithic, as an asymmetrical dispersion, then all utterances are potentially splintered, formally open to contradictory uses.'[50] Ezeulu is so keen to assert the monolithic nature of his power and knowledge that he will not allow for any polarity in either; for him, dispersed power is no power at all. Examples of this monological concept of power can be drawn from both his private and public lives.

As a father, Ezeulu is authoritarian and uncompromising in his opinions. Ezeulu's only fault, according to a diseased wife:

> was that he expected everyone – his wives, his kinsmen, his children, his friends and even his enemies – to think and act like himself. Anyone who dared to say no to him was an enemy. He forgot the saying of the elders that if a man sought for a companion who acted entirely like himself he would live in solitude. (p. 92).

What is revealing about this passage is that Ezeulu's behaviour is contrary to the doctrines of his culture which seems to allow indeed, celebrate an oppositional perspective. As his friend Akuebue reminds him, although the culture bestows a lot of power and authority on the father (p. 99), it is the pride of Umuaro 'that we never see one party as right and the other as wrong . . . in all great compounds there must be people of all minds' (p. 100). Ezeulu is, of course, deaf to a doctrine that promotes plurality.

The purpose of the narrative, as far as questions of language, power and knowledge are concerned, is to expose the disjunctive relationship between Ezeulu's monological perspective and the plurality of the Igbo world view. In many of his public speeches, the majesty of Ezeulu's oratory is not matched by the results; he tells good stories but he does not win the argument. His voice could be compared to that of the ancient Ikolo which calls Umuaro according to an 'ancient order' (p. 69) even when evidence shows that this order has been

The Language of the Dancing Mask

superseded by another. As I have already suggested, Ezeulu's problem lies precisely in a temporal paradox which he is aware of, but refuses to confront openly: he knows that the ancient order has been broken, and yet he wants to invoke this order to augment his powers. Nowhere is this paradox as apparent as in Ezeulu's tenuous relationship to white power. On one hand, he acknowledges the reality of white power. By sending one of his sons to the colonial school, he seems to have accepted a point which other people resist – 'there is no escape from the white man' (p. 84). On the other hand, he adamantly refuses to subordinate his priestly functions to colonial authority: 'Tell the white man that Ezeulu will not be anybody's chief, except Ulu' (p. 175). This statement, of course, refutes Nwaka's charge that Ezeulu is simply searching for personal power; it confirms JanMohammed's conclusion that the priest's desire for authority 'is not based entirely on egotism; it also stems from his view of the importance of his *religious* office.'[51]

However, in searching for a third discourse between Umuaro and the colonial government, whose interests does Ezeulu serve? What authorizes his actions? Can he articulate a new discourse that evokes a 'modern' Igbo culture outside the diminished African mode of production and the colonial political economy? The truth is, there is no epistemological consistency in Ezeulu's quest for a new power/knowledge relationship and his insight into colonial culture is only achieved through what de Man has called the 'rhetoric of blindness.'[52] For example, when he is imprisoned by the colonizer for refusing to become a warrant chief, Ezeulu is overcome by 'a feeling of loss which was both painful and pleasant':

> He had temporarily lost his status as Chief Priest which was painful; but after eighteen years it was a relief to be without it for a while. Away from Ulu he felt like a child whose stern parent had gone on a journey. But his greatest pleasure came from the thought of his revenge which had suddenly formed in his mind as he sat listening to Nwaka in the market place ... His quarrel with the white man was insignificant beside the matter he must settle with his own people ... Let the white man detain him not for one day but one year so that his deity not seeing him in his place would ask Umuaro questions (p. 160).

Blindness and insight seem to go hand in hand here: away from Umuaro, Ezeulu truly recognizes – no doubt unconsciously – that in relation to Ulu he is just a child, thus answering the question he posed earlier in the book (p. 3) as to the nature of his power. But when his thoughts turn to revenge, Ezeulu misrecognizes his functions, assumes that he has transcendental power over Umuaro, and that Ulu is his, rather than the community's, deity. It is as if in his quest for new forms of knowledge and interpretation, Ezeulu thinks he can beat his drum against the *ayaka* – the communal spirit chorus.

VI. The Silencing of the *Ayaka*

How do we explain this misrecognition? Is Ezeulu so consumed by his ego and hurt that he forgets one of Umuaro's simple civic lessons – that the six villages which came together to form Umuaro also created Ulu, the god he serves? Achebe argues that Ezeulu's 'priestly arrogance' tempts him into 'confusing his thinking with the thinking of the god.'[53] Indeed, Ezeulu's decision to 'wrestle' with his own people is predicated on his belief that he acts on behalf of Ulu, a point which the god himself challenges. But we can understand Ezeulu's motives more clearly if we push our blindness metaphor a bit further and examine the priest's role as an interpreter, keeping in mind de Man's famous claim that 'interpretation is nothing but the possibility of error.'[54] My claim here is simple: Ezeulu's whole relationship with his god and his community, the two entities he is supposed to minister to, is based on errors of interpretation which he refuses to acknowledge lest they invalidate his desire for power and the grievance that camouflages this desire.

Consider the role of the scapegoat which Ezeulu adopts when he is released from prison: walking in the rain, the priest feels elated, despite the threat this poses to his health, because he wants to appropriate nature as 'part of the suffering to which he had been exposed and for which he must exact the full redress. The more he suffered now the greater would be the joy of revenge. His mind sought out new grievances to pile upon all others' (p. 182). Well, like Lear in the hearth, Ezeulu is a man more sinned against than sinning; suffering will bring out his nobility and hence justify the punishment he metes on his adversaries. But the perceptive reader is also meant to see Ezeulu's self-representation as a form of projection – because of his narcissism, the priest has created an illusionary image of himself to deal with desires which cannot be rationalized. Thus, we can detect the selectivity involved in Ezeulu's self-representation: nowhere in the above scene does he take any responsibility for his suffering – he sees this suffering as the consequence of other people's actions. At the same time, when the narrator notes that Ezeulu's mind 'sought out' new grievances, we realize that these grievances could also be imagined.

Certainly, the function of the imaginary here alerts the reader not only to the possibility of error in Ezeulu's discourse, but also the fabrications involved. In other words, the priest has erected a stage and written a script in which he will play the tragic hero: 'He must first suffer to the limit because the man to fear in action is the one who first submits to suffer to the limit' (p. 184). The certainty that informs the tragic scenario which Ezeulu 'writes' for himself is only possible because of the priest's misinterpretation of the problematic of power which Achebe raised at the beginning of the novel: does he have real power or is he merely a watchman? (p. 3). In *Arrow of God*, almost every scenario in which power play is involved could actually be read as an attempt to answer this question. And since every attempt Ezeulu has made to use his linguistic and religious powers to bend Umuaro to his will has failed, then he awaits a final scene in which a conclusive answer will emerge. But as I have already suggested in my discussion above, Ezeulu's problem is one of historical belatedness: he would like to believe that he has the same power as other chief priests before him, but the context in which he functions makes this highly unlikely.

This problem is shown clearly in a skillfully juxtaposed scene in which Achebe reproduces Ezeulu's thoughts and, at the same time, exposes the limits of the priest's argument. Soon after his return from prison, or what he prefers to call exile, Ezeulu reflects on the responsibilities of his office and relives the anxieties shared by his precursors as to the nature of their power:

> What power had he in his body to carry such potent danger? But his people sang their support behind him and the flute man turned his head. So he went down on both his knees and they put the deity on his head. He rose up and was transformed into a spirit. His people kept up their song behind him and he stepped forward on his first and decisive journey, compelling even the four days in the sky to give way to him (p. 189).

What is crucial here is the context in which Ezeulu's reflections occur: he has decided to go to war against his people and yet he realizes that no Ezeulu has ever carried 'danger' without the support of the community; indeed, in the above quotation, the people have put the deity on Ezeulu – thus transforming him into a spirit – and the priest appears to have no power without the communal song behind him. In the circumstances, why would Ezeulu think that he can triumph over his people – the source of his empowerment?

A possible answer to this question is suggested a few moments later when the priest, overcome by the above thoughts, calls in his son Oduche and reminds him of another kind of power whose source is not in Umuaro: 'When I was in Okperi I saw a young white man who was able to write his book with the left hand. From his actions I could see that he had very little sense. But he had power; he could shout in my face; he could do what he liked. Why? Because he could write with his left hand' (p. 189). This assertion is a perfect example of what I earlier referred to as Ezeulu's epistemological inconsistency: he recognizes that there is a new power associated with the white man and that this power is connected to the mastery of writing; but he also misunderstands the connection between writing and power because by interpreting them from an Igbo perspective he assumes that the white man's power derives not from what he writes, but how he writes!

Ezeulu's misunderstanding of white power brings us to a theme that seems to preoccupy Achebe toward the end of his novel: the chief priest increasingly becomes alienated from his community, but he has no point of entry into colonial culture; he hence functions in a space of marginality in which the problems raised by the text cannot be resolved. Of course, throughout the novel Ezeulu has been cast as a man already alienated in his culture, a man defined more often than not by his temporal displacement rather than any mode of identification with his community, as the mandate of his office would seem to require; he is a discontented man who believes that 'the world is spoilt and there is no longer head or tail in anything that is done' (p. 27). Ezeulu's quest for a new discourse about his culture is motivated by his believe that the world may be spoilt, but 'Ulu is not spoilt with it' (p. 27). His transcendentalism hence depends on his ability to isolate Ulu from a spoilt world; he mistakenly abstracts his god from Umuaro and tries to transform him into what Achebe calls 'a world God.'[55] By isolating Ulu from cultural practices which he does not like, such as the shooting of guns to scare spirits (p. 112), Ezeulu claims the authority – exhibited in earlier times by his grandfather (p. 132) – to change traditions.

But the uniqueness of Ulu as a god, as Nwoga has informed us, is that his authority and function is not fixed or determined by taboo; this god has 'built-in cracks to be exploited by any crucial stresses.'[56] My contention here is that Ezeulu's ideology is founded on the belief that these cracks make Ulu a malleable god who can be shaped to serve a different age. After all, transformation is a doctrine dear to the priest; he believes that '[a] disease that has never been seen before cannot be cured with everyday herbs; (p. 133), and that 'a man must dance the dance prevalent in his time' (p. 189). Once more, Ezeulu's problems arise not so much because his doctrine is questionable, but because he refuses to allow for any resistance to the ideology he promotes, a resistance which the text dramatizes powerfully to counter the priest's assumption that he holds a monopoly on the truth. So if Ezeulu believes that the absence of taboo in Ulu's practices endow the chief priest with the license to carry out his planned-for punishment of Umuaro, the text shows the same 'crack' to be the priest's Achilles heel.

Because Ezeulu believes that doctrines must change to account for temporal shifts, his community will try to persuade him to find a way to eat the remaining yams so that the harvest can be saved; they will use a logic which the priest himself would use: 'We know that such a thing has not happened before but never before has the white man taken the Chief Priest away. These are not the times we used to know and we must meet them as they come or be rolled in the dust' (pp. 207–8). But Ezeulu is impervious to an argument which coheres to his own doctrine on cultural change (p. 209) because his actions have become forms of duplicity; he even consults the god to confirm an opinion he has already formed. Henceforth, as the people flock to the Christian church to save their harvest, Ezeulu will be a passive

The Language of the Dancing Mask

observer as his ideology becomes fractured and his authority is rendered useless.

Significantly, the moment of closure in *Arrow of God* returns us to the figure of the mask which opened my discussion. Initially, the mask raised the different ways in which the self could be connected to the community on a deeper level; as the Afikpo Igbo say, 'the process of masking is a conscious and deliberate attempt to produce *mma* in the person, to connect the person with the spirit of the secret society.'[57] However, at the end of *Arrow of God*, the mask has come to embody the trauma of separation, of Ezeulu's inability to engage with his community. In the ritualistic climax to the novel, as we noted earlier, two of Ezeulu's sons (Edogo and Obika) witness and participate in the ceremonial coming out of a new mask (both 'were intimately concerned with the Mask that was to come' [p. 194]), a gesture that is intended to give the community an opportunity to affirm its ties to ancestral forces even as it empowers a new generation. Because the mask embodies the spirit of the group, its integrity must be protected against evil forces and other pollutants; on this particular occasion, the latter are embodied by Otakekpeli, the 'wicked medicine man' (p. 196).

The important point, though, is that the 'purity' of a mask signifying the continuity of time and generational connections is threatened by other unseen forces. There are clear premonitions of this threat during the masking ceremony itself. We see it in Obika's rash confrontation with the wicked medicine man (p. 198) and Obikwelu's failure to sever the head of the sacrificial ram with the first stroke of his machete. These episodes prefigure or preface the final crisis of interpretation in the novel – Ezeulu's refusal to eat all the ritual yams and to call the harvest. Ezeulu's position as a priest divided from his congregation and isolated from his communal functions is clearly illustrated in the actions and fate of Obika, now clearly shown to be the father's double. As he runs the *Ogbazulobodo*, Obika is described as a man 'at once blind and full of insight': 'He did not see any of the landmarks like trees and huts but his feet knew perfectly where they were going; he did not leave out even one small path from the accustomed route. He knew it without the use of his eyes' (p. 226). Ezeulu, too, follows the path established by tradition and refuses to eat the ritual yams; but his insight into what tradition demands is a form of blindness because it leads to the shifting of ritual authority from Igbo religion to Christianity. Obika knows the accustomed route in his run; but this knowledge is precarious because it does not allow for new hazards and obstacles that might have arisen in the interim.

And so as Ezeulu's son enters the arena in what was predicated to be a moment of triumph, he collapses; the *ayaka* chorus which was preparing itself to welcome him pours cold water over his face and body and tries to revive him in vain. In the circumstances, the narrator notes, '[T]he song of the *ayaka* had stopped as abruptly as it had started. They all stood around unable yet to talk' (p. 227). A more deadlier form of silence will befall Ezeulu on the news of his son's death: his quest for power and knowledge will end in living death ('it was as though he had died' [p. 228]); the insight into the future he had sought to control so much is foreclosed from him, too, for 'there was no next time' (p. 228). As power shifts from Igbo shrines to Christian churches, the priest's madness is posited as a merciful 'act of malevolence': 'It allowed Ezeulu, in his last days, to live in the haughty splendour of a demented high priest and spared him knowledge of the final outcome' (p. 229). The final outcome is played out in Achebe's narratives of nationalism and postcolonialism.

4
Writing
in the Marginal Space

No Longer at Ease

Marginality designates the intermediate space between so-called African tradition and the projected modernity of colonialism ... This space reveals not so much that the new imperatives could achieve a jump into modernity, as the fact that despair gives this intermediate space its precarious pertinence and, simultaneously, its dangerous importance.

— V.Y. Mudimbe, The Invention of Africa

Margins and boundaries are always dangerous.

— Jean Franco, Plotting Women

I. The Problems of Realism and Reality

In *No Longer at Ease*, Achebe returned to the dangerous zone of 'occult instability' between the African and colonial cultures which the African writer was condemned to traverse sooner or later if he or she was to narrate the final outcome of the colonial encounters discussed in the previous chapters. And judging from the mixed reviews and critical commentaries which Achebe's second novel has received, the task of narrating the transition from colonialism to national identity must have been more perilous and difficult than he had expected. Nevertheless, Achebe must have been aware that in moving away from the themes of culture and domination which characterized *Things Fall Apart*, he was leaving behind traditional and time-tested narrative techniques – and thus stable instruments of producing meaning – which had secured his international reputation.

Achebe was certainly aware that the subject of *No Longer at Ease* – the struggle to forge a new Nigerian cultural and national identity – was contemporaneous with the act of writing itself. By the time the novel was published in 1960, the year of Nigerian independence, the discourse of national identity was still seeking forms through which to express itself; writing about the cultural and social pressures which young Nigerians encountered at the dawn of independence required multiple forms of experimentation with narrative techniques. Critics who have rushed to compare *No Longer at Ease* with *Things Fall Apart* have found the former wanting in 'depth,' 'coherence,' or 'vision' precisely because they have not payed enough attention to its contemporaneous and experimental nature, to the improvisorial element in its modes of representation.[1]

Now, of the many qualities which had impressed readers of Achebe's first novel, his use of binary oppositions (tradition/modernity, Igbo/European, orality/writing) has been the most admired; clearly, many readers have found such contrasting themes to be the source of narrative power in *Things Fall Apart*. And although I argued in Chapter Two that such binaries are not always sustained, there is no doubt in my mind (and this is the usual response of readers to the text) that Achebe's success in evoking the oppositions between the African and colonial traditions was the most memorable aspect of his first novel. The Igbo world may appear to be built on an unstable cosmological system in which a multiplicity of forces seem to be in contention ('When something stands, something else stands beside it'), but far from undermining the structure of society and knowledge, such oppositions would seem to stabilize the Igbo way of life. Dualism – a central theme in Igbo thought – is appropriately defined by Cole and Aniakor as 'the dynamic relationship between opposites.'[2] In short, opposites lead to a stable semiotic system; oppositions, says Culler in another context, are 'a device for the production of meaning – among the most powerful we have.'[3]

And so the security the reader of *Things Fall Apart* feels, even as Okonkwo's world seems to collapse around him, derives from our ability to recognize and identify with particular thematic positions in the novel. Of course, some readers might have found other equally stabilizing elements in the novel, such as Achebe's masterful evocation of Igbo culture and its dynamism, the relationship between the cultural hero and his community, a linear plot, and the 'development' of a dynamic and 'fully-realized' main character. In all cases, however, *Things Fall Apart* has fulfilled many of the conventions of the traditional novel – in the 'realistic' mode – and our ways of reading such novels.

In contrast, *No Longer at Ease* either seems to contravene such traditional conventions of reading or writing, or sets out to evoke realistic situations about Nigeria but fails to fulfil reader expectations about realism and reality. The gap between Achebe's narrative strategies and reader expectations in this novel seems to rile many influential critics. With characteristic vehemence, Eustace Palmer declared (in 1972) that Achebe's second novel was 'greatly inferior to his first in range of conception and intensity of realization. The understanding with which he conveyed his people's predicament, the mastery of plot, and keen psychological insight seem to have deserted him.'[4] One could be tempted to argue that this complaint tells us more about the nature of Palmer's critical method and ideology than it does about Achebe's strategies of representation. Palmer adopts, and tries to actualize, a Leaviate 'great tradition' assumption that a novel should realize a reality and provide keen psychological insight.

The demand by critics of *No Longer at Ease* that Achebe should have realized a coherent social space, developed a 'rounded' character, and/or probed into his subjects' psychology or consciousness does not come out of the blue; in many ways, this novel seems to encourage such a demand, and when it fails to fulfil reader expectations, its 'weaknesses' become glaring. But there is another way of looking at this problem which I propose as my thesis for this chapter: Achebe sets out to do·for the contemporary Nigerian scene what he did for Umuofia in *Things Fall Apart* – to evoke the transparent and representative power of narrative language, a language which will make the world available to the reader as a knowable object; but the more he tries to evoke Nigerian realities as a referent for his text, the more the new nation resists domestication in the text and hence recuperation by the reader. For when everything is said and done, Achebe's generation is trying to invent a Nigerian nation and a Nigerian national consciousness from amorphous and unstable entities arbitrarily yoked together by the colonizer. Certainly the ways in which Nigeria is invented by the colonizer and reinvented by the African nationalists will be a major theme in the novel. But Nigeria will henceforth remain a central problem in Achebe's quest for a stable historical referent.

The assumption that 'the truth of language lies in its referents', says Culler in one of the best discussions of representation in fiction, 'is of capital importance, not only because of the diverse narrative modes to which it ministers, but because of the strategy of reading it entails. To read the text is to identify with the world to which it refers. To read is to recognize.'[5] Achebe's struggle to capture the Nigerian scene in the 1950s and to dramatize the travail of what, for all practical purposes, is a post-colonial situation will keep on returning to some elementary questions: What is the Nigerian nation? What is the place of the individual subject in this entity? And what formal elements signify it? In *Things Fall Apart*, Achebe could fall on master codes of Igbo culture (the proverb, the market); in *Arrow of God*, he could trace this culture's loss of power and legitimacy through the devalorization of its central symbols (the new yam, the ikenga, the python); but in *No Longer at Ease*, national symbols were not yet available for the writer, and he had either to invent them or develop a negative genealogy, one which traced their loss and absence.

Indeed, the title and epigraph of the novel already hint at the central problematic that motivates Achebe's text: both come from a verse in T.S. Eliot's 'The Journey of the Magi,' a poetic rumination on the pilgrims' desire to return to a fixed place they could call home ('our places') and their ultimate realization that after a pilgrimage such a place no longer exists, that the old dispensation has been disturbed, that death is the only certainty in a world where the worship of new gods has destroyed the old spiritual framework. The 'Journey of the Magi' thus prefigures Obi Okonkwo's struggle to rediscover his place in the 'new' Nigeria, and the real and imaginary problems that block this process. As we will discover later in this chapter, Obi's desire for a nation could not be fulfilled because Nigeria in the 1950s had yet to evolve linguistic and cultural figures for a new national consciousness, and he had been forced to confuse his (imaginary) romance of the nation with the national community.

From a purely narrative perspective, the problems which Achebe faces in *No Longer at Ease*, and the strategies he develops to overcome them, arise from the fact that his referents resist organization into any simple textual framework. Achebe may well declare, as he does in 'The writer and his community,' that fulfillment involves the subordination of the self to the 'reality of otherness'[6] – including the idea of a national community – but at every stage in the novel, the reader is reminded of the difficulties that arise the moment Obi Okonkwo tries to identify with the 'new' Nigeria. Needless to say, his illustrious ancestor, Okonkwo, never had problems identifying with Umuofia in *Things Fall Apart*; as we saw earlier, he was to die defending what he thought were his community's ideals. Obi finds it difficult, if not impossible, to synthesize his desires with those of his country.

My emphasis here is not so much on this crucial split between self and community, which will certainly become important later in my discussion, but on the dangers Achebe faces in his desire to represent what Benedict Anderson has succinctly termed 'a special kind of contemporaneous community which language alone suggests.'[7] For Achebe's subject in *No Longer at Ease* is contemporaneous in two senses of the word: he is writing the novel in the 1950s and also about the 1950s. The author's proximity to his subject does not raise problems in itself; nevertheless, the contemporaneous community is a community in the making; it is not accessible to us in terms of established structures and institutions, but of anticipated linguistic and symbolic configurations; one of the key themes in this novel is Nigeria's search for a national idiom that might express its collective will.

But there is still another dimension to contemporaneousness in this novel: the 1950s is the period of transition from colonialism to national independence, a period in which, as any casual reading of the novel clearly shows, colonialism is giving way to a post-colonial situation; Nigerians are now forced to negotiate the claims of both colonial modernity and their previously degraded African mode of life. The period of transition is one in which binary oppositions (colonial/ African, modernity/tradition) seem to be collapsing, unveiling what Mudimbe calls 'the strong tension between a modernity that often is an illusion of development, and a tradition that sometimes reflects a poor image of a mythical past.'⁸ In *No Longer at Ease*, where the terms which defined the African experience in the colonial context have been destabilized by nationalism, mere oppositions are not enough to produce meanings; narration seems to take place in a hiatus, that marginal space which Mudimbe calls 'the locus of paradoxes that called into question the modalities and implication of modernization in Africa.'⁹

If the writer functions in a space in which there is no tangible matter to organize into an intelligible world, or when attempts to organize the world in terms of narrative language are doomed to failure because of the fluidity of this world, writing becomes a process of turning such problems into the subject of narration itself. In short, Achebe will try to realize a Nigerian community and a Nigerian character, but the meaning of his novel becomes the problems he encounters in trying to make this world accessible to us through narrative language. This does not mean that Achebe has given up on his attempts to represent a world which his readers can identify. What else can explain the excitement with which certain critics have commented on Achebe's portrayal of the Lagos scenes and 'the language which the author uses to portray the hybrid culture of modern Africa.'¹⁰ In an important discussion of language in the novel, Gakwandi has declared that 'One of the things on which Achebe's reputation rests is his ability to create a special idiom for the social setting which he is trying to depict.'¹¹ However, my contention is that the process of representation, what has been defined as 'the repetition or imitation in language of a lived experience and of a reality, physical or psychological'¹² does not come easily to Achebe in this novel.

Let's consider some examples of how Achebe tries to organize his world by appealing to the 'reality effect' and the problems he encounters in the process. In an important scene at the beginning of the novel, Mr. Green, Obi's former boss has retired to his club's bar after a game of tennis, and the narrator is trying to provide us with descriptions to reconstruct the world and vision of European expatriates in Lagos:

> Mr. Green had a light-yellow sweater over his white shirt, and a white-towel hung from his neck. There were many other Europeans in the bar, some half-sitting on the high stools and some standing

in groups of twos and threes drinking cold beer, orange squash or gin and tonic.[13]

Here, Achebe has set a context in which he can explore Green's attitudes towards the African, but the description is anchored on signs whose significance is not apparent. The reader will certainly notice the white colours (which seem to be repeated for emphasis); the arrangement of the Europeans around the bar would seem to constitute a pattern, too – but what is the significance of all this? I think it would be fair to say that the above description does not enhance our understanding of Mr. Green and his companions. Achebe seems to realize this because he does not try to develop or sustain this description. Instead, he lets the Europeans speak for themselves, allowing Mr. Green to expound what will become a famous theory on Africa and Africans.

The gist of Mr. Green's discourse here is the importance of facing 'facts' about Africans, but what is interesting about his pronouncements, and what accounts for their effectiveness compared to the description above, is that they contradict the factuality which the speaker vaunts so much:

> Mr. Green was famous for speaking his mind. He wiped his red face with the white towel on his neck. 'The African is corrupt through and through . . . They are all corrupt,' repeated Mr. Green. 'I'm all for equality and all that. I for one would hate to live in South Africa. But equality won't alter facts' (p. 3).

But what exactly are the indisputable facts which, in Mr Green's view, explain the nature of the African? Mr. Green finds a ready answer in well-established clichés which exist on the surface of colonialist discourse: for example, 'the African has been the victim of the worst climate in the world and of every imaginable disease' (p. 3). The important point here is not merely that Mr. Green's assertions are so subjective and prejudiced that he ends up deconstructing his own notion of 'facts'; on another level, such pronouncements give us greater access to the expatriate mentality than any objective descriptions Achebe may offer. Thus what began as a technical weakness – Achebe's inability to sustain descriptions and produce meaningful signs – is actually a manifestation of the author's realization about the limits he has to contend with as he tries to narrate the space of marginality.

Of course, some readers might be tempted to argue that the above quotations exemplify Achebe's inability to represent the European mind. But such hackneyed notions will not do, for the success or failure of Achebe's narrative cannot be judged against things or subjects who exist as they really are; rather, our concern should be focused on the effectiveness of such representations not their authenticity. And my main point here is that although Achebe's desire for objectivity may tempt him to produce meanings by representing things to evoke their sense of reality, his narrative language seems to stall irrespective of the objects to be represented. Consider Achebe's description of the Umuofia Progressive Union's meeting called to consider Obi's trial early in the novel:

> Somewhere on the Lagos mainland the Umuofia Progressive Union was holding an emergency meeting. Umuofia is an Ibo village in Eastern Nigeria and the home town of Obi Okonkwo. It is not a particularly big village but its inhabitants call it a town. They are very proud of its past when it was the terror of their neighbours, before the white man came and levelled everybody down. Those Umuofians (that is the name they call themselves) who leave their home town to find work in towns all over Nigeria regarded themselves as sojourners. They return to Umuofia every two years or so to spend their leave. When they have saved up enough money they ask their relations at home to find them a wife, or they build a 'zinc' house on their family land. No matter where they are in Nigeria, they start a local branch of the Umuofia Progressive Union (p. 4).

Although this is one of the few sustained passages in the novel, the reader is still struck by its incompleteness and incoherence. The first sentence locates the meeting on the Lagos mainland but refuses to go into details about the meeting place; the sentence is then left to hang in mid-air as Achebe introduces some background about Umuofia; but, quite surprising, Umuofia's history is evoked in an almost casual and haphazard way, without a sense of pride or dynamism. Has Achebe lost all his powers of evocation so soon after his masterful portraits of Umuofia in *Things Fall Apart*? Obviously not; what is apparent from the above quotation is the evolution of a narrative strategy which is keenly sensed to the problematics of the world evoked. The most obvious example of this strategy in the above passage is the way the narrator deliberately distances himself from Umuofia. For example, in the third sentence of the passage, when we are told that Umuofia is 'not a particularly big village but its inhabitants call it a town,' the narrator seems to mock the Umuofians' view of themselves; and in almost every sentence that follows (in the quoted passage), the narrator distances himself from the Umuofians through the use of pronouns such as 'they' and 'those.' The point I want to emphasize here, because it will become important later in my discussion, is that the narrator and his subjects no longer seem to share the same values or view events from the same perspective. The narrator who identified with Umuofia, even when he might have questioned some of its values in *Things Fall Apart*, finds himself in a situation where he must simultaneously represent the Umuofian ethos and question it, too.

There is a simple ideological explanation for this divided narrative posture: while the Umuofian sense of group unity might be laudable in a pragmatic sense, it also works against the ideal of Nigerian unity which this text struggles to promote. For if Umuofians see themselves as 'sojourners' in other parts of Nigeria, obviously a Nigerian consciousness has no chance of evolving. Furthermore, if the whole notion of Nigeria is a locus of paradoxes, a crossroads of different forces and ideological claims, the narrator of *No Longer at Ease* has no authority to organize this world into a coherent whole. He is obliged to evoke the reality of places and things, since this still remains an important mandate of the novel, but he must also expose the inadequacy of any form that seeks to account for a world which is no longer at ease.

In view of the problems the narrator encounters in achieving a 'reality effect,' we may wonder why Achebe still strives to create specific social spaces (such as the city, the country, and the club) and even goes out of his way to represent the idiom used in each space. The questions involved here are large and bear on the very nature of fictive space and the narrative process: '[W]hat allows the notion of space to be used as constituent both of the physical world and of linguistic structures? What is the relation between space as the condition of phenomenal reality and space as a formal category?'[14] There is no doubt that space (rather than time) is the key to representation in *No Longer at Ease*, and the reason for this is actually not hard to find. In *Things Fall Apart*, Achebe set his novel in fairly limited spaces (Umuofia and Mbaino) because he wanted to focus more on the temporal process, the tragic transformation of history at the beginning of the colonial period; in *No Longer at Ease*, history and transformation are not as important as their consequences, the most important of which is the dispersal of the people of Umuofia in what we have already referred to as the marginal spaces symbolized by the nation and the city. Thus, even though the descriptions of such spaces as Lagosian sheds and slums (pp. 15–16) and rural villages (p. 43) may be sketchy, they allow the author to portray the different, and sometimes contradictory, social spaces that make up Nigeria. What emerges in the end is a world in which the relationships between the self, the community, and the nation, create as many problems of narration as they offer ideological possibilities.

The idea of Nigeria is, of course, one of the central – but certainly not obvious – causes of tension between Obi and the Umuofians. For while the latter see themselves as foreigners in the national community, as we saw in the passage above, the former's commitment to the idea and ideal of Nigeria is the very foundation of his ideology and morality. If we take Anderson's famous definition of the nation as an 'imagined community',[15] we will be better placed to see that Achebe is not merely involved in a process of trying to portray a Nigeria consciousness awaking to its destiny, but strives to narrate the conditions under which a Nigerian nation is reinvented and articulated by the new generation and the problems they encounter trying to do so. In this respect, Obi shares the author's commitment to a Nigerian national consciousness, but his notion of a Nigerian nation is based on a basic misunderstanding – his belief in the Azikwean notion that the nation will awaken to its destiny when the young generation is emancipated from the colonial mentality internalized by their elders.[16]

Consider Obi's theory on corruption in the Nigerian public service: he believes that this institution 'would remain corrupt until the old Africans at the top were replaced by young men from the universities' (p. 35). The problem here is not the validity or invalidity of such theories, but the error on which they are founded: there is no reflectiveness on Obi's part on the meaning of Nigeria, how its institutions came into being, and how people in the country have naturalized certain practices such as corruption as part of what it means to be Nigerian. Obi's blindness and naïvety here is astonishing for another reason – his assumption that Nigeria is a stable and knowable community, even when the narrative (and his own experiences) call attention to the unformed character of the national community. Clearly, Obi's Nigerian is a fantasy which the narrative challenges along the way. We are told, for example, that 'It was in England that Nigeria first became more than just a name for him' (p. 11). The suggestion here is that before he went to England, Nigerian existed in Obi's mind merely as an image or sign detached from its realities.

The irony, of course, is that England does not make Nigeria real for Obi; on the contrary, it replaces one image with another so that the Nigeria he returns to 'was in many ways different from the picture he had carried in his mind during those four years' (p. 11); the national community exists as a romantic image in 'a callow, nostalgic poem' (p. 14). Once more, the problem here is not that Obi imagines Nigeria as a modern arcadia, nor the fact that such romantic notions are bound, sooner or later, to be frustrated by reality; rather, what becomes problematic is Obi's construction of a theory of Nigeria built on a fantasy created to counter the colonial fantasies of Africa which I discussed in the previous chapters.

Achebe might, of course, be tempted to dismiss Obi's Nigerian fantasy early in the text and move on to more pressing issues, but the fact that he traces it for the whole length of the narrative suggests the value such fantasies play in nationalist texts. As a matter of fact, there is an extent to which one cannot have a subject such as Obi – who sees the gratification of his desires, and his quest for 'character,' as tied to the national interest – without giving value to the fantasy of the nation itself. In an important discussion of the ideology and semiotics of the nationalist text, Edmond Cros has drawn our attention to an important theoretical proposition pertaining to the 'insertion of the individual into the framework of a national community'; he asserts that national integration, 'perceived as the construction of and the quest for ontological wholeness, is presented as a vital necessity

allowing us to confront the threatening presence of the *nonself*.'[17]
With this assertion in mind, we can now see clearly that Obi's
ontological quest is predicated on two premises: (a) the postcolonial
self can only achieve wholeness within an integrated Nigerian
community and (b) Nigeria is a diseased body that needs to be cured
before it can provide support to the 'new man.'

'Dear Old Nigeria,' Obi moans when he is asked to pay a bribe on
his return to Lagos (p. 28); the statement expresses his melancholy at
the degeneration of the Nigerian ideal and the frustration of his desire
to identify with a national body that has been restored to full health.
However, Obi's quest for an ideal nation is doomed from the start; his
hope that governmental institutions might promote national unity is
based on a misunderstanding of people's relationship with such institutions; as we are told a few paragraphs later, in Nigeria 'the government
was "they." It had nothing to do with you or me. It was an alien institution and people's business was to get as much from it as they could
without getting into trouble' (pp. 29–30).

The distance between the people and their government is an example
of what Obi sees as the Nigerian disease; if only people could love 'dear
Old Nigeria' as much as he does, then the national body could be cured
of its ills, and individuals could have an integrated spiritual framework
in which they could fulfil themselves. In the end, Obi will, of course,
realize that his expectations about Nigeria – indeed his whole romance
of the nation – was an imaginary response to his lack of a community
while he was in England. Thus, the fantasy of Nigeria will be destroyed
at the height of the crisis of self which develops when the subject
discovers he cannot reconcile his ideals to 'the way Nigeria was built'
(p. 89, p. 137). When he begins to take bribes, Obi has given in to the
national disease.

II. Narration and Derealization

Clearly, what makes writing in the marginal space possible is the
author's awareness that his community, characters, and narrator are
caught in an unstable social position and the ill-defined space which
signifies so-called modernity. In Africa, the urbanized space is the
synecdoche of the modern, for here, as Samir Amin has observed,
'vestiges of the past, especially the survival of structures that are still
living realities (tribal ties, for example), often continue to hide the new
structures (ties based on class, or on groups defined by their position
in the capitalist system).'[18] As I have already noted, many readers
have admired Achebe's evocation of the 'realities' of Lagos; what has
not been sufficiently emphasized is that like the modernity it signifies,
the city is a place of vestiges rather than essences, a geographical space
which reveals and conceals elements of the new postcolonial culture

in the same vein. Thus, Lagos can be a fantasy, a city of lights and glamour which conceals its harsh realities (pp. 11-13). The city is a world which appears so knowable – because it has developed its own mythologies – until one approaches it and discovers its capacity to mask its other faces (p. 15). Above all, Lagos is both a place of opportunity and a den of sin (p. 74).

In this modern space, then, we can no longer take the referential function of language seriously, for signs (both colonial and African) have been displaced from their signifiers. For example, in Mr. Ikedi's urban space, wedding feasts have declined with the introduction of invitation cards; one cannot even attend a neighbour's wedding 'unless he was given one of these papers on which they wrote R. S. V. P. – Rice and Stew Very Plenty' (p. 9). This exemplifies the function of modernity as a no man's land between the African and colonial traditions: an invitation card contravenes the old rules of courtesy in which you attended your neighbour's wedding without invitation; the result is the decline of wedding feasts, moans Mr. Ikedi; but the card also seduces you, whets your desire for the sources of pleasure that are withheld from you. The modern space promises the fulfillment of those desires promised to those Africans who have rejected their traditions; but most of the confusion and frustration we witness in the novel arises from the failure of the new culture to guarantee pleasure and to provide meanings which the Africans themselves control.

In the old days, says an old Umuofian, you knew who your heroes were because the codes that defined the heroic were clear, but today 'greatness has changed its tune. Titles are no longer great, neither are barns or large numbers of wives and children. Greatness is now in the things of the white man' (p. 49). How can young men like Obi hope to escape from the prisonhouse of the colonizing structure if the ideology of colonialism determines the values by which they live and are judged by their elders? And to return to the primary question I posed at the beginning of this chapter, how do you organize a world in which the old dispensation has collapsed?

Students of narrative theory, notably Barthes and Culler, have proposed an alternative way of representing a world in which things have fallen apart and the subject is no longer at ease. This is a strategy of derealization in which the narrator, instead of trying to achieve the reality effect by presenting his readers with concepts by which they can recognize the world, falls back on what Barthes calls the indirect language of literature: 'the best way for a language to be indirect is to refer as constantly as possible to things themselves rather than to their concepts, for the meaning of an object always flickers, but not that of the concept.'[19] In this kind of indirect representation, the author can present his readers with things (the invitation card, for example) without attributing any essence to them. Then, says Culler, the world created 'will seem real but there will be nothing to be done with it';

meanings will sometimes evolve from the objects that constitute this world, but these meanings will be 'sufficiently detached from their objects that the arbitrariness of the connection will be evident.'[20]

This arbitrariness explains those moments in *No Longer* when, in Gakwandi's words 'the author seems to take local imagery as a substitute for clarity.'[21] My argument, however, is that Achebe's narrative strategy is geared toward creating incongruency rather than clarity. His use of metaphors is a case in point. In rhetorical language the metaphor is a figure of intelligibility: by comparing two things with similar qualities, meanings are amplified and clarified. However, in Achebe's novel, metaphors often confuse the process of producing meaning, emphasizing the arbitrariness of the relationship between the objects being compared. Consider the following example:

> Whenever Mr Justice William Galloway, Judge of the High Court of Lagos and the Southern Cameroons, looked at a victim he fixed him with his gaze as a collector fixes his insect with formalin. He lowered his head like a charging ram and looked over his gold-rimmed spectacles at the lawyer (p. 1).

The reader of this passage can be forgiven for wondering what the judge and the collector have in common, or for failing to find any grounds of equivalence. If we cannot establish any likeness between the lawyer and the insect, a task made more difficult by Achebe's unwillingness to even suggest ways in which the two concepts could be seen to be similar, then won't the process of producing meanings be destabilized and clarity lost?

Moreover, what are we to do with descriptions which don't appear to have any obvious significance? 'Going from the Lagos mainland to Ikoyi on a Saturday night was like going from a bazaar to a funeral,' the narrator says in a scene that is intended to dramatize the differences between the 'native' and the 'European' parts of the city (pp. 15–16). And yet nothing in the phrases that follow suggests the significance that is to be derived from the oppositions between 'bazaar' and 'funeral,' although the two terms initially appear so suggestive. Even the proverb, Achebe's master code in *Things Fall Apart*, often points to empty spaces rather than significant meanings; it now has to compete with Western figures of speech. Of course, a Christian such as Mary will throw in an Igbo proverb for good measure ('You have the yam and you have the knife; we cannot eat unless you cut us a piece') even as she invokes the 'God of Abraham, God of Isaac and God of Jacob,' but no one is left in doubt about the ultimate source of authority in her discourse (p. 8). Isaac Okonkwo has rejected everything about his father except 'one proverb', but this utterance is insignificant within his Christian apparatus of meaning (p. 9). The proverb is no longer the paramount trope in Igbo culture.

The reader who feels frustrated by the absence of significance in the examples cited above might well wonder what function such metaphors and proverbs serve in the text. Are they merely decorative, rhetorical figures? If so, why has Achebe cast an already alienated character in a world in which meanings only point to the emptiness of the world? This kind of derealizing strategy, says Culler, creates meanings indirectly; by creating 'arbitrary and unmotivated signs', the narrator ensures that 'neither reader nor character may experience the solace of organic synthesis or "natural" significance.'[22] In the African modernist space, grammar has gone astray and the adopted colonial language has been bent out of shape. The generation which still looks up to the colonizer as its model of behaviour, Coleman reminds us in his study of Nigerian nationalism, is characterized by 'the misuse or overuse of long words, in the use of pompous oratory, and in the ostentatious display of educational attainments.'[23] For this generation, simple grammar will not do; the value of words does not lie in their meanings but sound (consider 'osculate' [p. 13]); the authority of a phrase depends on its phonology. 'The importance of having one of our sons in the vanguard of this march of progress is nothing short of axiomatic,' says the Umuofian orator, using the kind of English his audience admires, 'the kind that filled the mouth, like the proverbial dry meat' (p. 29). In contrast, Obi's English 'was most unimpressive. He spoke "is" and "was"' (p. 29). And so the words that would seem to matter have no 'natural' significance because they don't impress.

As we will see in our discussion of *A Man of the People* in the next chapter, Achebe seems to have decided that his readers can best understand his world if they are defamiliarized from it. A key tactic in this respect is his use of convoluted plotting devices in *No Longer at Ease*, his structuring of the story through a process that defies conventions of order and synthesis. In *Reading for the Plot*, Peter Brooks has argued that plotting in the novel is often motivated by the desire for significance and order; plotting is the 'activity of shaping' and 'the dynamic aspect of narrative', the process which not only moves the story forward, but also 'makes us read forward, seeking in the unfolding of the narrative a line of intention and a portent of design that hold the promise of progress toward meaning.'[24] In the traditional novel, the plotting activity, by enabling the narrator to connect discrete elements, provides both readers and characters with a linear way of organizing and explaining the world.

But once Brook's proposition has been restated, an obvious question arises: in a situation where the world can no longer be organized and explained because traditional systems of knowledge have collapsed and the colonial episteme has yet to develop an integrated philosophical system, what role does plot play in the novel? In *No Longer*, the act of plotting is clearly posited as a process of regression, perversion and retardation; there is no clear line of meaning and intention to be pursued; plotting establishes meanings through gaps and detours, we come to learn of the significance of things in their negative connotation or absence. In other words, plotting is useful for retarding rather than advancing meanings. For example, at the beginning of the novel, the most common response to Obi's corruption trial is bewilderment or simple incomprehension. 'I cannot comprehend how a young man of your education and brilliant promise could have done this,' the judge tells Obi in his summation; 'I cannot understand why he did it,' the British Council man says, picking up the refrain (p. 2). Even people who claim to have answers to Obi's predicament are forced to fall back on dubious metaphysical or semantic games: Mr. Green explains it in terms of a corrupt African nature (p. 3), while members of the Umuofia union explain Obi's fall in terms of his strong will (p. 5).

In both cases, however, the narrator suggests that the case is more complex than it appears. So, the inaugural moment of the narrative is presented as a puzzle – why did an idealistic young man like Obi become corrupted? – and the plotting activity, by connecting various episodes in the subject's life, is supposed to move the reader to a resolution of the puzzle. But this is not how Achebe's plot works in the end: the narrative traces discrete moments of Obi's life but ends up restating the puzzle rather than providing a solution:

> Everybody wondered why. The learned judge, as we have seen, could not comprehend how an educated young man and so on and so forth. The British Council man, even the men of Umuofia, did not know. And we must presume that, in spite of his certitude, Mr Green did not know either (p. 153).

This conclusion is remarkable for the way it contravenes traditional notions of closure: there is no resolution here, the plot has not advanced any new meanings for we are still trapped where we started, in our ignorance; indeed, the claims of knowledge are debunked with both a gentle note of mockery ('and so on and so forth') and the sharp dismissal of Mr Green, the one man who claimed to have the answers to Obi's dilemma. It is significant that although the judge provides a summation in Obi's trial, the text does not tell us what the sentence is; and because the sentence is the final and conclusive word – in legal terms – its absence here leaves the story still suspended, its conclusion still hanging in the air in keeping with Obi's belief that 'real tragedy is never resolved' (p. 36).

There is still another complication to plotting in *No Longer*: the plot does not seem to have what Brooks calls 'desire as a dynamic of signification.'[25] Unlike *Things Fall Apart* and *Arrow of God*, this novel does not arouse any passion for meaning; the tone adopted by the narrator, as the above quotation shows, is one of boredom or cynicism. Indeed, plotting, instead of arousing desire for meanings (which is traditionally achieved when events are placed in a context in which time moves forwards), retards or confuses the temporal process. In other words, there is no logic in the way Achebe treats time. And this is not because of any weakness in the author's conception of plot; rather Achebe wants to show the reader how meanings are produced by a world which no longer has an authentic logic to sustain it, and how desires are frustrated when ideals are subverted by realities. So, time seems to move to and fro, aimlessly, without a centre of significance. The novel opens with a clear demarcation of time and place ('For three or four weeks Obi Okonkwo had been steeling himself against this moment') but quickly begins to jump about from place to place like a roving camera; we move from the courtroom to Mr Green's club (p. 2), to the Umuofian Union's gathering place on the Lagos mainland (p. 4).

Since each situation provides the reader with differing responses to Obi's dilemma, the plot jumps around to contravene the reader's desire for a monological perspective. Plotting disperses centres of meaning and geographical spaces or juxtaposes opposed situations: Obi's downfall is placed opposite the great promise he offerred when he became the first Umuofian to go to England (pp. 6–10); his desire for a romantic Nigeria acts as a counterfoil to his experiences in England (p. 11); his childhood image of Lagos is presented against his early encounter of the city on his way to England (p. 12) and his discovery of the city slums 'Some years later' (p. 13). As we can see, Achebe has moved through several time frames within the space of a few pages.

My concern here is the way in which Achebe's plot deliberately subverts the logic of promise and destiny which underlies Obi's quest. For even if Obi's demise appears so tragic because he offered so much promise as a young man, or even because it was his destiny to go to England (p. 32), the reader cannot fail to see how the plot questions notions of destiny and promise by stressing disappointment and reversal rather than fulfillment. England, the promised land, has no reality for the colonial subject, and is hence dealt with as a minor incident in a life; in this place in which the colonized self was supposed to fulfil its destiny, Nigeria dominates Obi's consciousness (p. 11). Many times in the novel, Obi's relationship with Clara comes closest to providing him with fulfillment and pleasure, but it always seems to fall apart at the crucial juncture (p. 25, p. 64).

However, the most telling example of the process of disappointment and reversal which underlies the plot of this novel, is Obi's homecoming (Chapters Five and Six), the symbolic return to the source. The narrator tells us that '[F]our years in England had filled Obi with a longing to be back home in Umuofia' (p. 45). This desire for the homeland resonates with nationalist sentiments, and once Obi has touched Umuofian soil, he looks back at his isolation in England with defiance: 'Let them come and see men and women and children who knew how to live, whose joy of life had not yet been killed by those who claimed to teach other nations how to live' (p. 45). In the next chapter, however, we begin to see how the returning hero's concept of the homeland fails to cohere with 'ground reality': 'Obi's homecoming was not in the end the happy event he had dreamt of. The reason was his mother. She had grown so old and frail in four years that he could hardly believe it' (p. 50). The withering of the mother – the symbol of the homeland and the source of life – already points to Obi's tenuous state in Umuofia; his rejection of his father's God (p. 51) signals his rebellion from the paternal authority. Back home in Umuofia, Obi cannot reconnect with things as they were before his departure for England.

From a plotting perspective, as many readers of the novel are bound to recognize sooner or later, Achebe's narrative cannot be moved forward by evoking its contemporaneousness. Episodes drawn from the contemporary situation always seem to need a fragment from the past to propel them. For example, Obi's trial for corruption is not unique in itself; it becomes dynamic only when it is compared to his 'promise' in the past, his pioneering status in Umuofia, and his idealism in England. Moreover, the constant interpolation of past and present has an ironic function which helps Achebe generate meaning in his text. Consider the way the narrator explores the relationship between Obi and his boss Mr Green: instead of exploring the tensions between the two men directly, the narrator establishes a detour which takes us back to Obi's first day in 'the bush mission school' where the headmaster had knocked down a white inspector of schools who had slapped him. In those days, we are told, '[T]o throw a white man was like unmasking an ancestral spirit' (p. 58). It appears that the author has taken this detour to show us how times have changed: 'That was twenty years ago. Today few white men would dream of slapping a headmaster in his school and none at all would actually do it. Which is the tragedy of men like William Green, Obi's boss' (p. 59).

The point here is that the character has not changed but the context has, and Mr Green's frustration arises from his inability to function as a proper colonial. But there is another import, too: the confused African products of colonialism, such as Mr Omo, have not changed either. So, the values of the Ikedi/Jones episode from Obi's childhood highlight the strange conjunction of change and stasis that defines contemporary Nigeria. This is the kind of ambiguity expressed by the Hon. Sam Okoli in his attitude to the colonizer: 'I respect the white man although we want them to go' (p. 62). Plotting is one of the activities by which Achebe tries to sustain this ambiguity; it is also used as a device to explore the volatile relationship between self and world.

Now, in the traditional nineteenth century novel (Balzac is the often cited example), the ambitious hero is often conceived as a 'desiring machine' whose presence in the text 'creates and sustains narrative movement through the forward march of desire, projecting the self onto the world through scenarios of desire imagined and then acted upon.'[26] What happens to plot when this desire skids, when the scenarios imagined by the subject cannot be acted upon or are frustrated by the world? We will return to this question in more detail in the next section. What I want to stress here is how plotting in *No Longer* exposes the ways in which the unfolding of Obi's desires is hindered by unexpected, or unimagined, situations. Obi goes to attend a meeting of the Umuofia Union expecting to use the amicability of the situation to borrow more time to repay his loan (p. 74), but because he never imagined that the association that has actually invented him could be interested in what he considers to be his personal business, the meeting ends in an uproar (pp. 75-6). Indeed, the occasional dramatic moments in the novel arise when Obi's strict moral codes are either given frontal assaults (as in the bribery and inducement offered by Mark and his sister in Chapter Nine), or when he is ambushed by mundane practices (such as paying car insurance) which he did not anticipate.

In another sense, since Obi's desires are retarded because he fails to develop a proper perspective or effect proper communication with other important sectors in his life, the plotting activity is intended to indicate the gaps in his perspective and communicative situation; he rarely allows for another way of looking at, or doing, things. Thus, he had not told his family that Clara was *osu* because '[O]ne didn't write about such things. That would have to be broken very gently in conversation. But now it appeared that someone else had told them' (p. 105). After all, communication is still possible outside Obi's framework and language. Furthermore, Obi will come to learn that systems of thought and modes of discourse often derive their power from their erratic nature, not by conformity to a fixed structure.

For example, Obi assumes that he can win his parents consent to marry Clara by appealing to their Christian doctrines. When he speaks to his father about *osu*, he adopts the words and thoughts he assumed his father would have spoken, contrasting the Igbo world of 'darkness and ignorance' with 'the light of the gospel' (p. 120). As the narrator notes in emphasis, 'Obi used the very words that his father might have used in talking to his heathen kinsmen' (p. 121). But things will not work out as expected, for Obi's father has made a tactical manoeuver which the son didn't anticipate – the old man reverses himself and speaks in defence of Igbo doctrines on *osu* and from knowledge acquired through suffering ('Because I suffered I understand Christianity' [p. 125]). Obi thought he could elicit greater understanding from his mother, forgetting that she still has a keen sense of Igbo traditions which will not allow her to yield on this issue (p. 123). In the end, when Obi has been overtaken by the corruption he had tried to evade, the reader recognizes how Achebe's plot has perverted the subject's ideals and the march of his desires toward pleasure and fulfillment. But one question still needs to be answered: why does Obi, as a desiring subject, fail to project his self into the world, to act on those ideals that defined his promise in the first place?

III. The Generation of a Postcolonial Subject

Undoubtedly, many of the problems confronting Obi Okonkwo arise from his uneasy situation in the space between a diminishing colonialism and an emerging Nigerian nation. Like many members of the nationalist generation of the 1940s and 1950s, he struggles for a sense of character, the thing which colonialist discourse assumes is missing from the educated African, a forceful sense of self which will at once propel him beyond the prisonhouse of colonialism to recapture what Coleman terms 'a significant measure of identity with [his] lineage and with African culture.'[27] Obi will, of course, discover that while it is easy to renounce the colonial ideology embodied by Mr Green, it is far more difficult to recapture his African culture. Indeed, his tragedy is aggravated by the fact that the Igbo community – of which the Umuofia Union is an important synecdoche in the novel – is no longer the custodian of a distinctive Nigerian or African culture; the values of 'tribe' promoted by the union run counter to the Pan-Nigerian vision or consciousness which Obi tries to promote.

Thus, in No Longer at Ease, the dialectic of self and community, which is central to the shape of narrative in general, becomes a struggle between individual and group fantasy. As John Brenkman has noted, in narrative processes. '[T]he experience of the subject, who is constituted by and constituting through language, is lived within the struggle between the unrealized community and those social institutions which, deriving from the divisions of the community, shape the situations, interactions, and arrangements of everyday life.'[28] Clearly, Obi's social agenda was bound to conflict with that of his community, represented here by the Umuofia Progressive Union. For while such unions are formed to defend ethnic and regional interests, Obi is fighting for the yet unrealized Nigerian community in which cultural, linguistic, and ethnic differences are overcome or harmonized, and the integrity of the national body is established. It often appears (as in the case of Obi's quarrel with the union over Clara) that for the subject to achieve his individuality, and hence inscribe himself as a Nigerian, he must reject kinship and regional ties. The only problem with this proposition is that Obi is an invention of his kinsmen: they have educated him to serve their communal interests and thereby projected their own fantasies onto him.

This does not mean that Obi does not struggle to release himself from what he sees as the prisonhouse of Umuofia; what needs to be stressed is how his attempts to rebel against the community are always based on a misconception of the relationship between individual and group fantasies. Umuofians sent him to England to read law 'so that when he returned he would handle all their land cases against their neighbours. But when he got to England he read English; his self-will was not new. The Union was angry but in the end they left him alone. Although he would not be a lawyer, he would get a "European post" in the Civil Service' (p. 6). Obi gets his way, but Umuofia does not erase its fantasy; rather, the union just transfers its expectations in the belief that an investment can always be made to pay dividends in another function.

Obi miscontrues Umuofia's strategic retreat on the choice of his subject as an acknowledgment of his self-will. But the function of the narrative is to point out how alienated he is from the norms that govern his community, his failure to comprehend how his individuation is predetermined by communal institutions, and his inability to understand that the community also has the right to nurture its fantasies about him. Thus everybody comes to welcome Obi 'properly dressed in *agbada* or European suit except the guest of honour, who appeared in his shirtsleeves because of the heat' (p. 28). The narrator goes on to comment on this attitude: 'That was Obi's mistake Number One. Everybody expected a young man from England to be impressively turned out' (p. 28). Later, we are told that Obi's English was 'most unimpressive' (p. 29).

In effect, Obi has failed to live up to the image and function Umuofia created for him; for this reason he will become further isolated from his community, while the Nigerian identity he desires still remains unrealized. Now, another question arises: does Obi have a community he can identify with? As a nationalist, he has revolted against the colonial ideology; as a would be Nigerian, he has loosened ethnic and regional ties; as an African in search of his traditions, he values Igbo culture even when he cannot live by its prescriptions. He cannot abandon any of the above ties completely, nor can be embrace any of them wholly, for the two social centres that defined him – namely, colonialism and Igbo culture – are what Victor Turner has called communitas, 'a generalized social bond that has ceased to be and has simultaneously yet to be fragmented into a multiplicity of structural ties.'[29] Turner would hence characterize Obi's passage in the novel as a rite of passage through 'a cultural realm that has few or none of the attributes of the past and the coming state'; he exists in 'liminal' entities which 'are neither here nor there,' but are rather 'betwixt and between the positions assigned and arrayed by law, custom, convention, and ceremonials.'[30]

Nowhere is Obi's state of liminality as apparent as in the scene when he returns home to Umuofia after four years in England: he no longer believes 'in the father's God' (p. 51), but he cannot dissent from paternal ideology openly. At this juncture, it becomes clear that Obi's education and the construction of his identity has always been split between his father's Christian doctrine and his mother's (clandestine) Igbo culture, between the authority of the written word and orality. Obi's father 'believed utterly and completely in the things of the white man. And the symbol of the white man's power was the written word, or better still, the printed word' (p. 115); but for young Obi to succeed even in the colonial school, he needed to have some knowledge of his people's oral culture (p. 53). What these examples indicate, among other things, is the futility of any attempt, by the 'new' African, to negate either the claims of tradition or of colonial modernity in a narcissistic celebration of selfhood. Of course, Obi refuses to acknowledge that the community has rights over him: 'don't you dare interfere in my affairs again,' he tells the President of the Umuofia Union (p. 75). But it is precisely this claim to have a certain realm of self (one which is strictly private) that accentuates his monetary problems and eventually leads to his corruption. More importantly, since the community can only realize its fantasies through the individual, it will always lay claim to Obi even against his will: they will come to commiserate with him on the death of his mother and they will even hire a lawyer to defend him in his corruption trial.

What I have suggested so far in this section is the need to examine the tension between self and community as one possible way in which the reader can approach Obi as a postcolonial subject. My assumption here is that critics of the novel have not always found mechanisms for engaging Obi as a subject. One critic bemoans our inability to get into the character's mind and to grasp the significance of his vision, arguing that Obi 'does not come alive as a unique individual'[31]; another asserts that the hero is 'weak and insufficiently realized . . . for a central consciousness he is too uninteresting and vaguely portrayed.'[32] While these responses accrue from the conventions of reading which these critics adopt, I would like to suggest, following the line I have been pursuing in this chapter, that Achebe never set out to stress Obi's uniqueness as a character, a central consciousness, or as the kind of 'tragic hero' which Palmer would have preferred. Rather, Achebe conceives Obi as what JanMohammed suggestively calls 'a rather quixotic idealist.'[33] What does it mean, in both ideological and formal terms, for a character to be quixotic? This is a question we need to address in order to comprehend Obi and his function in the novel.

Let us begin by reflecting on the problematic of the 'quixotic' as it has been presented by Foucault in *The Order of Things*. Don Quixote's adventures, says Foucault, 'mark the end of the old interplay between resemblance and signs and contain the beginnings of new relations,' for he now lives in a world in which the relationship between words and things, signs and objects, is no longer defined by association and dissociation; he travels across the familiar plain of analogies (one in which signs were supposed to be intelligible because they could be connected to things) 'without ever crossing the clearly defined frontiers of difference, or reaching the heart of identity.'[34] Don Quixote's struggle is to realize a world that exists only in books, so that all the signs he has traced from the books he has read ('those extravagant romances') must be shown to tell the truth, to speak the language of the world. The quixotic hero sets out to decipher the world but also to force it to fulfil the ideal 'promise of the books', and each exploit is 'an attempt to transform reality into a sign. Into a sign that the signs of the language really are in conformity with things themselves. Don Quixote reads the world in order to prove his books.'[35] The quixotic figure wanders in the space left when the 'written word and things no longer resemble one another,' and he tries to establish a reality based on language alone, for it is in language that this subject 'breaks off its old kinship with things'.[36]

Foucault's exposition is, of course, more complex than I have represented it here, but it offers three points which can help us to understand Obi. First of all, he is a man entrapped in the dialectic of difference and identity; he finds that he cannot completely dissociate himself from the colonial culture which he has inherited from his father, nor can he totally identify with the Igbo culture of his ancestors. Secondly, Obi's ideals are based on 'books' in the sense that they are never shown to derive from the realities of the country, but are rather conceived in his imagination as moral codes which can be imposed on reality. Thirdly, the reality which Obi tries to construct is based on narcissism and reflects his inability to see himself as a subject who has an autonomous life outside his imaginary existence and the unrealized ideals that mark his desires. The most obvious quixotic elements of Obi's character derive from his need to be different, to break through the boundaries of culture and convention in an attempt to transform realities into signs which are more conducive to his imagination. Obi wonders why, as a school boy, he sent a letter of support to Hitler: 'What was Hitler to me or I to Hitler? I suppose I felt sorry for him' (p. 33). However, there is another possible explanation for Obi's behaviour here: he tries to empower himself by acting contrary to established beliefs and conventions. For this reason, his stubborn decision to marry Clara is equated to the act of a man challenging his chi (p. 37).

Killam has argued that the core of No Longer is 'the moral dilemma in which Obi finds himself and the conflict in the novel is produced by the clash between the strength of his moral awareness on the one hand and his almost total lack of moral courage in sustaining it.'[37] This conclusion is only possible to sustain if the reader accepts the reality of Obi's moral codes. But if we leave aside the question of Obi's honesty and moral commitment, there is no doubt that his moral system is constructed around imaginary concepts. As Deleuze and Guattari have observed, although 'the individual fantasy is itself plugged into the existing social field,' it apprehends this field 'in the form of imaginary qualities that confer on it a kind of transcendence or immortality under the shelter of which the individual, the ego, plays out its pseudodestiny.'[38] What this means, in regard to Achebe's character, is that Obi was only able to construct his moral scheme by refusing to see those realities that might have questioned his desire for transcendence, especially his sense of superiority, his belief that he can exist outside the corruption that he sees around him.

Obi refuses to recognize the validity of those experiences that exist outside his moral – and no doubt imaginary – scheme of things. Consider the incident in which Obi, on his way home to Umuofia, travels in a lorry which is stopped by two policemen expecting a bribe from the driver. Readers of the novel will remember how Obi is chastised by the driver of the lorry for having disrupted the transaction; we will also remember Obi's condescending (though private) reaction to the whole episode:

> 'What an Augean stable!' he muttered to himself. 'Where does one begin? With the masses? Educate the masses?' He shook his head. 'Not a chance there. It would take centuries. A handful of men at the top. Or even one man with vision – an enlightened dictator. People are scared of the word nowadays. But what kind of democracy can exist side by side with so much corruption and ignorance? Perhaps a half-way house – a sort of compromise.' When Obi reached this point he reminded himself that England had been as corrupt not so long ago. He was not really in the mood for consecutive reasoning. His mind was impatient to roam in a more pleasant landscape (p. 40).

Like the erotic dream of Clara that follows it, the above passage is a manifestation of Obi's narcissism: his conception of Nigeria as an 'Augean stable' does not allow for any other perspective; corruption here is thorough and only Obi Okonkwo has the cure for it; the uncorrupt individual exists independently of the corrupted social institutions. Of course, the narrator distances himself from this limited perspective because he realizes that it is not based on moral insight but on Obi's inability to understand the society in which he functions. Hence the stress the narrator places on the inconsonant nature of Obi's reasoning; his use of England as a model makes us sceptical of his moral crusade, for to the ordinary Nigerian, England is an entity that exists only in books. Like Don Quixote, Obi dreams that this fictional sign can be actualized in Nigeria.

In any case, Obi needs to sustain his imaginary notions of Nigeria because he finds it difficult to comprehend and hence project himself into the 'real' world; in effect, one might add, he is forced to create an illusion of his country because its realities remain out of his control. If Obi seems bent on creating a new, purer world, out of language and the imagination (remember his poem on Nigeria), it is because he cannot find a language with which to transform reality into a sign. Some of the most remarkable moments in the novel arise when Obi searches for a language to represent Nigerian realities, in his own way, or to project himself into the Nigerian scene; then he faces blockage and psychological censorship. For example, when his thoughts turn to the erotic, Obi could say 'any English word, no matter how dirty, but some Ibo words simply could not proceed from his mouth. It was no doubt his early training that operated this censorship, English words filtering through because they were learnt later in life' (p. 41). That Obi is also alienated in his language becomes clear a few moments later when he discovers that it is only by translating an Igbo song into English that 'its real meaning dawned on him' (p. 42). If he had tried to retain the integrity of his self in England by speaking Igbo (p. 45), what language will he now use to create or project a Nigerian reality? What language will Obi speak when he is caught between the desires of the self and the demands of the community?

In the scene where the President of Umuofia brings up the issue of Clara's *osu* identity, Obi trembles with rage; but like his illustrious grandfather Okonkwo, 'words always deserted him' at such times (p. 75). And in a kind of perverse way, when Obi becomes corrupted in the end, his spirit seems to have been released from the moral fantasy with which he had enshrouded himself; corruption seems to have liberated him from his fixed image of otherness and transcendentalism. Once he starts taking bribes, Obi has become aware of the illusory nature of his previous existence. Indeed, the greatest change that takes place in Obi at the end of the novel is his recognition that the self he thought was unique and original, not to mention moral, was a projection of other's desire – the union, his parents, the colonial culture, the nationalist movement, the collective desire for a new Nigeria – and now that he has recognized the imaginary nature of this existence, he can engage Nigeria on its own terms. But as we will see in the next chapter, for Achebe to transform the realities of Nigeria into a subject of narration, he must continuously alter his strategies to meet the challenge of the times.

5

The Realities
of the Nation

A Man of the People

The native intellectual who wishes to create an authentic work of art must realize that the the truths of a nation are in the first place its realities. He must go on until he has found the seething pot out of which the learning of the future will emerge.

– Frantz Fanon, 'On National Culture', *The Wretched of the Earth*

The work does not develop at random, in undiscriminating freedom; it grows because it is precisely determined at every moment and at every level.

– Pierre Macherey, A *Theory of Literary Production*

I. Writing, Improvisation, and Necessity

With the publication of A *Man of the People* in 1966, Achebe was to find himself imprisoned in the murky politics of postcolonial Nigeria as he tried to establish a hermeneutics for the dazzling and often confusing world ushered in, or unleashed by, independence, and as he struggled to find an appropriate form to represent the contradictory impulses of the postcolonial situation. As we saw in the last chapter, by the time Nigerian nationalism reached its fruition in the early 1960s, Achebe was beginning to acknowledge, and seriously reflect on, the problems that were going to accompany the country as it tried to seek the norms and values which would define its nationhood and as it sought what Fanon calls 'the seething pot out of which the learning of the future will emerge.'[1] But so long as the character of Nigeria and its nascent national consciousness was sought and defined in relation to the dominant colonial culture and the political institutions of the British colonizer, questions of group identity, ideology, and idiom could be postponed until after independence.

So long as Achebe was writing about the encounter between Africa and the West, his narratives could always be generated by the Manichean relation between Igbo traditions, on one hand, and colonial institutions on the other hand; so long as his subject was 'where the rain began to beat us', his ideology could be determined by the author's desire for a third meaning between the hegemonic culture of the colonizer and the repressed traditions of the colonized. However, in tracing Achebe's career from the beginning of the modern nationalist period (the late 1940s and early 1950s) to the year of Nigerian independence (1960), we have seen the progressive collapse of binary oppositions as the destiny of Africa becomes more localized and hence less determined by Europe. By the time *No Longer at Ease* was published – significantly in the year of Nigerian independence – social and cultural transformation was no longer determined by a conflict between self and other; on the contrary, Nigeria's transition to independence and nationhood was determined by complex forms of contradictions which left 'new' Nigerians like Obi Okonkwo unsure about their status in society. The realities of the 'new' Nigeria also alienated such characters, thus forcing them to question and even debunk the idealized and romantic image of the nation which had previously motivated their nationalist quests.

Initially, Achebe's literary ideology, like that of many other African writers, was motivated by the Fanonist belief that the act of writing, and hence the fight for national culture, 'means in the first place to fight for the liberation of the nation, that material keystone which makes the building of a culture possible.'[2] Consequently, the question which Achebe had to confront once independence had been achieved was simple: what is the function of the writer in the new nation, and is there a fundamental relationship between nation and narration? In 1964 Achebe could still assert that the primary function of the postcolonial writer was the liberation of his country from the prisonhouse of colonialism, especially as it was embodied in the colonial mentality. The writer could not eschew the daily realities of African life, Achebe would assert in 'The role of the writer in a new nation,' but the 'fundamental theme' had first to be disposed of: 'This theme – put quite simply – is that African people did not hear of culture for the first time from Europeans.'[3]

Thus, four years after Nigerian independence, Achebe still saw his task as archaeological: narration was geared toward the recovery of the nation's history; the contemporary realities of the nation, however pressing they may be, had to await a future time. But what made the realities of Nigeria so dramatic was the very fundamental irony that would henceforth determine Achebe's poetics – the future was already written in the present. Indeed, even as Achebe was arguing that the author's priority was the 'fundamental theme' of restoring the African character to history, in his own fiction this theme was being submerged under the weight of the very contemporary issues ('about politics in 1964, about city life, about the last *coup d'etat*') which he had considered secondary.[4] To understand the nature and function of ideology and narrative form in *A Man of the People* we must speculate on the forces that prompted Achebe to change his emphasis and strategy.

The most probable reason for Achebe's turn toward the contemporary situation might have been his realization that he could not draw a clear line between historical and contemporary subjects because, as he told Robert Serumaga, the postcolonial situation was one in which 'the worst elements of the old are retained and some of the worst of the new are added on to them.'[5] In effect, the African writer was trapped in a political impasse, caught between a colonial culture he thought independence would transcend, and a new political culture which seemed to magnify the worst of the colonial inheritance. In the quotation I use for my first epigraph, Fanon had challenged African intellectuals and artists to realize the realities of the nation in their works because he had assumed that the nation had a fundamental history which colonialism had repressed, and once this history had been brought to the surface of the nationalist text, the meaning of the nation and its future learning would emerge.

But once Achebe and his contemporaries sought the signs and values of the nation, so that they could make them the subjects of their works, they discovered that not even the resuscitation of repressed African histories could account for its depressing realities. Clearly, narration in the postcolonial situation could not be predicated on the evocation of a precolonial past nor a postcolonial future; rather the writer had to develop forms to account for, and represent, a historical period which was still in the making. As I will argue below, writing, rather than being determined by an archaeological gesture toward the past, or a prophetic evocation of the future, becomes a form of improvisation determined by contemporary political necessity.

But there is another reason why the atmosphere that generated *A Man of the People* needs to be examined more closely: most criticism and commentary on this novel has been based on what I consider to be a fundamental misunderstanding of the relationship between the text and its world. Because of what appeared to be the novel's prophetic nature, especially its anticipation of the first Nigerian coup, a theory developed during the civil war that Achebe was one of the planners of the coup.[6] Of course, as Achebe has been at pains to stress, and Lindfors has demonstrated so carefully, signs of the Nigerian crisis were evident everywhere and the novelist did not need prophetic powers to encapsulate them.[7] Achebe has noted that when he was writing his novel the Nigerian political machine had been 'so abused that whichever way you pressed it, it produced the same results; and therefore you wanted another force, another force just had to come in.'[8] But what was this new force? What form could it take in narrative?

Obviously, narrative could offer a space in which the problems of the postcolonial state could be explored and questions about the future might be raised even when ideological solutions and answers might appear remote. While a new postcolonial narrative might not celebrate the national ideals that motivated Achebe's earlier texts, it could derive its force from the political necessity that prompted it. For Achebe, the postcolonial text is clearly determined by the parting of ways between the writer and the politician in regard to the future of the nation: 'Having fought with the nationalist movements and been on the side of the politicians, I realized after independence that they and I were on different sides, because they were not doing what we had agreed to do. So I had to become a critic.'[9] Now writing functions as a form of critique prompted by the writer's estrangement from the realities of the nation – 'Political independence had come. The nationalist leader of yesterday . . . had become the not so attractive party boss.'[10]

In a bitter indictment of Nigeria at the height of the civil war, Achebe captured the problematic of the writer in the new nation more clearly still than he had in his 1964 lecture:

> The point I want to make here is that the creative writer in independent Nigeria found himself with a new, terrifying problem on his hands. He found that the independence his country was supposed to have won was totally without content. The old white master was still in power. He had got himself a bunch of black stooges to do his dirty work for a commission. As long as they did what was expected of them they would be praised for their sagacity and their country for stability (MY, 83).

What made this new situation terrifying, leaving aside the political problems it created, was that it left the writer confused about the nature and function of his art. The moment of independence was supposed to usher in the future in which all the historical contradictions generated by colonialism in the past could be resolved. But when the new nation state became an instrument of repressing identities, even as it propagated colonial values, the writer found it difficult to find new narrative forms to express the 'terrifying problem on his hands.'

Nevertheless, Achebe's quest for narrative forms that would measure to the pressures and contradictions of independence draws our attention to a crucial contradiction in his attempts to develop a theory of writing in the postcolonial situation: how do we explain the fact that in the 1964 lecture, he had argued that the province of the African writer was the fundamental rehabilitation of the African character from colonialist discourse, that contemporary history was secondary, even as he was busy writing *A Man of the People*, a novel which was obsessed with the realities of its moment of writing? There is even a further question to ponder here: if Achebe's earlier texts had been generated by what I call nationalist desire – the need to develop a narrative of liberation – what could generate a text in which the new nation had become an instrument of domination and repression? Clearly, independence had forced the writer to confront a question which he might have taken for granted in the colonial period – what is the necessity of the text in the reconstruction or invention of the new nation?

As we saw in the introduction, Achebe has the tendency to depreciate his art by tying it to concepts of representation in which the narrative reveals an original experience or affirms a natural truth. The fiction of literature, he asserts in a convocation lecture at the University of Ife in 1978, 'is not like the canons of an orthodoxy or the irrationality of prejudice and superstition. It begins as an adventure in self-discovery and ends in wisdom and humane conscience' (HI, 105). However, the notion of fiction as a form of adventure is based on the questionable notion that writing is a spontaneous act. But as my reading of Achebe's texts has shown so far, his works do not develop at random in what Pierre Macherey would call 'undiscriminating freedom'; rather, the work 'grows because it is precisely determined at every moment and every level'. Furthermore, the value of a work of art is determined by its status as a product 'at the point where several lines of necessity converge' and by our perception of its transformations and contradictions.[11]

Clearly, many critical discussions of *A Man of the People* have been limited by the failure, of most critics of the novel, to pay closer attention to the ideological environment in which it was produced, to highlight Achebe's struggle to account for an irrupting national reality, and his tortured quest for an ideology to account for a new 'Kleptocracy' (MY, 82). It sometimes pays to read a narrative in its own terms; otherwise, we may be tempted to impose on it patterns it never sought in the first place. Case in point: Eustace Palmer thought he was dismissing the novel when he called it 'a tract for the times' in which the author's 'didactic mission' failed 'to create situations, characters, and a plot which can convincingly carry the message.'[12] But the novel's relationship to its times is actually profound: Achebe was writing in a historical situation which was still incoherent; the form and ideology of his novel was bound to carry the contradictions and confusions of the times, and if the novel fails to carry the 'message' it is precisely because the message is still forming as Achebe writes.

In any case, the theoretical problem which needs to be resolved before we read the novel is this: what is the relation of the text to its context? Or as Frederic Jameson wondered in a famous attempt to explicate the dilemma of interpretation – 'is the text a free-floating object in its own right, or does it "reflect" some context or ground, and in that case does it simply replicate the latter ideologically, or does it possess some autonomous force in which it could be seen as negating that context?'[13] Let me pose this problem even more specifically: did Achebe reproduce Nigeria's crisis of independence (and hence inevitably produced a tract for the times) or did he negate the realities of the nation in search of 'another force' that might better represent the 'learning of the future'? Clearly, there is no simple answer to this problem, but the text itself, in particular the narrative problems Achebe encounters as he tries to improvise strategies of representing Nigeria, and the solutions he proposes for such problems, provide a useful starting point.

II. The Quest for Emergent Forms

One of the most persistent themes in *A Man of the People* is the narrator's difficulties in articulating a master narrative which can be used to explain historical events and their implications for both individuals and societies. In his adventures through the postcolonial landscape, Odili struggles for a language that might enable him to present the realities of the new state in totality; he also seeks an ideological vantage point from which he might explain what has happened to his country since independence. But he is eluded by both a totalized and a privileged ideological perspective; it is only when he writes the story – in retrospect – that the contradictions of his country begin even to make sense. One of the reasons why Achebe adopted a homodiegetic (first person) narrative in this novel was to dramatize the problems we encounter the moment we try to make sense of a world which has yet to establish its groundings, a world in which temporal relationships have collapsed and causality eludes the interpreters, especially when they are actors in the drama of the nation.

In spite of his apparent control of the narrative (most evident in the tone he adopts and his frequent bursts of rhetorical confidence), Odili is often forced to represent himself and his world from within a Nietschean prisonhouse of language where he 'cannot reach further than the doubt which asks whether what we see is really a limit.'[14] Certainly, Odili tells his story in retrospect in the belief that by distancing himself from contemporary events he can represent them more comprehensively, if not objectively; however, throughout the novel he often discovers that he cannot see further than the realities that overwhelmed him as an actor in the postcolonial drama. In the end, Odili, as a narrator rather than a character, has to improvise his story as he tries to make sense out of the contemporary landscape and to find the appropriate level of narration.

As a form of mediation, narrative is ideally supposed to confer coherence on the story by allowing the narrator to move or modulate 'from one level or feature of the whole to another' and thus unify the social field 'around a theme of an idea.'[15] But the first chapter of *A Man of the People* is a perfect example of Odili's struggle and failure to establish coherence even in the presence of a unitary theme (political corruption). Consider how many levels of narration and temporality exist in this chapter alone. The first level is the moment of narration, the present in which the story is told: here Odili sets out to narrate events which took place a while ago from the privileged point of closure when the experiences being narrated are over, and everything now makes sense and can be fitted into a pattern. But retrospective narration is subject to a major qualification or caveat: unless the reader knew, or admits, that Chief Nanga was a man of the people, 'the story I'm going to tell will make no sense.'[16] In effect, the story is told from a stable present, but its meaning and value lies either in the past (when Chief Nanga was a man of the people) or a textual, rather than real, future when his fate will be revealed. However, making sense of the contemporary situation will continue to be a problem for both Odili and the reader.

This problem is further complicated by what I consider to be the second level of mediation in the novel: this is the moment when the narrator takes us back to that eventful afternoon when Odili renewed his acquaintance with Chief Nanga on the minister's visit to the Anata Grammar School. But instead of linking the events of that afternoon with the moment of narration (the first level of mediation), Odili immediately introduces another level which takes us still further back in time to sixteen years previously when Nanga was a poor school teacher and the narrator was one of his pupils. Further, this moment of mediation is followed by a fourth level in which we are brought forward to a more immediate past (1960) when a crisis in the government and the purge of intellectuals disillusioned Odili with post-colonial politics.

Why does the narrative roam from one level to the other and how are we expected to explain all these movements in time and space? We cannot say that the narrator is using temporal shifts to perplex us, since no reader will have difficulties following the transitions which Odili makes; we cannot even say that Achebe intends such shifts to estrange his readers from the events narrated since many of them are clear; in essence, such shifts are intended to underscore the problem Odili has in establishing causal relationships and in accounting for time periods and their meanings. As both a character and narrator, Odili would prefer to fit the truths and realities of the nation – and Chief Nanga's place in the collapse of the nationalist dream – into clear political, cultural and social categories, but the historical crisis in the new nation negates this desire for systematization. Odili would prefer, as he strenuously tries to do in the first chapter, to present us with Chief Nanga as a typological character, one whose development mirrors the different stages in the evolution of the colony into a nation. In this connection, the narrator strives to pigeonhole Chief Nanga in three categories: the innocent school master (p. 2), the nascent politician he admired (p. 3), and the party boss whom he came to detest (p. 5). To explicate and represent the pitfalls of national consciousness in Africa, the narrator wants us to read the rise and fall of Nanga as an allegory of the promise and betrayal of nationalism.

But Odili's attempt to cast Chief Nanga's life in terms that mirror the allegory of the nation confronts a basic problem: Chief Nanga never seems to have shared Odili's puritan dream and longing that independence would cure the country of its ills; the minister's corruption was never the result of a fall from a previous state of innocence or idealism. Odili has simply projected his own desire for such innocence and idealism to the man of power, and his attempts to fit Chief Nanga's life into an ideal scheme confronts the narrator with numerous problems of interpretation. As a consummate performer, Chief Nanga appeals to Odili's sense of the imaginary; he forces the young man to invest in fantasies which are not founded on any clear sense of the political masks with which the minister has surrounded himself; the 'man of the people' does not change in the course of the story, but he has the power to force those around him to portray him according to their interests and desires. Thus, when the minister cheerfully recognizes Odili in public at the beginning of the novel, the latter is made to feel as if he had become 'a hero in the eyes of the crowd' (p. 9).

In Chief Nanga's presence, realities which Odili thought were fixed begin to shift: 'Everything around me became suddenly unreal; the voices receded to a vague border zone. I knew I ought to be angry with myself but I wasn't. I found myself wondering whether – perhaps – I had been applying to politics stringent standards that didn't belong to it' (p. 9). This is an apt example of the problem Odili encounters when he tries to give meaning to events. First, there is the discovery that realities are fluid, that identifiable experiences don't always have clear meanings, thus everything around him, which appeared so transparent a few minutes before, appears vague and unreal. Secondly, when the world resists the narrator's attempts to fit it into a preconceived schema, the narrating self is disturbed and dismayed, especially because what he expected to be his natural reaction (anger) does not materialize. Finally, Odili is forced to question his authority – has his ideology been flawed and incomplete so far, has he applied unrealistic standards to the *polis*?[17] The tentativeness in the above quotation is no doubt a sign that Odili's perspective has been destablized by Chief Nanga's presence.

The failure of things to fit into a preconceived pattern, and Odili's increasing awareness of the incompleteness of his ideology, becomes troublesome to the narrator because, as I noted above, his desire is to present us with a complete perspective, one which will account for all the contradictory strands that went into the making and unmaking of the nation. Indeed, Odili's shifting strategies of representation can be seen as attempts to present the country as a totality and its history as a complete narrative. At the beginning of the novel, the narrator's desire for totality is such that it is not enough for him to cite his own experiences (in regard to the purge of intellectuals); he also needs collaborating sources. Therefore, he has gone out of his way to preserve documents from the period – in the form of an editorial from an official newspaper (p. 4) and a distorted report in the Hansard (p. 5) – to help him represent his country's *zeitgeist* during the first few years of independence.

What needs to be stressed here, however, is that not even such documentation provides us with an adequate framework for representing the truths and realities of the nation in those turbulent times. In view of the contradictory nature of those truths and realities, and of the narrator's incomplete knowledge of some key events, narration can only continue if Odili acknowledges that it is impossible 'to convey in cold print the electric atmosphere of that day' and that he cannot recall what his feelings were because 'You must remember that at that point no one had any reason to think there might be another side to the story' (p. 5). These comments could be applied to the problems of meaning which Achebe poses in *A Man of the People*, too: written narrative ('cold print') can never match the original experience; every story is limited in the sense that there is always another side which is not accessible to the reader, even when that reader (the 'You') has been an observer of the scene. If the story cannot be complete, because the events to which it refers are contradictory and the languages from which it draws its narrative power are polyglot, then what allows such a story to proceed is its ability to call attention to its own limitations, to the problematics of narration in the postcolonial moment. As we will see in the next chapter, this would later become the central theme in *Anthills of the Savannah*.

As far as *A Man of the People* is concerned, it seems to me that for narration to proceed in a situation where the narrator is in danger of being overwhelmed by historical events, and in view of the conflicting social realities the narrator has to deal with, especially those events that always seem to block the movement of the story, Odili must become cognizant of the dangers and challenges of story telling as a process. In this connection, narration becomes a form of meta-commentary, what Jameson defines as 'a commentary on the very condition of the problem itself.'[18] Consider, for example, how Odili's struggle to introduce Elsie into his story becomes a commentary on the problems of narration itself:

> Well, Elsie! Where does one begin to write about her? The difficulty in writing this kind of story is that the writer is armed with all kinds of hindsight which he didn't have when the original events were happening. When he introduces a character like Elsie for instance, he already has at the back of his mind a total picture of her; her entrance, her act and her exit. And this tends to colour even the first words he writes. I can only hope that being aware of this danger I have successfully kept it at bay. As far as humanly possible I shall try not to jump ahead of my story (pp. 23–4).

Odili's anxieties are twofold: First, he fears that in narrating events in which meanings only become apparent after the fact, then writing negates the necessity that motivated it in the first place, that is, the need to capture the confusion of the times. Secondly, retrospective narration is predicated on the problematic assumption that a narrator distanced from events in time and place can confer a sense of coherence on past experiences. This assumption is deceptive not only because the drama of the nation is still unfolding as Odili writes, but also because the value of the experiences he witnessed lay in their fragmental and unpredictable nature, rather than any artificial sense of narrative unity and temporal coherence. As a narrator, Odili can only content himself with the belief that by acknowledging, and even reproducing, the fragmentary and occulted nature of experience, he has avoided disguise and duplicity.

Of course, some readers may well wonder why Achebe concerns himself with such problems of narration. Wouldn't it be easier for the novelist to use a traditional heterodiegetic narrative in which the narrator, who is not a character in the situation and events recounted, dons the privilege of omniscience and hence has access to the total picture? One could respond to this question by showing how one of the main themes of *A Man of the People* is how, when we are involved in the 'original event', we cannot have a total picture of things, for our involvement in such events is also censored. As we will see later in this chapter, when Odili becomes a player in the theatre of contemporary history, his representation of events becomes distorted. Furthermore, Achebe uses a first person narrator to tell the story from within so that he can show how postcolonial subjects are caught up in a great ironic moment which also calls attention to their historical belatedness – independence was expected to be a break with the colonial past, but has become, instead, the apotheosis of colonialist ideology and rhetoric.

What are the narrative implications of this historical irony? For one, meanings – and indeed the organization of events – becomes only possible after the event. Several minor events illustrate this point well. As a young boy, Odili was kicked out of a friend's house (because of his father's vocation as an agent of colonialism) and was chastised by his father for being the victim; significantly, the value of this event, as a commentary on the relationship between father and son, would only become apparent years later: 'I was only fifteen then and many more years were to pass before I knew how to stand my ground before him' (p. 30). In another instance, Odili bought a watch believing it was 'everything-proof' (because it was advertised as such), but 'Now I know better' (p. 38). As a direct observer of events, Odili is not a good and reliable source because he is easily entranced by the magic of the moment or simply deceived by an overt rhetoric that conceals the reality of things. For example, although he has been a keen observer of his country's politics for many years, Odili observes, retrospectively, that it was only when he was living in Chief Nanga's house that he was able to gain insight into the affairs of the country and to sink his teeth in the 'hard kernel of fact':

> sitting at Chief Nanga's feet, I received enlightenment; many things began to crystallize of the mist – some of the emergent forms were not nearly as ugly as I had suspected but many seemed much worse. I was not making these judgements at the time, or not strongly anyhow. I was simply too fascinated by the almost ritual lifting of the clouds' (pp. 39–40).

The above commentary highlights both the benefits and liabilities of Odili as a narrator. He tells us that his stay with Nanga has been insightful and has lifted the mist that surrounds the postcolonial situation; as a result, the things he witnesses in the minister's household challenged his previous conception of things; in effect, the narrator functions as a source of insight into the political corruption surrounding the new men of the people. But Odili also tells us that he was not making any judgements when these things were happening because he was mesmerized by political ritual; the insights he gained only had value much later when the whole picture was clear; in this sense, what Odili conceived to be his insight, initially, was also a form of blindness; he could not turn his knowledge into practical value. As I will argue below, as a first person narrator, Odili allows Achebe to both expose the corrupt world of our politicians, but also the limited knowledge of the interpreters of this world – the intellectuals.

Furthermore, the dialectic of insight and blindness, which characterizes Odili's function as a narrator, enables Achebe to explicate the postcolonial condition as more occulted than it may appear to casual observers. For what we are dealing with here are not merely the transparent truths and realities of the nation, as Odili may be tempted to argue, but also the indeterminate *polis* of the postcolonial state, a world which will not allow for a monological, or authoritative form of narration because '[T]he surprises and contrasts in our country were simply inexhaustible' (p. 40). Odili's function as a character and narrator should be valued both for the insights he provides and the blind spot in which he is imprisoned. If we don't consider the latter situation closely enough, then we will be entrapped in the narrator's duplicity, erroneously believing, as Lindfors has, that Odili 'has managed to remain untainted amidst all the surrounding corruption and his clear vision provides an undistorted view of a warped society.'[19]

What is surprising about Lindfors's conclusion is that there is no evidence in the novel that Odili sees himself as an untainted man (maybe a reformed 'sinner'); there are also no grounds for characterizing the narrator's perspective as undistorted (although he may try to create the illusion of objectivity), for his narative is built around the impossibility of developing a true perspective in a world of so much duplicity and manipulation. As both a character and narrator, Odili is not immune from such duplicity: at one stage in the novel, he overhears Chief Nanga pouring scorn on 'our young university people' of which Odili is representative; the narrator's reaction is a perfect example of what I mean by duplicity: 'I knew I was hearing terrible things but somehow I couldn't bring myself to take the man seriously. He had been so open and kind to me and not in the least distrustful' (p. 65).

There is an element of duplicity here: at the beginning of the novel, Odili was bitter with Chief Nanga and his type for the way they had treated the university élite; now, in the comfort of the minister's house, such bitterness seems to have abated. We will return to Odili's duplicity later when we discuss his divided role as a narrator and character. What I want to emphasise here is the fact that Odili's attitude towards Nanga is not solely determined by personal interests or a lack of integrity, but is also the failure to develop an appropriate form of representation, a symptom of what Griffiths calls the inadequacy 'of relying on any single rhetorical procedure as a "grammar of values" by which to judge the events of the book.'[20]

A similar problem is encountered the moment Odili tries to account for acts and events which do not fit into his current scheme or ideology, his imaginary relationship to things. Consider his confused reaction when he overhears Elsie and Chief Nanga in an intimate moment: 'What went on in my mind at that time lacked forms and I cannot now set it down' (p. 69). It would appear that not even the passage of time will enable the narrator to capture an originally traumatic event in writing; the paralysis which the narrating self experienced during the original moment still functions as a form of censorship: 'I find it difficult in retrospect to understand my inaction at that moment' (p. 70). Discovering that Chief Nanga was actually sexually engaged with his lover, Odili feels angry and humiliated, but 'I tried in vain to find the kind of words I needed to speak to Chief Nanga' (p. 71). In all these examples, the narrative is built on Odili's failure to act, to express his feelings, or to find adequate words to deal with the situation.

As a result, Odili's narrative is built around censorship rather than elaboration. His surface rhetoric creates the impression that he understands himself (and the politics of his country), but events always seem to indicate that a deeper reality is foreclosed from the subject. As a matter of fact, after Chief Nanga's sexual encounter with Elsie, Odili becomes conscious of the extent to which surface language ('these weak and trivial thoughts') function as 'a sort of smokescreen behind which, unknown to me, weighty decisions were taking shape' (p. 75). Moreover, Odili is marginalized from the 'great and momentous events' which dominate his narrative. Such events often take place in his absence, away in Anata or in hospital; they are common knowledge ('As the whole world now knows'), but because Odili controls the narrative, his removal from such events forces us to question his authority as a narrator. Indeed, while the country plunges into political chaos, and while the resulting events 'become so widely known in the world at large' (p. 140), Odili lies unconscious in a hospital; because his knowledge of such events comes to him through secondary sources, his determinate conclusions must always remain suspect.

III. Ironic Discourse and The Art of Negation

Looking back at the circumstances in which he wrote *A Man of the People*, Achebe observed (in 1973) that the world ushered in by political independence had been one of estrangement and confusion for African peoples. Independence, noted Achebe, had begotten a pulverized reality in which the gap between nationalist rhetoric and political practice was becoming obvious, and it was difficult for people to get a grip of the 'new cloud' that had appeared on the African sky: 'one hears that the party boss is already conducting a whispering campaign. "Yo done see us chop," he says, "now you see *dem* chop. Which one you like pass?" And the people are truly confused' (MY, 70). In effect, the new politics had also created its own rhetoric, its order of discourse, a discourse of duplicity and repression, of division and domination. In the circumstances, it is not difficult to see why Achebe would want to reproduce this new political discourse in *A Man of the People*; but he was also keen to undermine the representative and authoritative claims of the discourse of power and domination. He wanted to evoke narrative opposition to the new official order of things.

My contention here is that Achebe's turn to an ironic mode of discourse and its related forms of negation in *A Man of the People* was prompted by his need to develop an alternative way of representing the postcolonial state. As Rainer Warning has observed, 'Irony has its historical position in times of transition between the old that has already passed on and the new that cannot yet be made out,' and is conceived in 'an epoch of historical upheaval and change'.[21] There is no doubt that when Achebe was writing *A Man of the People* historical upheaval and unprecedented political change had come to characterize Nigeria; but if ironic discourse is the rhetorical mode most closely associated with historical upheaval and political changes, we might wonder why Achebe had not used irony in representing the equally traumatic period of transition from autonomy to colonialism which we discussed in *Things Fall Apart* and *Arrow of God*.

The obvious response to this question is that in the earlier periods represented in these novels historical trauma is somehow distant from the moment of writing; there is also a clear understanding of what has been lost and the character of the new value system ushered in by colonialism. Furthermore, historical upheaval is introduced or catalyzed by external forces. In contrast, the movement from colonialism to national independence creates conditions for irony not only because the historical trauma is more recent, indeed contemporaneous with the act of writing, but also because we are now also responsible for the upheaval we decry so much. More significantly, ironic discourse is generated by the disjunctive rhetoric of postcolonialism: on one hand, we are being told that there has been a radical transition from colonialism to independence, but, on the other hand, the evidence on the ground seems to point to the continuity and consolidation of colonial institutions.

Ironic discourse – rather than ironic speech acts which are confined to words which mean the opposite of what they state – refers to the total strategy the novelist adopts to deconstruct dominant or official discourse and thereby expose the 'cold facts' which official rhetoric conceals. Thus, ironic discourse is predicated on a cultural critique of dominant institutional traditions. According to Richard Howey, irony is a cultural phenomenon dependent on specific historical references:

> Great irony is itself a cultural event of the first order of importance for it already implicitly contains a perspective which allows for another dimension or order of evaluation. That is to say, irony, which has as its object the cultural patterns and traditional institutions, has a positionality which places it 'outside' of these patterns and institutions and it is this positionality which through ironic juxtaposition brings a new evaluational perspective into play.[22]

Certainly, Odili's narrative is conditioned by his need to find a position of narration and social commentary outside the institutions of the postcolonial state. He finds himself in a world in which truth comes out too late, or when no one is listening (p. 4), a world of contradictions and speculation in which the national language has been reduced to a series of meaningless clichés. But on another level, such clichés are important because they symbolize, in language and speech, the values by which people may order their lives. Words such as 'never-never arrangement' (p. 43) might not make sense to Odili, but they are the key to a system of graft and corruption reaching to the highest echelons of the government. Such 'official' language masks deep political problems with the most harmless words. But as I hope to show in the following pages, Achebe develops ironic strategies which will help his readers explicate this world and, at the same time, distance themselves from it.

As a narrator, Odili represents events and spectacles in such a way that the reader cannot but sense his or her involvement in them; at the same time, however, he draws such scenes into what Warning calls 'ironic negativity'.[23] For Odili to disengage himself from the institutionalized political and cultural space (the scene of corruption), he must represent events as valuable to those who initiate them (the actors) but valueless to the narrator and his readers. Double irony becomes important here. For example, when members of the hunter's guild come out to perform for Chief Nanga at the opening of the book, they cause a stir because they 'never came out except at the funeral of one of their number, or during some very special and outstanding event' (p. 2). This statement is double-edged: on one hand, it is ludicrous that a secretive guild should consider the visit of Chief Nanga worthy of their attention; but on the other hand, this act shows how the new party boss has become a special person in the new cultural text. As a narrator Odili resorts to irony to play off these meanings aganist one another: occasionally one of the hunters will shoot at a branch to impress the crowds, but most of them 'reserved their precious powder to greet the minister's arrival – the price of gunpowder like everything else having doubled again and again in the four years since this government took control' (p. 2). The hunters are hence going to waste their gunpowder to greet a man responsible for their economic woes.

A more dramatic example of double irony in the novel is the ostensible poisoning of Chief Koko (pp. 32–5): when the minister thinks his cook has put poison in his coffee, his hysteria underlines the fear with which the new men in power live; it also exposes the emptiness of their rhetoric, for in this case the 'ironic twist' is that the 'poison' was just locally processed coffee, itself the subject of a massive government campaign to promote the use of 'locally made products' (p. 35), which the cook had used because he could not find the imported stuff which the minister prefers. Odili's attitude toward this event is also subject to double irony, too: while the two ministers run scared, the narrator adopts an almost indifferent posture as if their drama is of little significance to him; at the same time, however, he believes important lessons can be drawn from the episode, especially since Chief Koko's fear mirrors that of Chief Nanga.

Since Odili is the one who draws our attention to the ironic implications of the above events, his method of narration functions, to borrow Warning's words, counterfactually 'taking as event something that in the cultural text has lost its eventful character, or, on the other hand, interpreting as nonevent something that in the cultural reference text has the full status of an event.'[24] If we remember that the cultural text refers to society or experience, while the real text is what takes place in the book, it is not difficult to figure out the ironic disjuncture between what takes place outside the narrative and how it is represented by Odili. In short, an ironic mode of representation becomes the 'hero's' strategy of transgressing the boundaries established by institutions. Warning observes, in an important revision of Yuri Lotman's theory on topological boundaries and hereditary social spaces, that this transgression of the boundary can be resisted by the existing order, or it 'can just as well shake an existing order, destroy it, or lead to a new order.'[25] In A Man of the People, there is pronounced ambiguity in the way Odili transgresses boundaries in his quest for a new political order.

Of course, Odili becomes involved in politics ostensibly because he wants to change the existing order, but his motives are not entirely pure, and there is always a lingering suspicion, in both his and the reader's mind, that politics is the weapon he will use against Nanga for stealing Elsie. Indeed, there is a sense in which Odili's political commitment is ironic because it is not sanctioned by his stated intention. Moreover, the reader cannot fail to see how Odili's political transgression is determined by the fictional rather than the cultural text; he has elevated politics to an aesthetic level because this is the only way he can engage with it and still retain what he considers to be his integrity. Thus, Odili is thrilled by the theatrical aspects of his political organization rather than their pragmatic function. Why, for example, does Odili write about his bodyguard as if the latter is a toy which has been given to a boy as a present? Because it is only by casting Boniface and his activities in poetic language that the narrator can confront the unsavoury political activities in which he has become involved in a quixotic bid to shake the existing order (p. 112).

To be managed, violent political drama has to become the subject of irony; only then can it be rewritten as aesthetics:

The fellows we ran into carried placards, one of which read: NANGAISM FOREVER: SAMALU IS TRAITOR. It was the first time I had seen myself on a placard and I felt oddly elated. It was also amusing, really, how the cowards slunk away from the roadblocks they had put up when Boniface reached out and grabbed two of their leaders, brought their heads together like dumb-bells and left them to fall to either side of him. You should have seen them fall like cut banana trunks. It was then I acquired my first trophy – the placard with my name on it. But I lost my windscreen which they smashed with stones. It was funny but from then on I began to look out for unfriendly placards carrying my name and to feel somewhat disappointed if I didn't see them or saw too few (p. 113).

Here, experience has become a game, a spectacle in which the distinctive values of the event (political campaign) and the nonevent (Odili's name on a placard) have become reversed. Later, Odili attends one of Chief Nanga's meetings in disguise, and instead of reflecting on the dangers of walking into enemy territory, he begins to exercise his fancy, projecting himself onto an imaginary scene before real events overtake him (p. 138). In his fancy, Odili had visualized a dialectical exchange between himself and Chief Nanga's supporters; when the crowds set upon him and beat him up, when reality overtakes fantasy, the narrator's perspective and authority have become undermined and negated.

Another important form of ironic negation in this novel takes linguistic forms, for the trope of irony, as Hayden White has observed, 'provides a linguistic paradigm of a mode of thought which is radically self-critical with respect not only to a given characterization of the world of experience but also to the very effort to capture adequately the truth of things in language.'[26] One of the reasons why it is so difficult to capture the truth of things in *A Man of the People*, is the instability of language itself, which, in turn, evokes a rhetoric of doubt. As a narrator, Odili's primary function is to capture a mode of language and narration that distances his readers from the corrupt world of Chief Nanga and his associates. Represented through clichés and empty phrases, the neocolonial world is shown to be either valueless, hopelessly imprisoned in the colonial structures which it mimics, or basically dishonest because it asserts what it does not intend.

Consider Grammarphone's representation of Nanga at the beginning of the novel: 'She was now praising Micah's handsomeness, which she likened to the perfect, sculpted beauty of a carved eagle, and his popularity which would be the envy of the proverbial traveller-to-distant-places who must not cultivate enmity on his route' (p. 1). There is always the chance that the singer's adoration of Nanga is genuine and she may mean every word she says, but her inflated discourse only succeeds in alienating the reader from the minister. An excellent example of mimicry is the *Daily Chronicle* editorial which attacks 'those decadent stooges versed in textbook economics and aping the white man's mannerisms and way of speaking', in a language and tone which has itself been picked from the English gutter press (p. 4). When the language of others is reproduced as cliché, its emptiness is made manifest, as it is lifted away from what Culler calls 'human praxis and intentionality in order to make it stupid.'[27]

How often does it appear to Odili that the ironies of the postcolonial world can only be comprehended if they are rendered as stupid as the language used to explain them away or to avoid dealing with their implications? After reading a notice on ways of disposing human excrement, inserted by the City Clerk of Bori in the *Daily Chronicle*, Odili asserts that '[T]he surprises and contrasts in our great country were simply inexhaustible. Here was I in our capital city, reading about pails of excrement from the cosy comfort of a princely seven bathroom mansion with its seven gleaming, silent action, water-closets' (p. 40). The bottom line is this: we cannot understand this world without distancing ourselves from it; because the narrator cannot organize such absurd realities through figures of logic and perception, ironic negation allows him to distance himself, and his reader, from the language he uses to represent the absurd situation.

The latter point becomes poignant if we recall that the power of dominant language derives from its ideological capacity to conceal its meanings and intentions from its interlocutors. It is brought home to Odili when he listens to the American, sent to advise his government on 'how to improve its public image in America' explain race relations in the United States:

> 'We have our problems,' he said, 'like everyone else. Some of my people are narrow as a pin – we have to admit it. But at the same time we have gotten somewhere. No one is satisfied, but we have made progress.' He gave some facts and figures about lynching which I don't remember now. But I do remember his saying that lynching was not racial in origin and that, up to a certain year like 1875 or something, there had been more whites lynched than negroes. And I remember too his saying that in five of the last ten years there had been no lynchings at all. I noticed that he did not say the last five years (p. 44).

In the above quotation, we see Odili's dual role as a character and an ironic narrator at work: he begins by quoting John directly, then he abandons this attempt to represent the other's speech directly, as if he has decided that the American's speech has no authenticity, credibility, or original value; in the last parts of the passage, John's language is recited selectively to underscore its duplicity and stupidity.

This shift from direct speech to re-citation is important to Achebe's narrative intentions: we can only be liberated from dead and duplicitous language if we dissociate ourselves from it; irony helps us realize how illogical and selective John's argument is; and yet, this stupid language has a certain kind of institutional power and hence cannot be dismissed. As a narrator, Odili must represent stupidity but also generate an ironic discourse that might allow his readers to escape the snare of deceptive rhetoric. For however much we might want to escape the stupidity that characterizes Odili's world, it is a stupidity which, because of the position of those who use it, has immense power. In essence, when even language itself has become corrupted, meanings are not produced by any evocation of the truth, but by the arbitrary attribution of linguistic signs to certain things. Thus, Jean, the American woman, might tend to overdo the 'waist wriggle' in the highlife dance, but her dancing, however erroneous it might seem to us, is possibly modeled on those 'breast-throwing, hip-jerking, young women which a neighbouring African state had made and was showing abroad as an African ballet' (p. 51). The reality of an African dance has hence been invented by a state.

IV. The Story and its Situation

If Achebe resorts to the kind of radical and disjunctive ironies which permeate *A Man of the People* to underscore the instability of the postcolonial situation, his use of Odili as an ironic narrator further undermines the process by which readers try to create meanings in the indeterminate politics of the African state after independence. In many ways, Odili's narrative posture, and his strategies of self-representation, call attention to his own uncertain position in the discourse he is supposed to control. Consequently, the narrator's use of language is not immune to the ironic paradigms which he triggers and others that he might not even be aware of; his discourse takes place in an ironic context in which 'figurative language falls back upon itself and brings its own potentials for distorting perception under question.'[28] True, Odili has adopted an authoritative narrative posture, but a closer scrutiny of his discourse shows that even his linguistic characterizations of reality are partial and incomplete, and hence not immune from the ironies he targets in the utterances of other subjects.

Take, for instance, the language the narrator adopts to represent the fall of Dr Makinde, the minister of finance: the intellectual is described as 'tall, calm, sorrowful and superior,' striking a demeanor in sharp contrast to the 'most unedifying spectacle' of the less-educated politicians; unlike the 'garbled version' in the Hansard, the minister's speech to parliament is clear and well-prepared, and its distortion drives Odili to tears 'and I don't cry all that easily' (p. 6). However, Odili's perception of Dr Makinde's ordeal is an act of verbal figuration that does not give the reader a better understanding of the political crisis that grips the country at this historical juncture: was the finance minister right because he was university educated? Wasn't there some validity to the cabinet's rejection of his austerity plan? The truth is, Odili adopts a language which is both inadequate and artificial because, in spite of his authoritative voice, the situation he represents is too complex to be reduced to the 'poetic' language which Odili adopts here. His authoritative tone aside, Odili functions as the vehicle of uncertainty and doubt; narrating from within the system of values and paradigms which his narrative is supposed to critique, he cannot be the source of an alternative perspective, and this forces us to question his objectivity.

While it is doubtful whether Odili ever seeks objectivity in his narration, it is quite clear that he does not allow for alternative perspectives in his discourse. For example, the only reason why the other teachers in his school don't support him in opposing the plan to line up to greet Chief Nanga is because they 'were all dead from the neck up' or, in the case of his friend and colleague Andrew Kadibe, they are tied to Nanga by 'Primitive loyalty' (p. 7). The words and phrases Odili uses to dismiss other perspectives points not only to the arrogance and sense of superiority which limits his way of organizing the world in narrative, but also shows how he is imprisoned in the same kind of superficial language he attacks in others. In his representation of events, the narrator bestows value on events and deprives them value in the same breath.

Consider, for example, the narrator's decision to join a new political party:

> I must say that I was immediately taken with the idea of the Common People's Convention. Apart from everything else it would add a second string to my bow when I came to deal with Nanga. But right now I was anxious not to appear to Max and his friends as the easily impressed type. I suppose I wanted to erase whatever impression was left of Max's unfortunate if unintentional presentation of me as a kind of pitiable jellyfish. So I made what I intended to be a little spirited sceptical speech (p. 78).

Here, Odili's representation of himself and others is determined by the simple need to protect his ego, to project a certain image of himself and to condition the way other characters view his condition. Important public events – the impeding collapse of the political situation in the country and the formation of a new political party – are secondary to private motives. One suspects that the narrator's scepticism towards the discourse of others is also a manifestation of doubts about his own subjectivity and confusion about his motives. However, Odili's difficulties as a narrator go beyond his own quest for an appropriate mode of self-representation: the narrator's self-centredness arises from his inability to extend himself to others, to a cause or a community.

Since Achebe believes that '[T]hose who have experienced fulfillment all attest to the reality of . . . otherness' (HI, 36), Odili's incompleteness will always be linked to his egotism, to his failure to extend himself to others. But this failure is also symptomatic of a larger breakdown between the self's relation to the other, whether this is a community or shared body of values. As a postcolonial subject, Odili exists in a context in which there is no shared and certain body of 'belief and norms of behaviour' (HI, 100), hence no system of values or thought into which he can extend himself and achieve fulfillment. Narration, rather than functioning as a process by which the narrator discovers and organizes a knowable world, becomes the process by which the subject relives the anxiety of colonial division and fragmentation and the failure of the postcolonial state to reintegrate the self into a community.

In Achebe's novel, such anxieties are exemplified, on the linguistic and syntactical level, by the failure of his characters to find a common national idiom, and Odili's inability to identify a national community which might symbolize his desire for a postcolonial identity. Like many people born in the nationalist period, Odili assumed that a national idiom would be the logical manifestation of a national consciousness; he is hence troubled by the representation of national identity through clichés and phrases which appeal to divisiveness. Early in the novel, Chief Nanga invites Odili to come to the capital and 'take up a strategic post in the civil service' because '[W]e shouldn't leave everything to the highland tribes. My secretary is from there; our people must press for their fair share of the national cake' (p. 12). The phrase 'national cake' is greeted with applause by the audience, which sees it as a symptom of the minister's learnedness, but the ironies of such superficial speech is not lost on the reader: the minister appeals to ethnic divisions but is applauded for his 'ownership of the white man's language' (p. 12).

Indeed, a few moments later Nanga asserts that he prefers to make his speeches in English because 'he had learnt from experience that speeches made in the vernacular were liable to be distorted and misquoted in the press' (p. 14). Above all, English is now posited as a unifying language bringing together 'all citizens of our great country whether they came from the highlands or the lowlands' (p. 14). Of course, none of the arguments which Nanga makes seem to be authentic given the superficial nature of his discourse; his pronouncements float around on the surface unconnected to commitments or disinterested motives. Detached from real signifiers and significant social referents, the rhetoric of the politicians matches the opportunism that drives the country to 'the verge of chaos' (p. 100).

Now, if we accept a common semiological premise that there is a homological relation between a sentence and a discourse (according to Barthes 'a discourse is a long sentence . . . just as a sentence . . . is a short "discourse" '[29]) and that sentences help writers organize scattered units into coherent meanings, then the failure of the nation state to find its own idiom is manifested in the degeneration of national language into petrified sentences. In spite of the many attempts Odili makes to organize 'the affairs of the nation' in a coherent manner, his discourse always flounders on his petrified syntax. Consider the following sentence: 'Max and some of his friends having watched with deepening disillusion the use to which our hard-won freedom was being put by corrupt, mediocre politicians had decided to come together and launch the Common People's Convention' (p. 77). Here we have an obvious disjunction between tone and vehicle: the narrator expresses a common sentiment – the urgent need for change and renewal – but his sentence reproduces the clichés used by the disgraced politicians. Thus, Odili expresses a genuine sentiment but undermines it through his semantic choices.

Indeed, Odili cannot even find the right words to express some of his most profound feelings; when we reflect on his reactions to dramatic scenes and situations, we are struck by the incongruency of his sentences. In an illustrative scene, Odili, watching Edna come out of a room, loses his composure, but he cannot find the words to express any sense of 'inner reality' to the reader: 'As she emerged into the front room all my composure seemed to leave me. Instead of holding out my hand still seated as befitted a man (and one older than she to boot) I sprang to my feet like some woman-fearing Englishman. She screwed up her face ever so slightly in an effort to remember me' (p. 90). Odili's chauvinism here is symptomatic of a larger problem: he throws up sentences which are so ill-considered, so enigmatic and inadequate to the situations they represent, that we cannot take him seriously; we are forced to distance ourselves from him in the same way we distance ourselves from Nanga's hackneyed language. This form of distancing is a key ingredient of Achebe's ironic discourse in the novel; to understand a world which is turned upside down we need to adopt a disjunctive posture toward it.

The final question to consider is Odili's deliberate adoption of an ironic framework as the only viable means of organizing his world: why does he decide to reorder his experiences in terms of a story in which the narrator's uncertain posture questions the authenticity of the events represented? At the beginning of the novel, Odili clearly defines his work as 'a story' (p. 1) which is intended to help the reader understand a highly contentious and confused time. Later, at a critical juncture in the novel, when Odili accompanies Chief Nanga to a book exhibition, he tells us that he had ambitions to write a novel (p. 58). Odili is attracted to the novel as a mode of representation because of what Culler calls 'the enabling convention' of the genre – 'the transparency and representative power of language.'[30] In its ideal and most traditional sense, the novel refers to a familiar world; the sentence gestures toward, and hence normalizes, realities which the reader is familiar with. But as we have already seen, an ironic discourse presents us with a world where there is a radical disjunction between words and things, a world of clichés and social fictions, in which the reader becomes as alienated as the narrator. And so, the question to pose here is this: why does Odili wade into a confused and murky world using narrative strategies which question his authority as a narrator?

To represent the realities of the postcolonial situation, Odili must fictionalize scenes and characters encountered in the past and in the process use his imagination to 'create for himself a different order of reality from that which is given to him' (HI, 96). Caught in the midst of disparate experiences, the narrating subject has no access to the pattern or significance of what he encounters; and so he seeks retrospective knowledge because this kind of knowledge cannot affect the turn of events – what is done in the past is done – the narrator can only hope for an imaginative recreation of the past as a lesson for the future. In this connection, it is important to underscore the differences between Odili as a character caught in the midst of things, and as a narrator armed with the kind of retrospective knowledge that makes ironic discourse possible. As a character Odili is imprisoned in 'emergent forms' (p. 39); he is a subject in a series of political spectacles which make it impossible for him to make strong judgements (p. 40). As we have already seen, his first response to many situations is spontaneous and his emotions are mixed.

The most obvious example of Odili's mixed or divided stance is his attitude toward Jailo, the nonconformist novelist. First, Odili forms a poor opinion of the novelist because the latter does not remember him from college; then when Jailo is scolded by the minister because of his dress, the narrator 'didn't know what to feel' (p. 62). What we see here is not simply Odili's inability to make judgements; he has affinities for Jailo, who shares a similar intellectual and cultural background which mocks the minister's 'illiteracy', but he is also under Nanga's powerful spell. As the novel progresses, it becomes apparent that the impetus for narration, as far as Odili is concerned, is the need to rewrite his self in order to understand it. While the early parts of the novel were concerned with external events – instances in which Odili is involved as a character but distanced from as a narrator – the second portion of the text becomes more introspective and self-analytical. As Chief Nanga's rival in politics and romance, Odili finds it imperative to confront his own motives in a gesture of 'self-analysis': 'I had to ask myself one question. How important was my political activity in its own right? It was difficult to say; things seemed so mixed up; my revenge, my new political ambition and the girl' (p. 108).

Odili's introspection, his desire to clarify things, leads to a recognition of his entangled motives; this recognition is a negative, hence ironic, mode of knowledge, which is nevertheless crucial because it helps the narrator understand his own implication in the affairs of the country. For Odili to think about the 'quick transformations' which have taken place in the country since independence, he must confront 'in particular' the changes of attitude in his 'own self' (p. 109). Before this point, creating meanings for Odili was a simple process of projection in which things had value only in relation to his ego and fantasies. For example, when he retells the affair between Nanga and Elsie to Max and his associates, Odili 'amends' his story because he is anxious to 'play down' his humiliation but even more because he 'no longer cared for anything except the revenge' (p. 76). The tone he adopts here is one of hurt and moral earnestness. Later in the novel, we know that his understanding has been transformed because he is able to mediate his own contradictions and to direct irony at himself:

> Many of us vowed then never to be corrupted by bourgeoisie privileges of which the car was the most visible symbol. And here I was in this marvelous little affair eating the hills like a yam – as Edna would have said. I hoped I was safe; for a man who avoids danger for years and then gets killed in the end has wasted his care (p. 109)

In the process of narration Odili has been able to grasp, and possibly understand, the gap that separates past ideals (the desire for change and transformation) with present realities (corruption and self-aggrandizement). His knowledge and perspective at the end of the novel is not fully cognizant of the cultural patterns and traditional institutions which lead to the pitfalls of national consciousness, but his ability to retrace the process by which the dream of national liberation was negated allows him to propose an ontological possibility for change and transformation. The great thing, we are reminded at the end of the narrative, 'is reminiscence; and only those who survive can have it' (p. 144). Reminiscence in narration is one strategy for confering significance on experience. And as we will see in the next chapter, memory is an important precondition for narration in Achebe's poetics.

6

The Story
& the Postcolonial World

Anthills of the Savannah

. . . you also have the storyteller who recounts the event – and this is one who survives, who outlives all the others. It is the storyteller, in fact, who makes us what we are, who creates history. The storyteller creates the memory that the survivors must have – otherwise their surviving would have no meaning.

Achebe, interview with Bill Moyers

I. Writing in the Postcolonial Moment

Achebe's concern with the power and authority of storytelling, of the function of the storyteller in the contemporary African situation, and the relationship of writers and intellectuals to the men of power in the postcolonial state, acquires its most urgent resonance in *Anthills of the Savannah*. For this novel, published after a gap of almost twenty years – during which the politics of Nigeria had unfolded through several military coups, a civil war, and endemic corruption – centres not so much on historical events and those who perform in the theatre of post-colonial politics, but on the form which the story of the nation takes and the interpretative problems its polis presents for those seeking concrete meanings to some of the most turbulent events on the African scene. In privileging the position of the storyteller, in comparison to 'the man who agitates, the man who drums up the people' and 'the warrior, who goes forward and fights',[1] Achebe is also calling attention to the need for his readers to look beyond the narrated events, which are grim and pessimistic, toward the future of renewal and rebirth suggested at the end of the novel.

The power of the storyteller, Achebe suggests in the epigraph that opens this chapter, does not lie simply in his or her mastery of the narrated event; rather, the narrator outlives the events he or she narrates and becomes the avatar of those memories which are crucial to the reinvention of our lives. In talking about the current political and socio-economic crisis in Africa, Achebe is not sure whether the journey we have taken since independence has been toward life or death. However, writing about this 'bad patch' as a 'segment of history' allows us to see beyond the limitations of the postcolonial moment:

> if you take the wide view of things, then you begin to see [the present crisis] as history, as human history over a long period of time, and that we are passing through a bad patch. It is not death. We are passing through a bad patch, and if we succeed, then even this experience of the bad patch will turn out to be an enrichment.'[2]

The way narrative recreates history and memory, and how this recreation gives meaning to moments of crisis and then transcends them to point out new vistas for the future, is a crucial theme in *Anthills*. In this novel, says Achebe, 'there is more of looking into the future, not just for women but for society generally; how, for example, we can use our past creatively.'[3]

In many ways, this concern with meanings and their realization in a future utopian moment is not new in Achebe's works; nor is his preoccupation with the ways in which the past can be made, through narration, to speak to the present. As we have seen in the previous chapters, all his novels can be read as one continuous quest for the meaning of the Nigerian nation in particular and the African experience in general. Achebe adopts different, and often experimental, narrative strategies, to explicate and dramatize the real and symbolic organization of the African world and to trace the evolution of certain discourses which determine the way we speak about the continent and its people. Nowhere can we find a better summary of Achebe's mission and vision as a writer as in his powerful introduction to the journal *African Commentary*, of which he is the publisher:

> We are ... committed to reclaiming the rich heritage of Africa, every inch of it, and redrawing the contours of African history which in the hands of others has been drawn, and is drawn, with great malice and lurid falsehood ... The perspectives will be many, reflecting the complexity of the problem but out of the welter will emerge a sound, clear vision of the way forward.[4]

What makes Achebe's ideological concerns and strategies of representation in *Anthills* so different from those in *No Longer at Ease* and *A Man of the People*, novels which basically deal with similar themes of political corruption, the absence of a national ethos, the pitfalls of national consciousness, and oppression and domination, is the simple fact that it is written twenty five years after independence in a post-colonial situation whose character and identity, in both the positive and negative sense, are no longer in doubt. For even when they appear to be dealing with the problems of the new or emerging nation, *No Longer* and *A Man* are narratives which use the postcolonial moment as what Edward Said calls the occasion 'for a retrospective reflection on colonialism, the better to understand the difficulties of the present in newly independent states.'[5] Such a retrospective examination of colonialism is not a priority in Achebe's writing agenda in *Anthills*: he does not dismiss our colonial past as a significant cause of our present problems, but he is fully aware of the interpretative and ideological limitations of positing colonialism as the sole origin of our present crisis.

True, Achebe still believes that the problems which all African countries face are, in an institutional and constitutive sense, traceable to colonialism and its systems: 'The withdrawal of the colonial powers was in many ways merely a tactical move to get out of the limelight, but to retain the control in all practical ways. In fact it turned out to have been even a better idea than running these colonies, because now you could get what you were getting before without the responsibility for administering it. You handed responsibility back to the natives, but continued to control the economy in all kinds of ways.'[6] But this kind of diagnosis raises several important questions which will come to determine, in crucial ways, the narrative strategies in Achebe's novel: what responsibility do Africans themselves bear for this crisis? Why have the ideologies and discourses of national consciousness, which provided clarity and vision in the nationalist period, failed to enlighten us about the postcolonial situation? Is it possible to redefine the contours of the African experience and how do we explicate those meanings that define the African world?

For narrative to dramatize and provide imaginary answers and resolutions to such questions and problems, for narrative to map a terrain in which diverse groups of Africans can speak about their condition and its problematics, it must clearly go beyond what Said calls a politics and rhetoric of blame, to come to grips and hence rethink the process of decolonization as the condition that has established the postcolonial society Achebe deals with in *Anthills*.[7] Although Achebe's narrative looks toward the future, it is also retrospective: most of the stories within it are told by narrators (Chris and Ikem) who are already dead by the time we read the novel; furthermore, these narrators are as obsessed with the past as they are concerned about the future. Indeed, the temporal conjunction between past and future allows Achebe to deal with two of his primary ideological concerns – the need to reinterpret the past to understand the present and his determination to break outside the vicious cycle of history to seek new possibilities beyond what he would call 'frozen time'.[8]

Achebe's diagnostic engagement with the past, and his quest for an unknown terrain beyond neocolonial reification, is part of a continuing effort to reinscribe and reinterpret Africa as 'the terrain contested with Europe'.[9] In this process of reinterpretation, as Said has forcefully argued, the present moment is 'a holding and crossing-over' between 'colonialism and its genealogical offspring'; it is a gap between a past which the writer must engage and transcend at the same time.[10] As a result, says Said, many postcolonial writers:

> ... bear their past within them – as scars of humiliating wounds, as instigation for different practices, as potentially revised visions of the past tending toward a future, as urgently re-interpretable and re-deployable experiences in which the formerly silent native speaks and acts on territory taken back from the colonialist.[11]

Indeed, in trying to map out new spaces for the nation, Achebe's main characters – Sam, Chris, Ikem and Beatrice – have to interrogate the past they shared, must often revise the meaning of that past in order to explain the choices they have made in the present. And in using different narrative voices, Achebe questions the three men's claim to speak for the African; the narrative redeploys the African space as heterogenous and multiple, defined by differences and contradictions, not homogenized into a singular national voice.

Achebe's rejection of a monological narrative voice, which I will explore in greater detail below, has important implications for the way he reconceives the postcolonial situation and for the way he posits narrative as a means of liberation and consciousness. This is particularly the case within the context of the independent African nation and the function of the new state as an instrument that represses rather than succours human freedom. In Fanon's theories of narrative, whose influence on Achebe's latter works cannot be underestimated, the function of narration in a colonial situation is to realize human freedom through the liberation of the nation. For Fanon, '[T]o fight for national culture means in the first place to fight for the liberation of the nation, that material keystone which makes the building of a culture possible.'[12] In Fanon's later work, as Patrick Taylor has noted, 'the liberated nation is the symbol of the totality of freedom in a temporal and spatial dimension ... Decolonization, as the entry into time and challenge to the colonizer's domination over history, transforms the lost space of the colony into the space, reconquered, of the new nation.'[13]

But the subsequent history of the postcolonial state has put Fanon's sanguine views on liberation and human freedom into question: the new nation does not always enable the constitution of a national culture or the transformation of history into a realm of freedom; on the contrary, the new nation has become an instrument of repressing cultural identity and of promoting, in one way or the other, the cultural values of the colonizer. In this sense, the new nation has betrayed its mandate and the desires and expectations of its populace. The African world, rather than follow the trajectory suggested by earlier narratives of liberation, has been turned upside down. Thus, Achebe looks at the world – 'the way it is organized' – and finds it 'inadequate': 'When you look at the possibility and then at what has been achieved, you can feel very, very bitter indeed.'[14] How can narrative liberate us from this grim, and – within the context of previous nationalist discourse – unexpected history?

Within the complexities and reversals of the postcolonial situation, Achebe's novel is plagued by doubts about its own relevance. This may appear strange, especially in view of Achebe's affirmative declarations on the power of art to rewrite history and to evacuate the self from the events that entrap it in frozen time. Nevertheless, as several reviewers have observed, *Anthills* is a novel which is haunted by (ostensibly) authorial digressions on the function of narration and writing in the postcolonial moment.[15] Such digressions often take the form of metacommentaries – commentaries on either the ideological environment in which the narrative is produced, or on the ways in which the work should be read, or even a discussion on the capacity of stories to conceal meanings. In Frederic Jameson's view, metacommentary is the process by which an act of interpretation engages itself with the strangeness of its situation; 'every individual interpretation must include an interpretation of its own existence, must show its own credentials and justify itself.'[16]

And so the initial question to pose here, as a form of entry into Achebe's text, is this: why does the author need to justify the function of his narrative and its concern with hermeneutics, the art of interpretation and critical reflection? We can possibly approach this problem by taking up Achebe's central premise about narrative, a premise articulated by the old Abazon elder in the middle of the novel:

> The story is our escort; without it, we are blind. Does the blind man own his escort? No, neither do we the story; rather it is the story that owns and directs us. It is the thing that makes us different from cattle; it is the mark on the face that sets one people apart from their neighbours.[17]

Here, narrative is presented as a form of insight (without it we are blind) and an agency with immense constitutive powers (it determines our movement, character, and identity). But this metacommentary on how narratives should be read and used already points to the crisis of meaning Achebe faces as a writer in a postcolonial situation; simply put, the old narratives of liberation, which assumed that the nation would be the fulfillment of human freedom, no longer have legitimacy. However, Achebe will not succumb to the postmodernist seduction which expresses its disappointment with the politics of liberation; he will not share the now common belief that narrative is 'no longer an adequate figure for plotting the human trajectory in society. There is nothing to look forward to: we are struck within our circle. The line is now enclosed within a circle.'[18]

On the contrary, Achebe is seeking ways of establishing new forms of narration that might have the power to liberate us from the circle of our postcolonial moment; he seeks a narrative that speaks about, but also transcends its historical imperatives. In the discourse on the story which is presented to us by the elder from Abazon, then, the power of narrative is that of an utterance, of a voice which carries within it compelling power and magic. Moreover, the old man isolates three functions of narrative which are clear indicators of the way Achebe would prefer to see his own postcolonial intellectual project: stories have dispersed (or plural) meanings, they are avatars of collective memories, and they have an erratic character.

In the first instance, the old man argues that all stories and the ideologies they support have a dialogic character; 'for what is true comes in different robes' (p. 123). If earlier nationalist narratives had assumed that the nation spoke one truth in one voice, in the postcolonial moment we are told to come to terms with the different voices and functions we play in our societies. Secondly, the power of the story is tied to its function as a depository of memories and its capacity for recall: recalling, says the old man, is greatest, because it allows the story to 'continue beyond the war and the warrior. It is the story that outlives the sound of war-drums and the exploits of brave fighters. It is the story, not the others, that saves our progeny from blundering like blind beggars into the spikes of the cactus fence' (p. 124). Clearly, the story seems to perpetuate historical events so that their meaning and significance will not be lost to future generations which might then be condemned to repeat the sins of their ancestors. At the same time, however, the story, in the process of recall, frees the subjects from the contigencies of the historical event; by abdicating the historical imperatives that evoked it in the first place, the story becomes timeless and hence acquires the power to direct our actions beyond the conditions that generated it. For Achebe, 'The storyteller appeals to the mind, and appeals ultimately to generations and generations and generations.'[19]

Third, the story has power precisely because of its complex, and even erratic character; the narrative threatens those in control because its agenda allows for different meanings. In his discourse on the power of stories, the old man evokes the name of the god Agwu, the patron saint of narrators who appears, unlike his brother Madness, to be a person of logic and control: 'Madness unleashes and rides his man roughly into the Wild savannah. Agwu possesses his own just as securely but has him corralled to serve the compound' (p. 125). However, the logic that propels Agwu to corral the storyteller to serve the community conceals the record and imperative of struggle that informs every narrative as it seeks to establish an oppositional stance vis-à-vis the dominant structures. As Ikem will later assert, 'storytellers are a threat. They threaten all champions of control, they frighten usurpers of the right-to-freedom of the human spirit – in state, in church or mosque, in party congress, in the university or wherever. That's why' (p. 153).

Indeed, the story by rewriting history (by creating a timeless and autonomous version of events so that they can speak to future generations) contests the constant attempt, by powerful institutions, to repress those collective memories that threaten control, memories that are obliterated when official history is textualized. Achebe's concern with the character and functions of stories (he tells Rutherford that 'the very nature of the story is one of the key issues in this novel'[20]) arises from his need to valorize the capacity of narrative to resist power. The struggle between power and narrative establishes the terrain in which the function of the story as the escort of the people can be explored: 'You have the story, you have the story-teller, so it is an exploration of the story and the story-teller and the way in which those who commandeer power would wish to commandeer history and so would be afraid of story-tellers.'[21]

But my initial question still remains: why does Achebe find it necessary to make the story an issue in the text, and why does he take great pains to underscore the relevance and legitimacy of narratives of liberation? The possible answer to this question is suggested by a general problematic in interpretation – the fact that works need commentaries on the way they should be read because their meanings are often censored by the other historical factors that accompany the invention of narratives. In Jameson's words, metacommentary 'aims at tracing the logic of the censorship itself and of the situations from which it springs: a language that hides what it displays beneath its own reality as language, a glance that designates, through the very process of avoiding, the object forbidden.'[22] In a world which has been turned upside down, Achebe believes that reality itself is a forbidden object; thus, narrative must be geared toward the institution of an African hermeneutics that might help us recover the hidden objects of our contemporary history.

II. The Quest for an African Hermeneutics

Halfway through *Anthills* Ikem Osodi, no doubt Achebe's example of an African deeply involved in the intellectual project of post-colonialism, is gripped by doubts about his own notions of self, community, and social purpose. Significantly, this crisis becomes obvious when Ikem, witnessing the 'stubborn sense of community' that binds Elewa and the taxi driver, becomes aware of his own isolation in the social situations which, as the editor of the government newspaper and as a poet, he has sought to represent and influence. Reflecting on his isolation, Ikem wonders how he could partake 'of this source of stability and social meaning' (p. 142). The moment he raises this question, however, he recognizes how the problem of self-identity, which he assumes to be an important precondition for social commitment, is tied to larger questions of meaning and interpretation: 'What about renouncing my own experience, needs and knowledge? But could I? I could renounce needs perhaps, but experience and knowledge, how?' (p. 142). The dilemma of the intellectual in the postcolonial situation is both one of experience and knowledge: how can intellectuals extend their experiences to those excluded from the powers and privileges ushered in by independence and how can they develop a fundamental knowledge about the conditions of a populace so different from them?

As we have already seen, Achebe assumes that '[F]ulfillment is other-centred, a giving or subduing of the self, perhaps to somebody, perhaps to a cause; in any event to something external to it. Those who have experienced fulfillment all attest to the reality of this otherness.'[23] However, many of the characters in *Anthills* often find it impossible to experience this sense of otherness because, as intellectuals and officials, their constitution as subjects is already predicted on their elevation, and hence isolation, from the kind of community that might ensure their fulfillment. Ikem decides that he cannot renounce his experience and knowledge to become like the poor; there is no way he can become like the poor 'except by faking': 'What I know, I know for good or ill. So for good or ill I shall remain myself; but with this deliberate readiness now to help and be helped' (p. 142).

On another level, however, a mode of knowledge derives its authority from what it promotes, in terms of consciousness, as much as from what it represses or is foreclosed from it, and there is no guarantee that a character's knowledge will sustain the integrity of selfhood. For example, Beatrice's knowledge and success as a student and government official has been achieved through the repression of the traditions and legends of her people. She is educated in schools which had no place 'for her bearers and the divinities with whom they had evolved. So she came to barely knowing who she was' (p. 105). Beatrice may have a vague sense of another self inside the one constituted by the official colonial culture, but this other, priestly self, has no function in her new world. In this sense, her knowledge is always wanting, blind to the other self. Indeed, there is a suggestion that since all forms of knowledge about the postcolonial condition are condemned to be partial and even deracinated, 'knowing or not knowing does not save us from being known or even recruited and put to work' (p. 105). If the 'knowing subject' is just an agent of forces beyond its control, why do many of the characters in the novel seem to be obsessed with understanding their condition? Why is developing an African hermeneutics so important to Achebe? Why is it imperative that narrative be geared toward understanding the complexity of the African crisis and its many sources.[24]

We can confront these questions more limpidly if we recall the situation that triggers the necessity of understanding and interpretation in the tradition of hermeneutics as it is represented in the hermeneutical circle. As David Hoy has argued, the hermeneutical circle is 'a fundamental principle of man's understanding of his own nature and situation. Understanding, and with it the hermeneutical circle, becomes a condition for the possibility of human experience and inquiry.'[25] This circle is not proposed as a solution to the crisis of meanings that we face in the present moment; rather it 'aims precisely to provoke reflection, and to challenge the putative certainty of established methods.'[26] In *Anthills of the Savannah* the narrative is clearly geared towards the two hermeneutical functions discussed by Hoy: on the one hand, most of the characters in the novel reflect constantly on the ways their individual selves and identities have been constructed and on the historical moments that have lead to the postcolonial situation; on the other hand, Achebe brings different narrative strategies into play to challenge previous methods of explaining this condition and the ideological explanations it has spawned.

Indeed, from the moment the novel opens hermeneutical issues are shown to be imperative in explaining the African condition. Chris Oriko's concerns at the beginning of the novel are anchored around the need to understand 'a game that began innocently enough and then went suddenly strange and poisonous' (p. 1). As an interpreter of power games at the highest levels of the government, Chris feels it is important for him to establish a logic of causation, to identify 'a specific and decisive event and say: it was at such and such a point that everything went wrong and the rules were suspended' (p. 2). But he has not 'found such a moment or such a cause although I have sought hard and long for it' (p. 2). In the circumstances, the 'witness' is forced to reject any notions of significance in the historical process, to reduce everything to a game, and then renounce his previous methods of interpretation because they made him blind or too busy to notice the gamesmanship which he has now acknowledged.

Chris concedes that he can no longer postulate the fundamental elements that have created the crisis he writes about, nor can he adjudicate different interpretations on the postcolonial condition; nevertheless, he values his role as a writer, as an observer, and agent of historical memory. He may not be able to isolate the precise origins of the crisis he writes about, but he was there at the beginning and is thus uniquely qualified to bear witness to the past that has given birth to the present moment. If Achebe's primary concern, as we saw in the previous section, is to establish a fundamental relationship between writing and memory, then Chris's retrospective look at the past is an important attempt to show how his present understanding has evolved. For even as he reflects on how his attitude toward the monster he helped birth (p. 10) has changed, Chris is also questioning, even debunking his previous modes of understanding. What began as an attempt to earnestly participate in the formation of a nation, has now degenerated into a game: Chris represents himself sitting at 'this silly observation post making farcical entries in the crazy log-book of this our ship of state'; his disenchantment with the men of power 'turned long ago into a detached clinical interest' (p. 2).

Chris's movement from commitment to detachment is symptomatic of the problems intellectuals face the moment they try to find a voice to articulate the desires and yearnings, even the idealism, that motivated them at an earlier stage in the decolonization process. The tragedy of the intellectual in government, but without power or authority, lies in what Said calls 'the constitutive limitations imposed on any attempt to deal with relationships that are polarized, radically uneven, remembered differently.'[27] This tragedy is exemplified by Ikem's attempt to understand the African situation differently, to develop a logic for explaining a condition which appears illogical. Ikem argues that the best weapon against those in power 'is not to marshall facts, of which they are truly managers, but passion. Passion is our hope and strength, a very present help in trouble' (p. 38). But what exactly is the power of passion and why does it seem to have the capacity to rescind those narratives that are based on facts, that appeal to the authority of the factual?

In a situation where the real problem of understanding and interpretation 'is having no way of knowing from one day to another, from one minute to the next, just what is up and what is down' (p. 45), passion provokes spectacles and incidents, such as the public execution (pp. 39–45), which seem to speak louder than words. Thus, Ikem's method is based on creating scenarios which might penetrate 'through the chink' in the 'solid wall of court jesters' surrounding the president or the 'new make-believe' that masks the state of the country. Where Chris might have sought facts and words to explain situations, Ikem resorts to word games which underscore the scepticism that his passion conceals. For postmodernist philosophers such as Lyotard, such word games emphasize the fact that the great narratives – which appealed to the facts of history or the integrity of the speaking subject – have lost their function, direction and goal; such narratives have become dispersed. We live at the intersection of various forms of language, says Lyotard, 'but we do not necessarily establish stable language combinations, and the properties of the ones we do establish are not necessarily communicable.'[28] Of course, Ikem believes that language games, when they are informed by passion, can be communicated; yet he seems to doubt the veracity of narrative as a liberating praxis: ' "All gestures of resistance are now too late and too empty. Gin it shall be forever and ever, Amen." Jovial words, but there is not the slightest sign of gaiety in the voice or the face' (p. 54).

Ikem's tragedy is that he desires a narrative that provokes action, but he is condemned to play word games that mirror his own disappointment and inability to change his society. Now, if we recall that in the narrative of liberation, as it has be defined by Fanon, the truth of the nation is incarnated in an 'illuminating and sacred communication'[29], then Ikem's *angst* is a result of his failure to communicate his vision to others. His agnostic attitude develops from his bitter sense of belatedness, his recognition that the gestures of resistance that might have created a 'sacred communication' have yielded to language games. Nevertheless, Achebe still holds hope for those old narratives which escort us through time and space to a realm of freedom. Consider the discourse on daughters, for example: Idemili's narrative revolves around the mysteries that surround phenomenon and the vital connection between the word and the divinity that 'sponsors' it (p. 102). When it is informed by divinity, the word ameliorates the abuses of power; thus the Almighty sends down Idemili 'to bear witness to the moral nature of authority by wrapping around Power's rude waist a loincloth of peace and modesty' (p. 102).

Achebe seems to feel, as does Ikem, that power has triumphed precisely because it has released itself from the morality embodied by Idemili. In this sense, the act of telling stories is an attempt to recover the original relationship between authority and morality. This attempt to recover original meanings and intentions – to determine what Kermode calls the 'undetected latent sense' – seeks to penetrate the surface language of power to reveal 'a secret sense; to show what is concealed is what is proclaimed.'[30] The Almighty's original intention was to confer power and authority to his creations, but to adorn both with morality. However, from the very beginning, the balance between the two entities (secular power and moral authority) was imperiled by problems which are quite central to Achebe's discourse: Idemili's devotees increased and spread all over the country. The more they spread the more they faced the problem of retaining the original balance between power and morality: 'how could they carry to the farthest limits of their dispersal adequate memories of the majesty of the Pillar of Water standing in the dark lake?' (p. 103).

Attempts to recover the original secret are hence bound to disappoint:

> Man's best attempts to snare and hold the grandeur of divinity always crumbles in his hands, and the more ardently he strives the more paltry and incongruous the result. So it were better he did not try at all; far better to ritualize that incongruity and by invoking the mystery of metaphor to hint at the most unattainable glory by its

very opposite, the most mundane starkness – a mere stream, a tree, a stone, a mound of earth, a little clay bowl containing fingers of chalk (p. 103).

If we cannot retain an original moral sense to counter the destructive effects of power, and if our attempts to hold divinity are condemned to fail, then the best we can do is narrate about our failures (hence ritualize the incongruity between moral intention and rampaging power) and to use metaphorical representations as substitutes for a dispersed divinity. But are such metaphors and rituals enough to restore moral authority to the polis? It is significant that Beatrice, who is a modern representative of Idemili, exists in a world which has repressed the rituals and practices of her divinity. But as I have already suggested, Achebe's narrative serves precisely to expose the gap between what exists and is unknown and the 'grandeur of divinity' that might have allowed us to taper power.

The kind of narrative in which the word is informed by divinity appears anachronistic in Achebe's novel for another reason: the world recovered through legends and myths is represented through a meta-phorical language that assumes a coherent relationship between signs and signifiers (the tree or stream can hence stand for Idemili's divinity); but in the postcolonial world the relationship between words and things is often one of radical disjunction. Ikem, who seeks a metaphor-ical moral order that might explain and possibly overcome 'human failing', is often struck by the absurdity of his world. For example, he is condemned for leading a simple life 'without such trimmings as chauffeurs'; the absence of extravagance stamps him 'not as a modest and exemplary citizen but as a mean-minded miser denying a liveli-hood to one unemployed driver out of hundreds and thousands roam-ing the streets'; this paradox is 'so perverse in its implications as to justify the call for the total dismantling of the grotesque world in which it grows – and flourishes' (p. 138).

Similarly, Beatrice has a clear sense of the postcolonial world as a dispersed reality which can no longer be organized around a kernel of meanings; she hence sees writing as 'the challenge of bringing together as many broken pieces of this tragic history as I could lay on' (p. 82). Even with the right scenarios and episodes, Beatrice finds it difficult to find a way to begin her story – 'Anything I tried to put down sounded wrong – either too abrupt, too delicate or too obvious – to my middle ear' (p. 82). Like most other characters in the novel, she will struggle for the right words to create meanings out of incon-gruity and to deal with contradictions which, as Ikem says, have become 'the very stuff of life' (p. 100).

Writing is hence a retrospective moment which seeks to recapture a past of promise and to contrast it with a present of failure; at the postcolonial moment of narration, the narrators must contrast the

nationalist longing for a homogenized form and culture with the fragmentation engendered by the politics of power and betrayal. In other
words, Achebe's novel forces his readers to acknowledge the two sides
to nationalism and its narratives: on one hand, there is the narrative
that willed the colonized peoples entry into history and hence freedom
and liberation; on the other hand, there is what Aijaz Ahmad has
called the 'nationalism of mourning' which has unleashed violent forces
of division and dismemberment.[31] The two movements of nationalism are highlighted in Ikem's poem 'Hymn to the Sun' (pp. 30–1).

The poem is, of course, defined by its strong elegiac tone; it is a
sustained lament for the death of the nation and the catastrophe that
has come over its people. The poem seeks a reason for present suffering
from the Almighty and wonders why attempts at sacrifice and expia-
tion have failed: 'Look, our forlorn prayers, our offerings of concilia-
tion lie scattered about your floor where you cast them disdainfully
away; and every dawn you pile up your long basket of day with the
tools and emblems of death' (p. 30). But apart from mourning the death
of the nation and its abandonment by the divinities, the 'hymn' is a
form of commemoration in which the poet evokes the power of
memory to decipher what Vernant calls 'the invisible, a geography of
the supernatural.'[32] In a poem dominated by metaphors and images of
death and suffering, Ikem seeks possibilities of going beyond the
present decay and to look forward to 'the season of renewal': the
destruction is such that 'the songbirds left no void, no empty hour
when they fled because the hour itself had died before them. Morning
no longer existed'; but this evocation of death, a way of conquering
the past with memory, carries the poet into the future.

Recounting legends of death and decay – during which time itself is
obliterated – allows the poet, in Vance's words, 'to recover, in the
name of a collectivity, some being or event either anterior in time or
outside of time in order to fecundate, animate, or make meaningful
a moment in the present.'[33] Ikem's poem seeks to recover, on behalf
of the Abazon delegation, the past of legend as a mirror in which the
present polis can look at itself; in the same moment of commemoration, the past is 'seen as a dimension of the beyond':

> And now the times had come round again out of story-land. Perhaps
> not as bad as the first times, yet. But they could easily end worse.
> Why? Because today no one can rise and march south by starlight
> abandoning crippled kindred in the wild savannah and arrive
> stealthily at a tiny village and fall upon its inhabitants and slay them
> and take their land and say: I did it because death stared through
> my eye (p. 33).

Ikem becomes concerned with death and decay in an attempt to point
out the absence of a community of spirit and a moral tradition; he
wonders whether the values that motivated the people in 'story-land'

can be revitalized in the present moment. He concludes that the situation might get worse because the conditions in which the legendary quest took place have become transformed. For this reason, the poet cannot recommence the past, nor can he acquiesce to the demands of the present; rather, his poetic quest is for what Michael M.J. Fischer calls 'revelations of traditions, re-collections of disseminated identities and of the divine sparks from the breaking of the vessels'; retrospection allows the poet 'to gain a vision for the future' and to function as a powerful critique 'of several contemporary rhetorics of domination'.[34]

III. Narrative and the Failure of National Language

At the beginning of the novel, as we have already seen, Chris tries to map the exact moment when the nationalism of restoration gave way to the nationalism of mourning. However, at the moment when Chris and his associates try to write the tragic history of the nation, even the unifying language which earlier nationalists thought would bring the nation together proves hard to grasp. In Achebe's novel, official language (in the form of decrees) co-exists with the poetic language and intellectual discourse of Ikem, which in turn rubs shoulders with the 'market' dialect of Elewa and the taxi drivers. While each language might appear valid in its own situation, what seems to bother Achebe is the loss of the ideal or mythology of the nation as a common frame of reference.

In *The Trouble with Nigeria*, Achebe speaks of his country as gifted by Providence but betrayed by those in charge of its destiny. But Achebe's agonizing over Nigeria – 'our corruption, gross inequalities, our noisy vulgarity, our selfishness' – is written with the knowledge that the nationalist desire for 'a pan-Nigerian vision' was possibly buried by Awolowo's 'success' in the Western House of Assembly in 1951.[35] 'Perhaps it was an unrealistic dream at the best of times, but some young, educated men and women of my generation did dream it,' says Achebe of the dream of the Nigerian nation.[36] Since this dream has not faded from Achebe's consciousness, one of the primary issues raised in the novel is how it can be reimagined and possibly resuscitated in imaginary terms. What narrative forms and styles can tell the story of a national dream that has disintegrated?

Achebe's use of heterogenous discourse and narratives in the novel is connected to important questions on national language and identity. Historically, as Timothy Brennan has argued, the development of the novel as a genre 'accompanied the rise of nations by objectifying the "one, yet many" of national life, and by mimicking the structure of the nation, a clearly bordered jumble of languages and styles.'[37] The novel was supposed to create a textual space in which, in the words of Bakhtin, 'the word becomes polyglot, once and for all and irreversibly. The period of national languages, coexisting but closed and deaf to each other, comes to an end.'[38] For Bakhtin, national culture is essentially the cohesiveness of a system of linguistic norms – the 'generative forces of linguistic life' – and a struggle 'to overcome the heteroglossia of language force'; national language is the desire for ideological unification and cultural centralization.[39]

But the reverse seems to be the case in the modern languages of the novel in general and in the postcolonial world in particular; while a heterogenous national language and culture is what is sought, at least on the manifest level, the policies and practices of the élite mitigate against such a language and culture; the uses of stories to animate a past of collective memory and a unified mythos pits utopian desires with the tragedies of history. Chris talks about the history of the country as if it were the history of Ikem, Sam and himself, but as Beatrice intimates, the belief that the history of the country can be encapsulated in the lives of three individuals, however influential they might have been in the shaping of its history, is based on conceit. Chris is thus forced to concede that the history of the nation – and hence its narrative – is multivalent and heterogenous: 'We tend sometimes to forget that our story is only one of twenty million stories – one synoptic account' (pp. 66–7). Achebe's anxiety, one suspects, is how these other stories can be incorporated into the narratives controlled by the élite.

Edward Said has asserted that '[O]ne way of getting hold of the commonest post-colonial debate is to analyze not its content, but its form, not what is said as how it is said, by whom, where, and for whom.'[40] For even where there might be ideological agreement on the process of decolonization and a common understanding of the problematics of the postcolonial condition, varied enunciative strategies conceal different modalities as to the reconfiguration of the national space in the moments of crisis. This is what Chris has in mind when he tells Beatrice that 'there is nothing concrete on which Ikem and I quarrel. What divides us is style not substance. And that is absolutely unbridegeable' (p. 118).

On further examination, however, this difference in style has important implications; style is a mask for intransigent theoretical and ideological positions. It is this 'strangeness' of style which Chris tries to explain to Beatrice:

> You see, if you and I have a quarrel over an orange we could settle it by dividing the orange or by letting either of us have it, or by handing it over to a third party or by throwing it away. But supposing our quarrel is that I happen to love oranges and you happen to hate them, how do you settle that? You will always hate oranges and I will always love them; we can't help it (p. 118).

In the circumstances, we cannot hope for a unitary system of values, a coherent ideology, or a formal language that will resist our hetero-glossia. In Bakhtin's words, language is heteroglot in nature because 'it represents the co-existence of socio-ideological contradictions between the present and the past, between differing epochs of the past, between different socio-ideological groups in the present, between tendencies, schools, circles and so forth, all given a bodily form.'[41] By telling his story from the perspective of different characters – a fact which some critics have criticized – Achebe is trying to give 'bodily forms' to the contradictions that inform the nation.[42]

In analyzing the different narrative styles adopted by different char-acters in the novel, we are also exploring paradigms and ideologies in contention. As Bakhtin has noted, '[T]he speaking person in the novel is always, to one degree or another, an *ideologue*, and his words are always *ideologemes*. A particular language in a novel is always a particular way of viewing the world, one that strives for a social signif-icance.'[43] Achebe's novel is anchored around three characters – Chris, Ikem, and Beatrice – who are also narrators and ideologues in the sense Bakhtin has used the word. Although the narratives of the three characters are concerned with common themes – the condition of the nation, issues of power and domination, the failure of national con-sciousness – their approach to these themes is distinctive in three respects: in the way the narrators strive for social significance in a fragmented and even disintegrating world, their quest for an appropri-ate style to narrate the postcolonial condition and knowledge to explain it, and on the kind of reflections they direct on themselves as witnesses of the unfolding drama of the nation.

In their quest for social significance, these characters draw their authority primarily from the fact that they have been witnesses to the rise and fall of the new ruling class. None of the three narratives qualify as a conventional *testimonio* (the narrators are not really excluded from authorized representations nor do they speak in the name of a collective), but they share three important aspects of the testimonio narrative as it has evolved in the last thirty years. First, all three stories are 'told in the first person by a narrator who is also the real protagonist or witness of the events he or she recounts, and whose unit of narration is usually a 'life' or a significant life experience.'[44] Secondly, the *testimonio* is a 'powerful textual affirmation of the speaking subject'; the dominant formal aspect of this narrative is 'the voice that speaks to the reader in the form of an "I" that demands to be recognized, that wants or needs to stake a claim on our attention.'[45] Thirdly, as witnesses, the narrators not only seek to represent the vera-city and truth effect of what they have experienced but also to evoke, in the reader's imagination, 'a sensation of *experiencing the real*.'[46]

But in discussing how these aspects are brought to play in each narrative, we need to stress that Achebe's storytellers, unlike the arche-typal narrators of *testimonios*, are not marginalized in the linguistic and power systems they are writing about; on the contrary they assert their authority as witnesses by showing the ways in which they affected the events which they narrate. In this sense, as Millet has noted, the discourse of a witness is not simply a reflection of his or her experience 'but rather a refraction determined by the vicissitudes of memory, intention, ideology.'[47] Indeed, Chris's narrative mirrors the other two in the ways it seeks a beginning by reflecting on the relationship between the subject – as a character and narrator – and the historical events he narrates. As we have already seen, Chris's narrative is motivated by the need to overcome anxieties about his own position in the history of the nation and especially the evolution of Sam as a dictator. His striving for social significance is futile without a clear cognition of the relationship between self and other, and the narrator's own implication in the situation that now represses him.

To be a credible witness, Chris must pre-empt questions about his own involvement in the tragic history of his country; he does this by taking responsibility for having invented some of the men who now surround the president; his 'clinical detachment' cannot conceal the fact he was 'personally responsible for recommending nearly half of them for appointment' (p. 2); as to the reputation of Professor Okong, the most notorious of the courtiers, it was Chris who built him up as a leading African political scientist and ended up 'fostering a freak baby' (p. 11). But no sooner has Chris acknowledged his implications in the tragic history of the nation than he seeks the imperative to distance himself by reflecting on the changes and transformations he has undergone; as a witness, Chris begins by informing us of the sources of his authority and veracity – we can trust him because he is right in the centre of the events he narrates. For example, while reflecting on the apologies he makes to the president, Chris makes the following observation: 'A year ago I would never had said it again that second time – without doing grave violence to myself. Now I did it like a casual favour to him. It meant nothing at all to me – no inconvenience whatever – and yet everything to him' (p. 1).

Furthermore, Chris detaches himself from the raw experiences of history and re-expresses them as stories to be read and observed; he hangs around the discredited politicians so that he can observe and write about them. Having placed himself in a position where he is both involved and detached, Chris claims the authority of the ironic gaze that can penetrate the masks of power. Consider, for example, the general wisdom, in circles of power, that 'the trouble with His Excellency is that he can never hurt a man and go to sleep over it' (p. 3). To represent such an absurdity as it exists and yet detach himself from it, the narrator resorts to irony:

That's one refinement, by the way, we've not yet lost: we do wait for his back to be turned. And some will add: That's a pity because what this country really needs is a ruthless dictator. At least for five good years. And we will laugh in loud excess because we know – bless our dear hearts – that we shall never be favoured with such an undeserved blessing as a ruthless dictator (p. 3).

If we recall that there have been 'unconfirmed rumours of unrest, secret trials and executions in the barracks,' then Chris's ironic tone is an important tool for exposing the duplicity which informs the language of the courtiers around the presidency and official discourse in general. Whereas official language (especially when it has become militarized) seeks monological meanings, Chris has adopted a discourse that plays with words to expose their double meaning: the word 'dissociate' terrorizes the cabinet because, in their militarized minds, it suggests death and annihilation (p. 5).

In his disenchantment, Chris can no longer take the generative structure of words seriously; he does not aspire for the kind of deep meanings which Professor Okong seeks; rather he seems to suggest that significance can only be skimmed on the surface of language; real meanings emerge from play not earnestness. Indeed, whereas Ikem would suggest that the only way to understand Sam is to psychoanalyze him, thereby establishing the unconscious motives for his actions, Chris prefers to represent the head of State as a performer: his excellence is often shown in dramatic scenarios; he is a man pleased with his dramatic performances; when he takes out his neatly-folded silk handkerchief out of his breast pocket, he dabs his eyes 'daintily like a fat clown' (p. 22). Ironically, by deciding to stay in the halls of power to witness the tragic unfolding of his nation's history, Chris too has become a performer; as he rightly observes, his reflections on Ikem and Sam are also a form of self-reflection: 'We are all connected. You cannot tell the story of any of us without implicating the others. Ikem may resent me but he probably resents Sam even more and Sam resents both of us vehemently. We are too close together, I think' (p. 66).

But this is only one perspective, a singular form of reflection. When we turn to Ikem's narrative, we find the basic or 'real' history may be the same, but the strategies of narration and the forms of knowledge they proffer are significantly different. As a 'second' witness, Ikem is intended to call into question the conclusions of the first; his narrative inevitably calls attention to the ambiguities, silences, and absences which exist in both the official discourse and Chris's version of things. The most important aspect of Ikem's narrative language is its extreme subjectivity – he is a master of free indirect discourse and the interior monologue. For example, when Ikem observes his neighbours, his primary concern is not the accurate observations of the world around him but the ways in which he can reinvent experiences to fit his state of mind. He thinks of the neighbour who works with the Post and Telegraphs corporation and begins to weave a scenario whose significance is not that it might fit into a scheme of reality but might satisfy the observer's state of mind:

> So it was Mr So Therefore, the notorious Posts and Telegraphs man in the next flat. He crawled through the third door. Perhaps he will beat his beautiful wife tonight; he hasn't done it now in months. Do you miss it then? Confess, you disgusting brute, that indeed you do! Well, why not. There is an extraordinary surrealistic quality about the whole thing that is almost satisfyingly cathartic (p. 34).

In effect, Ikem projects himself into ordinary reality and tries to transform it into a surreal form as if by doing so he can capture the inner, or rather invisible, nature of things. When he wakes up in the morning, he is not sure how much of what he 'witnessed' had actually happened 'and how much I had dreamt up on my own' (p. 35); in a world of mixed metaphors, he seeks significance in the deep structures (of the dream and the occult) which Chris has renounced; facts are no guarantee that you can know 'just what is up and what is down' (p. 45).

Ikem's attraction to the spectacle as a mode of mediating experience is predicted on the belief that when reality is projected or reinvented it yields those truths which have been repressed by official doctrines based on the marshalling of facts (p. 38). As we have already seen, spectacles such as public executions bring forth and dramatize the uncomfortable truths which facts try to repress. For instance, we cannot understand the perverted nature of authority if we read the official decrees it issues; authority reveals itself better in the 'ritual obscenities' it perpetrates; during the public executions, Ikem notes, '[A]uthority and its servants far exceeded my expectations that day on the beach' (p. 41). Ikem is attracted to dramatic scenarios because they seem to provide him with insights which are not based on facts or logic: at the execution, for example, he notices how the populace laughs 'so blatantly at their own humiliation and murder' (p. 41); incidents or scenarios in the market place (where 'one thousand live theatres' go on at once [p. 47]) provide an alternative handle on reality.

But in spite of his attraction to the dramatic narrative, and his refusal to be seduced entirely by the language games that have created what he calls 'the new make-believe' (p. 48), and in spite of his smugness and sense of moral superiority, Ikem fails to find fundamental explanations for events and phenomena from some of the most important and threatening performances, those connected with the exercise of power. This failure is most apparent in Ikem's representation of Sam. Now, we have already seen how Chris presented Sam as a performer, a man better understood in terms of his acts rather than beliefs; for Chris, a performance does not have value in itself, but in what it tells us about the performer and his or her audience; instead of dismissing the power play as a harmless game in which Sam is just a mere clown, Chris did allow his subjects some conflicting, ulterior, and complex motives. In contrast, Ikem presents Sam as a clearly knowable subject, '[N]ot very bright but not wicked' (p. 49).

For Ikem, the president is a harmless performer in a drama which cannot be harmful in itself; what makes Sam 'enormously easy to take' is his sense of theatre, a mode of performance detached from any real significance:

> He is basically an actor and half of the things we are inclined to hold against him are no more than scenes from his repertory to which he may have no sense of moral commitment whatsoever . . . Of course one may well question the appropriateness of these attitudes in a Head of State. But quite frankly, I am not troubled by that. In fact the sort of intellectual playfulness displayed by Sam must be less dangerous than the joyless passion for power of many African tyrants. As long as he gets good advice and does not fall too deeply under the influence of such Rasputins as Reginald Okong we may yet avoid the worst (p. 50).

But Ikem's view of Sam as a harmless jester cannot be taken seriously; we have already seen, this time from Chris's perspective (which is positioned closer to the presidency) that the man of power is not simply a victim of bad advice; he is a subtle manipulator who masks his authoritarian intentions behind a mask of benignity. Ikem's image of his school friend is based on a basic misunderstanding of the workings of power in his country; as a result, this portrait is not important for what it tells us about Sam, but for its indictment of Ikem's mode of knowledge, the limits of his sentimentality, and his political naïvety.

At his famous lecture at the university, Ikem appears as the master of the dialectic and the perfect student of universal human nature. But what appears to be his insights into the failures of national consciousness is also a form of projection: he has invented a romantic image of the nation (as it should have been rather than as it is) and created a redeeming role for himself in this idealized space. In moments of exhilaration, especially after it appears that he might afterall have a real role to play in the redemption of the nation, Ikem thinks in strong 'even exaggerated images':

> He saw himself as an explorer who has just cleared a cluster of obstacles in an arduous expedition to earn as a result the conviction, more by intuition perhaps than logic, that although the final goal of his search still lies hidden beyond more adventures and dangers, the puzzles just unraveled point unambiguously to inevitable success (p. 140).

Here is Ikem the dreamer yearning 'to connect his essence with earth and earth's people'; bemoaning the 'failure of our rulers to re-establish vital inner links with the poor and dispossessed of this country, with the bruised heart that throbs painfully at the core of the nation's being' (pp. 140–41). The language and tone Ikem adopts here aligns him with the 'naive romantics' he assails in his editorials.

Nevertheless, Ikem's naïvety is an important corollary to his idealism and his moral indignation, and it would be a mistake to argue that Achebe underscores this character's romanticism to dismiss it. For let us not forget that romance is an imporant ideologeme for articulating contradictions and as a strategy which aims 'at the transfiguration of the world of everyday life in such a way as to restore the conditions of some lost Eden, or to anticipate a future realm from which the old mortality and imperfections will have been effaced.'[48] Ikem's self-representation as an explorer overcoming obstacles on the road to perfection and justice is analogous to the quest of the hero in what Frye has defined as the 'quest-romance' – 'the search of the libido or desiring self for a fulfillment that will deliver it from the anxieties of reality but will still contain that reality.'[49] Thus, Ikem simultaneously dreams of an utopian world in which the desires of nation and self might be fulfilled and turns his gaze to the realities (the adventure and dangers) that lie between him and 'the final goal of his search' (p. 140).

In his detailed representation of Beatrice, as both a narrator and character, Achebe also seeks to narrate a salvational perspective. The fact that Beatrice is the first sustained female subject in Achebe's fiction is important in itself, but what makes it still more significant is the author's desire to use the female character to offer what Jameson would call 'the possibility of sensing other historical rhythms, and of demonic or Utopian transformations of reality now unshakably set in place.'[50] In an interview with Anna Rutherford, Achebe makes a crucial connection between women as ideologemes and the 'radical new thinking' that is required to rescue the African subject from the postcolonial impasse and thus initiate the important task of 'looking into the future':

> In mapping out in detail what woman's role is going to be, I am aware that radical new thinking is required. The quality of compassion and humanness which the woman brings to the world generally has not been given enough scope up till now to influence the way the world is run. We have created all kind of myths to support the suppression of the woman, and what the group around Beatrice is saying is that the time has now come to put an end to that. I'm saying the woman herself will be in the forefront in designing what her new role is going to be, with the humble cooperation of men. The position of Beatrice as sensitive leader of that group is indicative of what I see as necessary in the transition to the kind of society which I think we should be aiming to create.[51]

For most of the novel, Beatrice exists as a projection of the desires of the men around her: for Chris, she is 'a perfect embodiment of my ideal woman, beautiful without being glamorous. Peaceful but very, very strong' (pp. 63–4); for Ikem, she is a reincarnation of the priestess

Idemili; for Sam, she is a convenient sexual object. And while one is not quite certain that Achebe, in trying to design a new role for this character, has escaped the mythologies that surround the lives and experiences of women (she is often defined by some quite stereotyped notions about women such as the power of intuition over thought, feelings over reason [pp. 70–3]), his major achievement is to have allowed Beatrice to narrate her own experiences and to provide us with a third perspective on the history of the nation. In the latter function, which is most manifest in the representation of the head of state as 'host', Beatrice is able to articulate the social and historical contradictions that define the postcolonial moment; for Beatrice, minor gestures become metonymies for the neocolonial mentality of the men of power. In the party given by the head of state, for example, the masks of power and the militarized version of politics are stripped by the American girl who has become too familiar; and 'for these effronteries she got nothing but grins of satisfaction from the gentlemen in question,' notes Beatrice (p. 78).

But Beatrice is more important as a writer: it is in this role that she begins to point to the kind of future which Achebe's novel anticipates. Whatever their differences as writers and intellectuals Chris and Ikem never doubt or question the veracity of their project – they assume that so long as the right method can be found – then the troubled history of the nation will be represented. Beatrice cannot assume the same confidence in her method nor take her position as a witness for granted; in spite of her influential role in the affairs of the nation, Beatrice is marginalized because of her gender. As a result, her narrative begins by calling attention to its problematics, the failure to find appropriate beginnings, its circularity as it tries to establish vital connections. Writing often degenerates into 'discarded pages' which 'seemed like a necessary ritual or a sacrifice to whoever had to be appeased for this audacity of rushing in where sensible angels would fear to tread, or rather for pulling up one of those spears thrust into the ground by the men in the hour of their defeat and left there in the circle of their last dance together' (p. 83).

These remarks underscore two of the most important elements in Beatrice's narrative: first, there is the sense of doubt about her authority to write (she cannot undertake the task with the kind of audacity her male friends assume because she does not write from a position of power); secondly, she is positioned at a strategic moment of writing when the men are dead and only the women are left, like the proverbial anthills, to witness the past of drought and destruction. While Chris and Ikem were engaged in retrospective narratives which would end with their silencing, she begins from the moment of silence and looks toward the future. Furthermore, Beatrice realizes that the condition of the nation cannot be understood until the autobiography of the writing self has been written; the narrator must begin by understanding herself beyond the given images that have fixed her as a projection of other people's desires. Beatrice wonders whether writing can help the world understand 'what one insignificant female did or did not do in a calamity that consumed so many and so much'; she wonders whether writing serves her ego or a public service (p. 84). But she soon realizes that one cannot write about public events without interrogating the life of the writing self itself; before the self is extended into the historical sphere, she must counter her public image, especially those accounts which she will never get used to, such as her presumed ambition: 'Ambitious. Me ambitious! How? And it is this truly unjust presentation that's forcing me to expose my life on these pages to see if perhaps there are aspects of me I had successfully concealed even from myself' (p. 84).

Initially, Beatrice had not intended to write her autobiography, but there is no way she can provide an authentic account of the genealogy of postcolonial culture without reflecting on how she was constructed within it; the early history of the self foretells her future function in the public sphere. Thus, her recollections of her father and his insistence on the subordinated position of females in the household foretells her future marginalization in the political culture (p. 87). In different ways, both Ikem and Chris trigger contrary feelings in Beatrice; but she survives both men so that she can try and reconcile the two distinct styles they typify and their unfulfilled search for reconciliation.

Indeed, one could argue that Achebe intends Beatrice to be the proverbial anthill that survives to tell the tale of the drought, the ultimate witness to the tragic drama of the nation; she is also the voice that tries to reconcile the contrary forces and binary oppositions that define the postcolonial state. Chris's final journey on 'The Great North Road' is an allegorical journey through the national landscape. During the course of this journey, he is able to highlight the contraries that seem to be tearing the nation apart: the 'cocktail circuits' of the city are contrasted to the impoverished rural areas (p. 204), the forest is contrasted to the savannah, and the road itself tells 'its own story of the two countries' as the relatively wealthy South gives way to the desolate North. Chris makes a final journey through a terrain which reminds us how economic and political inequality and neglect have contributed to the negation of the nationalist dream of one nation, one culture; he meets his death as a witness to this failure.

But Achebe is eager to transcend the 'oppressive realistic representation'[52] which dominates his novel; he is adamant that he will not allow the oppressiveness of the present to have the upper hand for '[A]rtists should not be the ones to offer despair to society.'[53] Indeed, one could argue that Achebe's primary concern in this novel is to write an ending to the colonial and neocolonial narratives of African history, thereby hallowing a new discursive space for a genuinely postcolonial beginning. He believes that '[W]e have to work with some hope that there is a new generation, a group of survivors who have learned something from the disaster. It is very important to carry the message of the disaster to the new dispensation.[54]

The last chapter of the novel suggests that the new dispensation depends not only on a radical rethinking of the past but also a redesigning of the forms in which our cultures are represented. The naming of Elewa's new baby is a narrative (imaginary) resolution to the paradoxes and problems of 'an alienated history'; it is a symbolic gesture 'to appease an embittered history' (p. 220). Significantly, history is not appeased by any return to a mythical tradition, but by a radical questioning of tradition itself; the new dispensation includes the license to name and rename differently, hence the boy's name given to Elewa's baby. Clearly, the narratives of our postcolonial future must reconceive all the doctrines which have fixed Africans in alienated histories. Such narratives are needed 'to ensure that Africa and the rest of the Black world step into the next century with dignity and a rekindled optimism.'[55]

Notes

1

Nation Formation & the Novel

pages 1 to 23

1 Roland Barthes, *S/Z: An Essay*, trans. Richard Miller (New York: Hill and Wang, 1974), p. 15. According to Barthes the act of rereading is 'a deliberate contradiction in terms': if we *'immediately* reread the text, it is in order to obtain, as though under the effect of a drug (that of recommencement, of difference), not the *real* text, but a plural text: the same and the new' (p. 16).

2 V.Y. Mudimbe, *The Invention of Africa: Gnosis, Philosophy, and the Order of Knowledge* (Bloomington: Indiana University Press, 1988 and London: James Currey 1990), p. xi.

3 V.Y. Mudimbe, 'African Literature: Myth or Reality', in *African Literature: The Present State/L'état présent*, ed. Stephen Arnold (Washington, D.C.: Three Continents Press, 1985), p. 8.

4 *Ibid.*

5 Bill Moyers, Interview with Chinua Achebe, in *A World of Ideas*, ed. Betty Sue Flowers (New York: Doubleday, 1989), p. 333.

6 'Interview with Chinua Achebe', by Anthony Appiah, John Ryle and D.A.N. Jones, *Times Literary Supplement*, February 26, 1982.

7 Chinua Achebe, *Hopes and Impediments: Selected Essays 1965-1987* (Oxford: Heinemann, 1988), p. 96. Further references will be included in the text and flagged HI.

8 Pierre Macherey, *A Theory of Literary Production*, trans. Geoffrey Wall (London: Routledge, 1978), p. 48.

9 According to Edward W. Said, the representation of the Orient as 'an unconditional ontological category' is an example of a permanent vision which denies the 'other' 'the potential of reality for change'; in contrast, 'narrative is the specific form taken by written history to counter the permanence of vision.' See *Orientalism* (New York: Vintage, 1979), p. 240. For a discussion of the ways in which the discourse on Orientalism might apply to Africa, see Christopher L. Miller, *Blank Darkness: Africanist Discourse in French* (Chicago: The University of Chicago Press, 1985), pp. 13-23.

10 Quoted in Jonathan Ngate, *Francophone African Fiction: Reading a Literary Tradition* (Trenton: Africa World Press, 1988), p. 5.

11 Appiah et al, 'Interview with Chinua Achebe.'

12 'Chinua Achebe: accountable to our society', Interview by Pat and Ernest Emenyonu *Africa Report* 17 (May 1972), p. 25.

13 Macherey, p. 6.

14 *Ibid.*, p. 9.

149

15 Chinua Achebe, *Morning Yet on Creation Day: Essays* (London: Heinemann, 1975), p. 5. Further references will be included in the text and flagged MY.
16 Moyers, p. 343.
17 Appiah et al, 'Interview with Chinua Achebe.'
18 Chinua Achebe, 'The role of the writer in the new nation,' in *African Writers on African Writing*, ed. G. D. Killam (London: Heinemann, 1973), p. 8.
19 *Ibid.*
20 Frantz Fanon, *The Wretched of the Earth*, trans. Constance Farrington (New York: Grove Press, 1968), p. 233.
21 Interview with Donatus Nwoga in *African Writers Talking*, ed. Dennis Duerden and Cosmo Pieterse (London: Heinemann, 1972), p. 8.
22 Fanon, p. 233.
23 Kalu Ogbaa, 'An interview with Chinua Achebe,' *Research in African Literatures* 12 (Spring 1981), p. 13.
24 Jean Franco, 'The nation as imagined community,' in *The New Historicism*, ed. H. Aram Veeser (London: Routledge, 1988), p. 205.
25 Moyers, p. 339.
26 Mudimbe, 'African Literature', p. 9.
27 Said, *Orientalism*, p. 239.
28 *Ibid.*, p. 240.
29 *Ibid.*
30 Moyers, p. 337.
31 Jacques Derrida asserts that '[T]he sign is always the supplement of the thing itself.' See *Of Grammatology*, trans. Gayatri Chakravorty Spivak (Baltimore: John Hopkins University Press, 1976), p. 146.
32 Said, *Orientalism*, p. 21.
33 Chinua Achebe, 'Foreword: The Igbo world and its art,' in *Igbo Arts: Community and Cosmos*, by Herbert M. Cole and Chike C. Aniakor (Los Angeles: Museum of Cultural History, 1984), p. ix.
34 Edward Said, 'Intellectuals in the post-colonial world,' *Salmagundi* No. 70-1 (Spring-Summer 1986), p. 46.
35 In *Critics on Chinua Achebe*, ed. John Agetua (Benin City: John Agetua, 1977), pp. 30, 35.
36 Achebe, 'The Igbo World,' p. ix.
37 Emmanuel Obiechina, *Culture, Tradition and Society in the West African Novel* (Cambridge: Cambridge University Press, 1975), p. 3.
38 Mudimbe, 'African Literature', pp. 8, 11.
39 Michel de Certeau, *The Writing of History*, trans. Tom Conley (New York: Columbia University Press, 1988), p. 320.
40 Fanon, p. 38.
41 Edward Said, 'Reflections on exile', *Granta* 13 (Autumn 1984), p. 162.
42 Kwame Anthony Appiah, 'Out of Africa: topologies of nativism,' *The Yale Journal of Criticism* 2 (Fall 1988), p. 156.
43 Mudimbe, *The Invention of Africa*, p. 47.
44 Moyers, p. 333.
45 Interviews with Dennis Duerden and Robert Serumaga in *African Writers Talking*, pp. 11, 12.
46 Moyers, p. 333.
47 Henry Louis Gates, Jr., 'Editor's Introduction: writing "race" and the difference it makes,' *Critical Inquiry* 12 (Autumn 1985), p. 9.
48 Michel Foucault, 'What is an author?' in *Textual Strategies: Perspectives in Post-Structuralist Criticism*, ed. Josue V. Harari (Ithaca: Cornell University Press, 1979), p. 142.
49 Appiah, 'Out of Africa,' p. 155.
50 Victory W. Turner, *The Ritual Process: Structure and Anti-Structure* (Chicago: Aldine, 1969), pp. 95, 96.

52 Interview with Lewis Nkosi in *African Writers Talking*, p. 4.

53 See Dorothy Hammond and Alta Jablow, *The Africa That Never Was: Four Centuries of British Writing about Africa* (New York: Twayne, 1970) and *The Myth of Africa* (New York: The Library of Social Sciences, 1977); Miller's *Blank Darkness* and Abdul R. JanMohammed, *Manichean Aesthetics: The Politics of Literature in Colonial Africa* (Amherst: The University of Massachusetts Press, 1983); and George W. Stocking, Jr. *Victorian Anthropology* (New York: The Free Press, 1987).

54 *Blank Darkness*, p. 5.

55 Quoted in Helen Lackner, 'Colonial administration and social anthropology: Eastern Nigeria 1920-40,' in *Anthropology and the Colonial Encounter*, ed. Talal Asad (London: Ithaca Press, 1973), p. 134.

56 Appiah, 'Out of Africa,' p. 174.

57 Appiah et al, 'Interview with Chinua Achebe.'

58 On the function of 'the principle of difference, as the condition for signification,' see Jacques Derrida, *Margins of Philosophy*, trans. Alan Bass (Chicago: University of Chicago Press, 1982), p. 10.

59 *Ibid.*, pp. 10-15.

60 *Ibid.*, p. 213.

61 See *Igbo Arts*, p. 17.

62 Fanon, p. 209.

63 Achebe, 'The role of the writer,' p. 7.

64 de Certeau, p. xxvii.

65 Mudimbe, *The Invention of Africa*, p. 1.

66 *Ibid.*, p. xxvi.

67 Jonathan Culler, *Structuralist Poetics: Structuralism, Linguistics and the Study of Literature* (Ithaca: Cornell University Press, 1975), p. 189.

68 Homi K. Bhabha, 'The other question: difference, discrimination and the discourse of colonialism,' in *Literature, Politics and Theory: Papers from the Essex Conference 1976-84*, ed. Francis Barker et al. (London: Methuen, 1986), p. 156.

69 M.M. Bakhtin and P.M. Medvedev, *The Formal Method in Literary Scholarship: A Critical Introduction to Sociological Poetics*, trans. Albert J. Wehrle (Cambridge, MA.: Harvard University Press, 1989), p. 4.

70 *Ibid.*, pp. 16-17.

71 Claude Lévi-Strauss, *Structural Anthropology*, trans. Claire Jacobs and Brooke Grundfest (New York: Doubleday, 1967), p. 67.

72 Ogbaa, p. 2.

73 Quoted in Julia Kristeva, *Desire in Language: A Semiotic Approach to Literature and Art*, ed. Leon S. Roudiez, trans. Thomas Gora et al (New York: Columbia University Press, 1980), p. 109.

74 Frederic Jameson, *The Political Unconscious: Narrative as a Socially Symbolic Act* (Ithaca: Cornell University Press, 1981), p. 20.

2

Things Fall Apart

pages 24 to 50

There are several editions of *Things Fall Apart*; the text refers to London: HEB, 1962 (AWS, 1). Reset 1976. 150 pp.

Things Fall Apart

Things Fall Apart
London: Heinemann, 1958. 185 pp. cased
London: HEB, 1962 (AWS, 1). 187 pp. p/b (also available in Heinemann's New Windmill Series, 162). Reset 1976.
New York: Astor Honor, 1959, 215 pp.
Greenwich, Conn.: Fawcett, 1969 (Premier Book, T 450). 192 pp.

1 Interview with Donatus Nwoga in *African Writers Talking*, ed. Dennis Duerden and Cosmo Pieterse (London: Heinemann, 1972), p. 7.

2 Chinua Achebe, *Morning Yet on Creation Day: Essays* (London: Heinemann, 1975), p. 70. Further references will be included in the text and flagged MY.

3 Roland Barthes, *Writing Degree Zero and Elements of Semiology*, trans. Annette Lavers and Colin Smith (Boston: Beacon Press, 1967), p. 4.

4 Dorothy Hammond and Alta Jablow, *The Myth of Africa* (New York: The Library of Social Sciences, 1977), p. 13.

5 Harold Bloom, *The Anxiety of Influence: A Theory of Poetry* (New York: Oxford University Press, 1973), p. 5.

6 Lauren Jenny, 'The strategy of form,' in *French Literary Theory Today: A Reader*, ed. Tzvetan Todorov, trans. R. Carter (Cambridge: Cambridge University Press, 1982), p. 59.

7 The Negritudists, says Soyinka, 'did receive some unintentional bolstering from yet another category . . . best described as "unmediated exposition" – of which Chinua Achebe, the Nigerian novelist, may be held as the finest practitioner.' See *Art, Dialogue and Outrage: Essays on Literature and Culture* (Ibadan: New Horn, 1988), p. 180.

8 See Edward W. Said, *Orientalism* (New York: Vintage, 1979), p. 21.

9 See John Hearne, 'Introduction,' *Carifesta Forum: An Anthology of 20 Caribbean Voices* (Kingston: Institute of Jamaica, 1976), p. vii.

10 Chinua Achebe, *Things Fall Apart* (London: Heinemann, 1976). Further references will be included in the text.

11 David Carroll, *Chinua Achebe* (New York: Twayne, 1970), p. 16.

12 Quoted by Elizabeth Isichei, *The Ibo People and the Europeans* (London: Faber, 1973), p. 18.

13 Christopher L. Miller, *Blank Darkness: Africanist Discourse in French* (Chicago: The University of Chicago Press, 1985), p. 170.

14 For the relationship between Basden and the Achebe family, see Robert M. Wren, *Achebe's World: The Historical and Cultural Context of the Novels of Chinua Achebe* (Washington, D.C.: Three Continents Press, 1980).

15 G. T. Basden, *Among the Ibos of Nigeria* (London: Frank Cass, 1966), pp. 9–10. This book was first published in 1921.

16 Said, p. 21.

17 Elizabeth Isichei, *A History of the Igbo People* (London: MacMillan, 1976), p. 3.

18 Richard N. Henderson, *The King in Every Man: Evolutionary Trends in Onitsha Ibo Society and Culture* (New Haven: Yale University Press, 1972), p. 105.

19 See Georg Lukacs, *The Theory of the Novel*, trans. Anna Bostock (Cambridge, M.A.: The MIT Press, 1971), pp. 120–27.

20 Miller, p. 169.

21 Soyinka, *Art, Dialogue and Outrage*, p. 180.

22 V. Y. Mudimbe, 'What is the real thing?: psychoanalysis and African mythical narratives,' *Cahiers d'études Africaines* 107/108 (1988), p. 316.

23 Kalu Ogbaa, 'An Interview wth Chinua Achebe,' *Research in African Literatures* 12 (Spring 1981), p. 1.

24 Said, p. 21.

25 Michel Foucault, *The Order of Things: An Archeology of the Human Sciences* (New York: Vintage, 1973), p. xx.

26 See Gerald Prince, *Dictionary of Narratology* (Lincoln: University of Nebraska Press, 1987), p. 51.

27 Victor Uchendu, *The Igbo of Southeast Nigeria* (New York: Holt, 1965), p. 11.

28 Jacques Derrida, *Of Grammatology*, trans. Gayatri Chakravorty Spivak (Baltimore: John Hopkins University Press, 1976), pp. 11-12.

29 For a discussion of the circle of culture as I use it here, see Sterling Stuckey, *Slave Culture: Nationalist Theory and the Foundations of Black America* (New York: Oxford University Press, 1987) pp. 3-19.

30 Wole Soyinka, *Myth, Literature and the African World* (Cambridge: Cambridge University Press, 1976), p. 147.

31 David Couzens Hoy, *The Critical Circle: Literature, History, and Philosophical Hermeneutics* (Berkeley: University of California Press, 1982), p. vii.

32 Marshall Sahlins, *Culture and Practical Reason* (Chicago: University of Chicago Press, 1976), p. 206.

33 *A History of the Igbo People*, p. 32.

34 Marcel Mauss, *The Gift: Forms and Function of Exchange in Archaic Societies*, trans. Ian Cunnison (New York: Norton, 1967), p. 1. For a discussion of Mauss's work and the function of forms of exchange within the symbolic order, see Claude Lévi-Strauss, *Introduction to the Work of Marcel Mauss*, trans. Felicity Baker (London: Routledge, 1987).

35 Foucault, p. 174.

36 *Ibid.*, pp. 180, 202.

37 Isichei, p. 8.

38 Sunday O. Anozie, 'Structurology IV: the semiotics of the yam,' *The Conch* xii (1980), p. 131.

39 Amilcar Cabral, 'National liberation and culture,' in *Return to the Source: Selected Speeches of Amilcar Cabral*, ed. Africa Information Service (New York: Monthly Review, 1973), pp. 41-2.

40 Ross Chambers, *Story and Situation: Narrative Seduction and the Power of Fiction* (Minneapolis: University of Minnesota Press, 1984), p. 3.

41 John B. Thompson, *Studies in the Theory of Ideology* (Berkeley: University of California Press, 1984), p. 7.

42 Abiola Irele, 'The tragic conflict in the novels of Chinua Achebe,' in *Critical Perspectives on Chinua Achebe*, ed. C. L. Innes and Bernth Lindfors (Washington, D.C.: Three Continents Press, 1978), p. 14.

43 *Ibid.*

44 Kaja Silverman, *The Subject of Semiotics* (New York: Oxford University Press, 1983), p. 77.

45 Claude Lévi-Strauss, *Structural Anthropology* (New York: Anchor Books, 1967), p. 199.

46 Silverman, p. 77.

47 Harold Scheub, 'When a man fails alone,' *Présence Africaine* 74 (1970), p. 64.

48 Irele, p. 12.

49 Scheub, p. 63.

50 Louis Althusser, *Lenin and Philosophy and Other Essays*, trans. Ben Brewster (New York: Monthly Review Press, 1971), pp. 164-5.

51 See Louis Althusser, *For Marx*, trans. Ben Brewster (London: Verso, 1979), p. 144.

52 Scheub, p. 62.

53 See Silverman, p. 61.

54 Barthes, p. 15.

55 Caroll, p. 73.

56 C. L. Innes, 'Language, poetry and doctrine in *Things Fall Apart*' in *Critical Perspectives*, p. 112.

57 Prince, p. 66.

58 Oladele Taiwo, *Culture and the Nigerian Novel* (New York: St Martins Press, 1976), p. 112.

59 See Bernth Lindfors, 'The palm-oil with which Achebe's words are eaten,' in *Critical Perspectives*, pp. 67–85; Emmanuel Obiechina, *Culture, Tradition and Society in the West African Novel* (Cambridge: Cambridge University Press, 1975), p. 156; and Kenneth Harrow, 'Metaphor and proverb: master trope in *Things Fall Apart*,' Paper presented at the African Studies Association conference, October 28-31, Chicago, Illinois.
60 Michel Foucault, *The Archaeology of Knowledge and the Discourse on Language* trans. A. M. Sheridan Smith (New York: Pantheon Books, 1972), p. 216.
61 'Language and action in the novels of Chinua Achebe,' in *Critical Perspectives*, p. 68.

3
Arrow of God

pages 51 to 77

There are several editions of *Arrow of God*; the text refers to London: HEB, 1964, 1974 (AWS, 16). Revised Edition 230 pp.
Arrow of God
London: Heinemann, 1964. 304 pp. cased
London: HEB, 1965 (AWS, 16). 296 pp.
New York: John Day, 1967. 287 pp.
New York: Doubleday, 1969 (Anchor Book, A 698: with an introduction by Kenneth Post) 266 pp.
1 According to Frantz Fanon, '[T]he colonial world is a manichean world ... The native is declared insensible to ethics; he represents not only the absence of values, but also the negation of values.' See *The Wretched of the Earth*, trans. Constance Farrington (New York: Grove Press, 1968), p. 41. The best discussion of Fanon's manichean allegory and African literature is Abdul R. JanMohammed's *Manichean Aesthetics: The Politics of Literature in Colonial Africa* (Amherst: The University of Massachusetts Press, 1983).
2 See Chinua Achebe, 'Foreword: the Igbo world and its art,' in *Igbo Arts: Community and Cosmos*, ed. Herbert M. Cole and Chike Aniakor (Los Angeles: Museum of Cultural History, 1984), p. ix.
3 Chinua Achebe, *Hopes and Impediments: Selected Essays 1965-1987* (Oxford: Heinemann, 1988), p. 39. Further references will be included in the text and flagged HI.
4 Jonathan Peters *A Dance of Masks: Senghor, Achebe, Soyinka* (Washington, D.C.: Three Continents Press, 1978), p. 115.
5 Herbert M. Cole, *Mbari: Art and Life Among the Owerri Igbo* (Bloomington: Indiana University Press, 1982), p. 196.
6 Chinua Achebe, *Arrow of God*, revised edition (London: Heinemann, 1974), p. 46. Further references will be included in the text.
7 Dennis Duerden, *The Invisible Present: African Art and Literature* (New York: Harper and Row, 1975), p. 131. See also G. I. Jones, *The Art of Eastern Nigeria* (Cambridge: Cambridge University Press, 1984) and Simon Ottenberg, *Masked Rituals of Afikpo* (Seattle: University of Washington Press, 1975), p. 11.
8 Franco Monti, *African Masks*, trans. Andrew Hale (London: Paul Hamlyn, 1969), p. 15.
9 *Ibid*.
10 Phanuel Akubueze Egejuru, *Towards African Literary Independence: A Dialogue with Contemporary African Writers* (Westport: Greenwood Press, 1980), p. 127.

11 Wole Soyinka, *Myth, Literature and the African World* (Cambridge: Cambridge University Press, 1976), p. 91.

12 Garrett Stewart, 'Dickens, Gance and Blanchot,' *The Yale Journal of Criticism* 2 (Spring 1989), p. 147.

13 Jonathan Culler, *Flaubert: The Uses of Uncertainty* (Ithaca: Cornell University Press, 1974), p. 84.

14 Jonathan Culler, *Structuralist Poetics: Structuralism, Linguistics and the Study of Literature* (Ithaca: Cornell University Press, 1975), p. 189.

15 J.O.J. Nwachukwu-Agbada, 'An Interview with Chinua Achebe,' *The Massachusetts Review* (Summer 1987), p. 281.

16 Edward W. Said, *Beginning: Intention and Method* (New York: Basic Books, 1975), pp. 83–4.

17 *Ibid.*, p. 84.

18 Kalu Ogbaa, 'An Interview with Chinua Achebe,' *Research in African Literatures* 12 (Spring 1981), p. 13.

19 According to Gerald Prince, free indirect discourse represents a character's utterances or thoughts without the tag clause used in the representation of normal indirect discourse. See *Dictionary of Narratology* (Lincoln: University of Nebraska, 1987), p. 34.

20 Michal Peled Ginsburg, 'Pseudonym, epigraphs, and narrative voice: *Middlemarch* and the problem of authorship,' *English Literary History* 47 (1980), p. 550. See also Roy Pascal, *The Dual Voice: Free Indirect Speech and Its Functioning in the Nineteenth-Century Novel* (Totowa, N.J.: Rowman, 1977).

21 Culler, *Flaubert: the Uses of Uncertainty*, p. 109.

22 Said, *Beginning*, p. 84.

23 Christopher, L. Miller, *Blank Darkness: Africanist Discourse in French* (Chicago: The University of Chicago, 1985), p. 8.

24 Richard Terdimann, *Discourse/Counter-Discourse: The Theory and Practice of Symbolic Resistance in Nineteenth-Century France* (Ithaca: Cornell University Press, 1985), p. 210.

25 Roland Barthes, 'Introduction to the structural analysis of narratives,' in *A Barthes Reader*, ed. Susan Sontag (New York: Hill and Wang, 1982), p. 288.

26 Frederic Jameson, *Marxism and Form: Twentieth Century Dialectical Theories of Literature* (Princeton: Princeton University Press, 1971), p. 70.

27 Culler, *Flaubert: the Uses of Uncertainty*, p. 109.

28 Claude Lévi-Strauss, *Tristes Tropiques*, trans. John Russell (New York: Atheneum, 1971), p. 180.

29 Alexander Okwudor Attah, 'Okoroshi music,' in *Igbo Arts*, p. 212. ·

30 Emmanuel Obiechina, *Culture, Tradition and Society in the West African Novel* (Cambridge: Cambridge University Press, 1975), p. 238.

31 JanMohammed, p. 170.

32 *Ibid.*, pp. 170–71.

33 Pierre Bourdieu, *Outline of A Theory of Practice* (Cambridge: Cambridge University Press, 1977), p. 169.

34 Simon Gikandi, *Reading the African Novel* (London & Postsmouth, N.H.: James Currey/Heinemann, 1987), pp. 149–65.

35 David Carroll, *Chinua Achebe* (New York: Twayne, 1970), p. 118.

36 Michel Foucault, *The Order of Things: An Archaeology of the Human Sciences* (New York: Vintage, 1973), p. 44.

37 Simon Ottenberg, 'Ibo receptivity to change,' in *Continuity and Change in African Cultures*, ed. William R. Bascom and Melville Herskovits (Chicago: University of Chicago Press, 1959), p. 134.

38 Obiechina, p. 235.

39 See Charles Segal, *Interpreting Greek Tragedy: Myth, Poetry, Text* (Ithaca: Cornell University Press, 1986), p. 48.

40 V.N. Volosinov, *Marxism and the Philosophy of Language*, trans. Ladislav Matejka and I.R. Titunik (Cambridge, MA.: Harvard University Press, 1986), p. 10.

41 See Gikandi, *Reading the African Novel*, p. 156.
42 *Igbo Arts*, p. 30.
43 T. Uzodinma Nwala, *Igbo Philosophy* (Lagos: Lantern Books, 1985), p. 214. An intriguing discussion of the relationship between the Ikenga and Igbo systems of thought can be found in A. E. Afigbo, *Ikenga: The State of Our Knowledge* (Owerri: Rada Publishing Company, 1986).
44 'Interview with Chinua Achebe,' in *Palaver: Interviews with Five African Writers in Texas*, ed. Bernth Lindfors et al (Austin: African and Afro-American Research Institute, 1972), p. 8.
45 Egejuru, p. 27.
46 Edmond Cros, *Theory and Practice of Sociocriticism* (Minneapolis: University of Minnesota Press, 1988), p. 38.
47 Jack Goody, *The Interface Between the Written and the Oral* (Cambridge: Cambridge University Press, 1987), p. 148.
48 Herbert M. Cole, 'Ibo art and authority,' in *African Art and Leadership*, ed. Douglas Fraser and Herbert M. Cole (Madison: University of Wisconsin Press, 1972), p. 84.
49 See J. L. Austin, *How To Do Things With Words* (London: Oxford University Press, 1962).
50 John Frow, *Marxism and Literary History* (Cambridge, MA.: Harvard University Press, 1986), p. 63.
51 JanMohammed, p. 170.
52 See Paul de Man, *Blindness and Insight: Essays in the Rhetoric of Contemporary Criticism*, Second Edition (Minneapolis: University of Minnesota Press, 1983), pp. 102–41.
53 *Palaver*, p. 9.
54 de Man, p. 140.
55 Egejuru, p. 127.
56 D. Ibe Nwoga, 'The Igbo world of Achebe's *Arrow of God*,' *Research in African Literatures* 12 (Spring 1981), p. 20.
57 Simon Ottenberg, *Masked Rituals*, p. 12.

4

No Longer At Ease

pages 78 to 100

There are several editions of *No Longer at Ease*; the text refers to London: HEB, 1963 (AWS, 3). Reset 1975. 154 pp.
No Longer at Ease
London: Heinemann, 1960. 170 pp. cased
London: HEB, 1963 (AWS, 3). 176 pp. p/b
New York: Astor Honor, 1960. 170 pp.
Greenwich, Conn.: Fawcett, 1969 (Premier Book, T 449). 159 pp.

1 This is the basic assumption underlying the following influential studies of the novel: G. D. Killam, *The Novels of Chinua Achebe* (London: Heinemann, 1969), pp. 35–58; David Carroll, *Chinua Achebe* (New York: Twayne, 1970), pp. 65–88; and Eustace Palmer, *An Introduction to the African Novel* (New York: Africana, 1972), pp. 63–71.
2 See Hebert M. Cole and Chike C. Aniakor, *Igbo Arts: Community and Cosmos* (Los Angeles: Museum of Cultural History, 1984), p. 17.

3 Jonathan Culler, *Flaubert: The Uses of Uncertainty* (Ithaca: Cornell University Press, 1974).
4 Palmer, p. 63.
5 Culler, p. 83.
6 Chinua Achebe, *Hopes and Impediments: Selected Essays 1965-1987* (Oxford: Heinemann, 1988), p. 36. Further references will be included in the text and flagged HI.
7 Benedict Anderson, *Imagined Communities: Reflections on the Origins and Spread of Nationalism* (London: NLB, 1983), p. 131.
8 V.Y. Mudimbe, *The Invention of Africa: Gnosis, Philosophy, and the Order of Knowledge* (Bloomington: Indiana University Press, 1988 and London: James Currey, 1990), p. 5.
9 *Ibid.*
10 Shatto Arthur Gakwandi, *The Novel and the Contemporary Experience in Africa* (London: Heinemann, 1977), p. 32. A useful discussion of the Lagosian influence in the novel can be found in Robert M. Wren's *Achebe's World: The Historical and Cultural Context of the Novels of Chinua Achebe* (Washington, D.C.: Three Continents Press, 1980), pp. 61-76.
11 Gakwandi, p. 32.
12 Michal Peled Ginsburg, *Flaubert Writing: A Study in Narrative Strategies* (Stanford: Stanford University Press, 1986), p. 1-2.
13 Chinua Achebe, *No Longer At Ease* (London: Heinemann, 1987), p. 2. Further references will be included in the text.
14 Alexander Gelley, *Narrative Crossings: Theory and Pragmatics of Prose Fiction* (Baltimore: Johns Hopkins University Press, 1987), p. 38.
15 For Anderson, the nation 'is an imagined political community – and imagined as both inherently limited and sovereign' (p. 7).
16 James S. Coleman, *Nigeria: Background to Nationalism* (Berkeley: University of California Press, 1963), pp. 146-7.
17 Edmond Cros, *Theory and Practice of Sociocriticism* (Minneapolis: University of Minnesota Press), pp. 163, 165.
18 *Ibid.*
19 Quoted in Culler, p. 108.
20 Culler, p. 108.
21 Gakwandi, p. 36.
22 Culler, p. 108.
23 Coleman, p. 146.
24 Peter Brooks, *Reading for the Plot: Design and Intention in Narrative* (New York: Vintage, 1984), p. xiii.
25 *Ibid.*, p. 37.
26 *Ibid.*, pp. 40-41.
27 Coleman, p. 158.
28 John Brenkman, *Culture and Domination* (Ithaca: Cornell University Press, 1987), p. 174.
29 Victor W. Turner, *The Ritual Process: Structure and Anti-Structure* (Chicago: Aldine, 1969), p. 96.
30 *Ibid.*, pp. 94, 95.
31 Carroll, p. 88.
32 Palmer, p. 68.
33 Abdul R. JanMohammed, *Manichean Aesthetics: The Politics of Literature in Colonial Africa* (Amherst: The University of Massachusetts Press, 1983), p. 174.
34 Michel Foucault, *The Order of Things: An Archaeology of the Human Sciences* (New York: Vintage, 1970), p. 46.
35 *Ibid.*, p. 47.
36 *Ibid.*, pp. 48, 49.
37 Killam, p. 50.

38 Giles Deleuze and Felix Guattari, *Anti-Oedipus: Capitalism and Schizophrenia*, trans. Robert Hurley et al (Minneapolis: University of Minnesota Press, 1983), p. 62.

5

A Man of the People

pages 101 to 124

There are several editions of *A Man of the People*; the text refers to London: HEB, 1966 (AWS, 31). Reset 1975. 149 pp.

A Man of the People
London: Heinemann, 1966. 166 pp. cased
London: HEB, 1966 (AWS, 31). 176 pp.
New York: John Day, 1966, 167 pp.
New York: Doubleday, 1967 (Anchor Book, A 594: with an introduction by Kenneth Post), 141 pp.

1 Frantz Fanon, *The Wretched of the Earth*, trans. Constance Farrington (New York: Grove Press, 1968), p. 225.

2 *Ibid.*, p. 233.

3 Chinua Achebe, 'The role of the writer in the new nation,' in *African Writers on African Writing*, ed. G. D. Killam (London: Heinemann, 1973), p. 8.

4 *Ibid.*

5 Interview with Robert Serumaga in *African Writers Talking*, ed. Dennis Duerden and Cosmo Pieterse (London: Heinemann, 1972), p. 8.

6 Chinua Achebe, *Hopes and Impediments: Selected Essays 1965-1987* (Oxford: Heinemann, 1988), p. 104. Further references will be included in the text and flagged HI.

7 'Interview with Chinua Achebe,' in *Palaver: Interviews with Five African Writers in Texas*, ed. Bernth Lindfors et al (Austin: African and Afro-American Research Institute, 1972), p. 8.

8 *African Writers Talking*, pp. 14-15.

9 *Palaver*, p. 8.

10 Chinua Achebe. *Morning Yet on Creation Day: Essays* (London: Heinemann, 1975), p. 70. Further references will be included in the text and flagged MY.

11 Pierre Macherey, *A Theory of Literary Production*, trans. Geoffrey Wall (London: Routledge, 1978), pp. 39, 42.

12 Eustace Palmer, *An Introduction to the African Novel* (New York: Africana, 1972), p. 84.

13 Frederic Jameson, *The Political Unconscious: Narrative as a Socially Symbolic Act* (Ithaca: Cornell University Press, 1981), p. 38.

14 Quoted by Frederic Jameson, *The Prisonhouse of Language* (Princeton: Princeton University Press, 1972), frontispiece.

15 Jameson, p. 28.

16 Chinua Achebe, *A Man of the People* (London: Heinemann, 1988), p. 1. Further references will be included in the text.

17 See Jonathan Culler, *Flaubert: The Uses of Uncertainty* (Ithaca: Cornell University Press, 1974), p. 86.

18 Frederic Jameson, 'Metacommentary,' in *The Ideologies of Theory: Essays 1971-1986* (Minneapolis: University of Minnesota Press, 1988), p. 5.

19 Bernth Lindfors, 'The palm-oil with which Achebe's words are eaten,' in *Critical Perspectives on Chinua Achebe*, ed. C. L. Innes and Bernth Lindfors (Washington, D.C.: Three Continents Press, 1978), p. 62.
20 Gareth Griffiths, 'Language and action in the novels of Chinua Achebe,' in *Critical Perspectives*, p. 77.
21 Rainer Warning, 'Irony and the "order of discourse" in Flaubert,' *New Literary History* 13 (Winter 1982), pp. 264-5.
22 Richard Lowell Howey, 'The Dialectics of Irony,' *Nietzsche-Studien Band* 4 (1975), p. 46.
23 Warning, p. 274.
24 *Ibid.*, p. 275.
25 *Ibid.*
26 Hayden White, *Metahistory: The Historical Imagination in Nineteenth Century Europe* (Baltimore: Johns Hopkins University Press, 1973), p. 37.
27 Culler, p. 166.
28 White, p. 37.
29 Roland Barthes, 'Introduction to the structural analysis of narratives,' in *A Barthes Reader*, ed. Susan Sontag (New York: Hill and Wang, 1982), p. 256.
30 Culler, p. 80.

6

Anthills of the Savannah

pages 125 to 148

There are several editions of *Anthills of the Savannah*; the text refers to London: William Heinemann, 1987. 233 pp.
Anthills of the Savannah
New York: Doubleday, 1988.
Oxford: HEB, 1988 (AWS) 240 pp.

1 Bill Moyers, Interview with Chinua Achebe, in *A World of Ideas*, ed. Betty Sue Flowers (New York: Doubleday, 1989), p. 337.
2 *Ibid.*, p. 343.
3 Anna Rutherford, Interview with Chinua Achebe, in *Kunapipi* 9 (1987), p. 4.
4 Chinua Achebe, 'Our Mission,' in *African Commentary* 1 (October 1989), p. 4.
5 Edward Said, 'Intellectuals in the post-colonial world,' *Salgamundi* 70-71 (Spring-Summer 1986), p. 45. Achebe says that his novel took such a long time to complete because, in trying to 're-create' recent African history in fictional terms, he had been forced to rethink this history by the Nigerian civil war: 'This horrendous experience was, for me, the end of an epoch, and it really drew a curtain across modern African history ... I needed to sit back and reflect before saying anything more.' See Kim Heron, 'A risky and dangerous relationship,' *The New York Times Book Review*, February 21, 1988.
6 Moyers, p. 338.
7 Said, pp. 45-47.
8 Moyers, p. 343.
9 Said, p. 54.
10 *Ibid.*
11 *Ibid.*, p. 54-5.

12 Frantz Fanon, *The Wretched of the Earth*, trans. Constance Farrington (New York: Grove Press, 1968), p. 233.

13 Patrick Taylor, *The Narrative of Liberation: Perspective on Afro-Caribbean Literature, Popular Culture, and Politics* (Ithaca: Cornell University Press, 1989), p. 82.

14 Moyers, pp. 336, 338.

15 For example, John Povey argues that Achebe 'falls into a pattern of writing in which he explains and discusses rather than represents . . . The author's personal presence is continuous and extended.' See his review of *Anthills* in *African Arts* 21 (August 1988), p. 22. A rather misplaced review of the novel is one by Bruce King in *The Sewanee Review* 96 (Fall 1988), pp. 84–5.

16 Frederic Jameson, 'Metacommentary', in *The Ideologies of Theory: Essays 1971–1986* (Minnneapolis: University of Minnesota Press, 1988), p. 5.

17 Chinua Achebe, *Anthills of the Savannah* (New York: Doubleday, 1988), p. 124. Further references will be included in the text.

18 See Said's discussion of Foucault's and Lyotard's rejection of the narratives of liberation, p. 50.

19 Moyers, p. 337.

20 Rutherford, p. 5.

21 *Ibid.*

22 Jameson, p. 16.

23 Chinua Achebe, *Hopes and Impediments: Selected Essays 1965–1987* (Oxford: Heinemann, 1988), p. 36. Further references will be included in the text and flagged HI.

24 Achebe, *African Commentary*, p. 4.

25 David Couzens Hoy, *The Critical Circle: Literature, History, and Philosophical Hermeneutics* (Berkeley: University of California Press, 1982), p. vii.

26 *Ibid.*

27 Said, p. 45.

28 Jean-Francois Lyotard, *The Postmodern Condition: A Report on Knowledge*, trans. Geoff Bennington and Brian Massumi (Minneapolis: University of Minnesota Press, 1984), p. 52.

29 Quoted in Taylor, p. 81.

30 Frank Kermode, *The Genesis of Secrecy: On the Interpretation of Narrative* (Cambridge, MA.: Harvard University Press, 1979), pp. 4, x.

31 Aijaz Ahmad, 'Jameson's rhetoric of otherness and the "national allegory," ', *Social Text* 17 (Fall 1987), p. 22.

32 Jean Pierre Vernant, *Myth and Thought Among the Greeks* (London: Routledge, 1983), p. 80.

33 Eugene Vance, 'Rolands and the Poetics of Memory,' in *Textual Strategies: Perspectives in Post-Structuralist Criticism*, ed. Josue Harari (Ithaca: Cornell University Press, 1979), p. 374.

34 Michael M.J. Fischer, 'Ethnicity and the post-modern arts of memory,' in *Writing Culture: The Poetics and Politics of Ethnography* ed. James Clifford and George E. Marcus (Berkeley: The University of California Press, 1986), p. 198.

35 Chinua Achebe, *The Trouble with Nigeria* (Enugu: Fourth Dimension, 1983), pp. 2, 5.

36 *Ibid.*

37 Timothy Brennan, *Salman Rushdie and the Third World: Myths of the Nation* (New York: St Martins, 1989), p. 8.

38 Mikhail Bakhtin, *The Dialogic Imagination*, ed. Michael Holquist and Caryl Emerson (Austin: University of Texas Press, 1981), p. 12.

39 *Ibid.* pp. 270–71.

40 Said, p. 46.

41 Bhaktin, p. 291.

42 Achebe says that he uses different perspectives in his novel 'to indicate that nothing is simple and that we must not aim for naïve simplifications. We must accept life with all its complexities . . .' See Rutherford, p. 6.

43 Bakhtin, p. 333.
44 John Beverley, 'The margin at the centre: on *Testimonio* (Testimonial narrative),'
Modern Fiction Studies 35 (Spring 1989), p. 13.
45 *Ibid.*, p. 16.
46 *Ibid.*, p. 22.
47 Quoted in *Ibid.*
48 Frederic Jameson, *The Political Unconscious: Narrative as a Socially Symbolic Act*
(Ithaca: Cornell University Press, 1981), p. 110.
49 Quoted in *Ibid.*
50 *Ibid.*, p. 104.
51 Rutherford, p. 4.
52 Jameson, *The Political Unconscious*, p. 104.
53 Moyers, p. 338.
54 *Ibid.*, p. 339.
55 Achebe, *African Commentary*, p. 4.

Index

Index

Althusser, Louis, 41, 42
Amin, Samir, 87
Anderson, Benedict, 81, 85
Aniakor, Chike, 21, 68, 79
Anozie, Sunday, 37
Appiah, Kwame Anthony, 14, 17
Awolowo, Obiafemi, 138

Bakhtin, M. M., 22, 23, 139, 140
Barthes, Roland, 2, 23, 25, 44, 88, 121, 149
Basden, G. T., 28
Bloom, Harold, 25
Bourdieu, Pierre, 67
Brennan, Timothy, 138
Brooks, Peter, 90, 91

Caroll, David, 27, 44, 67
Cabral, Amilcar, 38
Cary, Joyce, 18, 27
Cole, Herbert, 21, 53, 68, 79
Conrad, Joseph, 27, 63
Coleman, James, 90
Cros, Edmond, 86
Culler, Jonathan, 22, 57, 60, 80, 88, 91, 122

de Man, Paul, 72, 73
de Certeau, 14
Deleuze, Giles, 98
Derrida, Jacques, 11, 20, 33
Duerden, Dennis, 16, 53

Eliot, T. S., 81

Fanon, Frantz, 7, 51, 101, 102, 103, 128
Fischer, Michael M. J., 138
Franco, Jean, 78
Foucault, Michel, 17, 32, 36, 48, 67, 97, 98

Gakwandi, Arthur Shatto, 82, 89

Gates, Henry Louis, 16
Goody, Jack, 70
Griffiths, Gareth, 49
Guattari, Felix, 98

Hammond, Dorothy, 18, 25
Harrow, Kenneth, 47
Hoy, David Couzens, 35, 133
Howey, Richard, 114

Innes, C. L., 44
Irele, Abiola, 39, 41
Isichei, Elizabeth, 35, 37

Jablow, Alta, 18, 25
Jameson, Frederick, 64, 106, 109, 129
JanMohammed, Abdul, 18, 66, 72, 97

Kane, Cheikh Hamidou, 17
Kermode, Frank, 51, 135
Killam, D. G., 98
Kimoni, Iyay, 4

Lévi-Strauss, Claude, 23, 40
Lindfors, Bernth, 47, 103, 112
Lukacs, George, 30
Lugard, Lord, 27

Machery, Pierre, 5, 101, 105
Mbari, 12, 52
Miller, Christopher, 18, 27, 30, 62
Miller, Richard, 149
Mofolo, Thomas, 2, 6
Monti, Franco, 54
Moyers, Bill, 1, 3, 125
Mudimbe, V. Y., 3, 13, 21, 78, 82

Ngugi, wa Thiong'o, 5
Nwala, T. Uzodinma, 69
Nwachukwu-Agbada, J. O. J., 57
Nwoga, Donatus, 7, 24, 75

CPSIA information can be obtained
at www.ICGtesting.com
Printed in the USA
JSHW032147050920
7671JS00002B/154